Library of
Davidson College

THE CARIBBEAN IN THE PACIFIC CENTURY

THE CARIBBEAN IN THE PACIFIC CENTURY

Prospects for Caribbean-Pacific Cooperation

Jacqueline A. Braveboy-Wagner
with
W. Marvin Will
Dennis J. Gayle
Ivelaw L. Griffith

Lynne Rienner Publishers • Boulder & London

Published in the United States of America in 1993 by
Lynne Rienner Publishers, Inc.
1800 30th Street, Boulder, Colorado 80301

and in the United Kingdom by
Lynne Rienner Publishers, Inc.
3 Henrietta Street, Covent Garden, London WC2E 8LU

© 1993 by Lynne Rienner Publishers, Inc. All rights reserved

Library of Congress Cataloging-in-Publication Data
Braveboy-Wagner, Jacqueline Anne.
  The Caribbean in the Pacific century: prospects for Caribbean-Pacific cooperation/Jacqueline A. Braveboy-Wagner, with W. Marvin Will, Dennis J. Gayle, and Ivelaw L. Griffith.
  Includes bibliographical references and index.
  ISBN 1-55587-195-X (alk. paper)
  1. Caribbean Area—Foreign economic relations—East Asia 2. East Asia—Foreign economic relations—Caribbean Area. I. Title.
HF1496.5.318B73 1992
337.72909—dc20   92-17082
                                                            CIP

British Cataloguing in Publication Data
A Cataloguing in Publication record for this book
is available from the British Library.

Printed and bound in the United States of America

The paper used in this publication meets the requirements
of the American National Standard for Permanence of
Paper for Printed Library Materials Z39.48–1984.

Contents

List of Tables and Figures	vii
Preface	ix

PART 1 ▪ ASIA PACIFIC AND THE CARIBBEAN: BACKGROUND AND LINKAGES — 1

1. Global Transformation: Asia Pacific into the Twenty-first Century, *Jacqueline A. Braveboy-Wagner* — 3
2. Asia Pacific: Intraregional Relations, *Jacqueline A. Braveboy-Wagner* — 15
3. The Caribbean: Intraregional Relations, *Jacqueline A. Braveboy-Wagner* — 33
4. Japan, East Asia, and the Caribbean: Economic Linkages, *Jacqueline A. Braveboy-Wagner* — 45

PART 2 ▪ DEVELOPMENT: WHAT CAN THE ENGLISH-SPEAKING CARIBBEAN LEARN FROM ASIA PACIFIC? — 73

5. Applying the East Asian Development Model to the English-speaking Caribbean, *Dennis J. Gayle* — 75
6. Security for Development: Caribbean–Asia Pacific Regional Mechanisms, *Ivelaw L. Griffith* — 101

PART 3 ▪ THE SMALL STATES OF THE PACIFIC AND THE CARIBBEAN: COMMON PROBLEMS AND POTENTIAL LINKS — 127

7. No Easy Choices: Comparing the Political Economies of the Newer Caribbean and Pacific States, *W. Marvin Will* — 129
8. Security Problems of the Newer Caribbean and Pacific States, *W. Marvin Will* — 171

PART 4 ▪ CONCLUSION — 195

9. Strengthening the Links, *Jacqueline A. Braveboy-Wagner* — 197

About the Author and Contributors	205
Index	207
About the Book	217

Tables and Figures

Tables

1.1	Intra-Pacific Exports of Major Caribbean Basin Countries/Groups	9
2.1	Basic Data, Independent Asian-Pacific Countries	16
3.1	Basic Data, Caribbean Basin States	35
4.1	Trade of Caribbean Basin Countries with Developing Asia	47
4.2	Trade Between Caribbean Basin Countries and Asian-Pacific Countries	48
4.3	Trade Between Caribbean Basin Countries and Japan and Ranking of Japan as Trade Partner	52
4.4	Japan's Trade by Region and Country	55
4.5	Japanese Direct Investment Abroad by Region	56
4.6	Geographical Distribution of Bilateral ODA	57
4.7	Japan's Bilateral ODA to Caribbean Basin Countries	60
5.1	Economic Growth Indicators, East Asian and Caricom States	88
6.1	Regional Initiatives Involving Third World Nations	108
6.2	Profile of ASEAN and Caricom	121
7.1	Economic Indicators for the Caribbean Community and Suriname	133
7.2	Economic Indicators of Independent and Freely Associated Pacific States	137
7.3	Economic Change in the Caribbean per capita GDP	138

Figures

1.1	Map of the Pacific Basin	6
3.1	Map of the Caribbean Basin	34
6.1	Structure of the Regional Security System	116
7.1	Map of Political Entities of the Pacific Islands	135
7.2	Estimated Economic Dependence and External Assistance in Selected Pacific States and Territories	141

Preface

This book grew out of a sustained interest in Japan and Southeast Asia on the part of the principal author, who lived and did research in Japan in the late 1970s and visited many of the Southeast Asian countries. In 1988, she returned to Japan as a visiting professor of political science at Tokyo Metropolitan University, under a grant from the City College of the City University of New York. In addition, contributors Dennis J. Gayle and Ivelaw L. Griffith have long had a strong interest in the Asian region, Gayle's specialty being Singapore and Griffith having visited the area as a working journalist. W. Marvin Will has been fine-tuning his interest in the complementary area of the Pacific for some time.

The writers of this volume are all, however, primarily Caribbeanists, and it is primarily to Caribbean scholars and policymakers that the work is aimed. In the 1970s, there was little interest in Asia Pacific on the part of Caribbean policymakers. But during the late 1980s and early 1990s, it has been impossible to ignore the growing trek of Caribbean (and Latin American) policymakers to Japan and the East Asian "dragons"—a new focus attributable to the dynamism of the Asian-Pacific region and to the search for diversified sources of aid and trade.

In May 1989, the principal author organized a panel on "Asia/Pacific–Caribbean Linkages: An Exploration" for the Caribbean Studies Association's annual convention in Barbados. Panelists agreed that the Caribbean needs to diversify its economic and political relations, especially in an era of keen economic competition for niches in the markets of the developed countries and preoccupation by traditional aid donors with more troubled regions of the world. Out of the discussion came the idea for a book that would represent a deeper exploration of the subject of Asian-Pacific–Caribbean relations. The resulting effort may be viewed by some readers as too broad in scope—the early part of the book touches on the entire Caribbean Basin and the book goes beyond the main Asian-Pacific region to a separate discussion that focuses on the Pacific islands—but the broad sweep represents a conscious attempt to uncover for Caribbeanists as many potential linkages as possible between the regions. Although the book is primarily aimed at Caribbeanists, it is hoped that Asian scholars might find something for themselves in these pages—an introduction to the Caribbean and its complexities and an understanding of the similarities as well as the more obvious differences between the regions. If the growing interest of Asian students at the City University of New York is any guide, the book should appeal to certain Asian-Pacific readers. The book is written with as little jargon as possible, on the assumption that readers will want basic information as well as informed yet uncomplicated analysis.

There are many people that Braveboy-Wagner wishes to thank for their assistance in this project, including but not limited to Nozomu Kawamura of Tokyo Metropolitan University, whose efforts contributed greatly to an intellectually stimulating stay in Japan; Kotaro Horisaka of Sophia University; Motoko Iwami (who went beyond the call of duty) and Ryuichi Fujita of the Long Term Credit Bank of Japan; a good friend, Masato Ninomiya of Brazil and Japan; Harue Ode, Mr. and Mrs. Mori, and young Mika Honike, who were helpful in very special ways; Naoko Ueda of the Economic Section of the Consulate General of Japan; Taina Glaude of the United Nations; and especially her spouse, Jeffrey Wagner, a Japanologist who introduced her to the East and has assisted her in everything from interpreting and translating to facilitating fax communication. Braveboy-Wagner also wishes to thank the contributors to this volume for their patience in making the large number of changes requested and willingly acquiescing in producing several drafts.

W. Marvin Will would also like to thank Pacific specialist Lamont Lindstrom, who coauthored the original paper on the political economy of the Caribbean and Pacific presented by Will at the Caribbean Studies Association conference in 1989. Lindstrom not only extended learned counsel, but also graciously permitted the use of some of his data, which are incorporated into Chapters 7 and 8. Sincere appreciation is also owed to the University of Tulsa for providing Dr. Will some research support, and to the National Endowment for the Humanities for a summer 1990 grant that made it possible to begin manuscript revision.

Jacqueline A. Braveboy-Wagner
W. Marvin Will
Dennis J. Gayle
Ivelaw L. Griffith

PART 1

ASIA PACIFIC AND THE CARIBBEAN: BACKGROUND AND LINKAGES

1

Global Transformation: Asia Pacific into the Twenty-first Century

Jacqueline A. Braveboy-Wagner

In the early 1990s, a new world order is being shaped from the ruins of the old order that was marked by ideological bipolarity and proxy conflicts. The rapidity of the changes that have taken place are captured in Nicholas Rizopoulous's description of a cartoon appearing in a 1990 *Cincinnati Enquirer*. The cartoon depicts a "bemused President Bush, sitting at his desk in the Oval Office, looking at his watch and thinking: 'Communism is dead, the Wall is down, Apartheid is falling, Mandela is free, the Sandinistas are ousted, Germany is reuniting, the Cold War is over. I've returned all my calls, and, heck, it's not even lunchtime!'"[1] Two years later, we can add that Panama's Manuel Noriega has been overthrown, Iraq has been defeated, the Soviet Union has been transformed into a shaky Commonwealth of Independent States, and the main challenges in U.S. foreign policy are primarily economic and intimately linked to a dismal domestic economic performance.

As the 1990s move forward, there are indeed new security challenges emerging around the globe: for example, concerns about the disposition of the nuclear arsenal of the former Soviet Union; the shift in the European balance of power toward a unified and more assertive Germany; and the intensification/reemergence of ethnonationalist conflict in Eastern Europe (particularly Yugoslavia), in the former Soviet Union, and in Africa. But most analysts agree that with the end of the Cold War, strategic concerns on the part of the great powers are now being matched by economic concerns. As one journalist writes: "Today, a country's balance of trade is as important an indicator of its status as its place in the balance of power."[2] In terms of the global economic structure, at least three major economic blocs (megablocs, according to some analysts) are forming in the 1990s: The European Community (EC) nations will eliminate trade barriers in 1992 and move thereafter to stronger monetary and political union. Stronger links with the members of the European Free Trade Area (EFTA) have already been forged, and newly liberated Eastern European states have been offered associate status. The second bloc is the North American Free Trade Area (NAFTA), which includes Canada, the United States, and Mexico. With an eye on the other megablocs, the United States has offered to negotiate free-trade arrangements with all the countries of the Western Hemisphere, and Chile, Venezuela, and Argentina are expected to enter into negotiations in the not-too-distant future. Finally, there is the Pacific bloc, an informal but powerful economic group with strong patterns of intraregional trade (though not free trade). The core nations of this bloc—Japan and the East Asian "tigers," or "dragons" (Korea, Taiwan, Singapore, and Hong Kong)—have chronic surpluses in trade with the United States and Europe and are the target of sustained efforts to persuade them to liberalize their economies. It is this Asia Pacific bloc of nations that is the particular focus of this book.

Well before the dramatic changes in Europe, analysts were focusing on the "Pacific Rim phenomenon," the emergence of the Asian-Pacific region as a major economic actor on the global scene. As one scholar noted not long ago: "As the twentieth century draws to a close, the Pacific is rapidly emerging as the world's most dynamic arena, and its peoples are driving forces of global economics and international politics."[3] According to another writer, "Predictions made in Teddy Roosevelt's era, when it was commonly expected that [the twentieth century] would be the 'Pacific Century,' have now been fulfilled. The region is now at the center of world economic growth, and much political attention as well."[4]

The globalization of the world economy in the twentieth century has been directly responsible for the rise of Japan and the East Asian nations, which positioned themselves to take advantage of increasing economic interdependence.[5] Indeed, there is reason to believe that the Pacific will be even more important to the future. First, Japan—the Pacific core—has begun to be viewed, and to view itself, as an equal partner (even a somewhat superior one, given U.S. economic problems) with the United States in the global economy and has also begun to assume—at least partly at the urging of the United States—a global role both as provider of economic assistance to developing countries and, more recently, to Eastern Europe, and as political broker in some Asian matters.[6] Second, the demise of the Cold War has brought economic and social issues to the forefront of global attention. A dubious sign of this is the results of a 1990 poll indicating that most U.S. citizens now seem to feel more threatened by Japanese economic power than by (former) Soviet military power.[7]

Indeed, the changes in communist Europe—like those in China earlier—have been in large measure impelled by economic considerations. Liberalization opens up opportunities for injections of Western financial assistance and for improved trade. Thus, a respected Sovietologist noted in 1989 that a liberalized Soviet Union was aiming to "compete with countries like Taiwan and South Korea in the export of expensive manufactured goods."[8] The comparison with Taiwan and South Korea was opportune because after the oil crisis of the mid-1970s slowed economic growth in the industrial world, the engines of growth of the world economy became the Asian-Pacific countries: first among these is Japan, the country with the largest trade surpluses; second, the East Asian newly industrializing countries (NICs), popularly termed the four "tigers"; and third, some of the countries of Southeast Asia that are also beginning to make their presence felt in what is called the "flying-goose" pattern of development.[9] It is the increasing importance of these countries that enables analysts to propose that the twenty-first century will be a Pacific century, at least as much as a European or, to a lesser degree, a North American one.

Indeed, in the 1970s and 1980s, there were those who predicted a Pacific century—beyond the twentieth—on the basis not only of the importance of the individual countries but also the possible institutionalization of cooperation within the Pacific Basin as a whole. The countries of the Basin include the members of the Association of Southeast Asian Nations (ASEAN)—Brunei, Indonesia, Malaysia, Philippines, Singapore, and Thailand—which are linked in a preferential trading arrangement and also a security community; the industrial nations of Japan, the United States, Canada, Australia, and New Zealand; South Korea, China, Taiwan; the numerous Pacific Island states (Cook Islands, Fiji, Kiribati, Nauru, Niue, Papua New Guinea, Solomon Islands, Tonga, Tuvalu, Vanuatu, Western Samoa); and the Latin America states of Chile, Peru, Ecuador, Colombia, Panama, Costa Rica, Nicaragua, El Salvador, Guatemala, and Mexico. A pact involving this many countries would be a formidable arrangement, whether formalized in a free-trade area or informally constituted for economic and environmental purposes. But the waxing and waning of support for more limited institutionalization shows that true Basin-wide cooperation is still a long way off, even though progress has been made.

The idea of a Pan-Pacific, or Pacific Basin, community was initially put forward by Japanese academics, in particular economist Kiyoshi Kojima, who in 1965 proposed the creation of a Pacific free-trade area. Japanese official interest led to a series of regional conferences, the Pacific Trade and Development Conferences (PAFTAD). PAFTAD conferences on Pacific economic cooperation have been attended by academics, policymakers, and businesspeople.[10]

A parallel development was the formation in 1967 of the Pacific Basin Economic Council (PBEC), which linked business organizations in the five developed Pacific countries. The membership of PBEC soon climbed to sixteen with the addition of a number of developing countries, and the organization has held annual meetings.[11]

As the Asian nations increased their economic strength in the 1970s, governmental interest in Pacific cooperation intensified. The authors of a 1979 U.S. Congressional Research Service report suggested the establishment of an Organization for Pacific Trade and Development

Figure 1.1 Map of the Pacific Basin

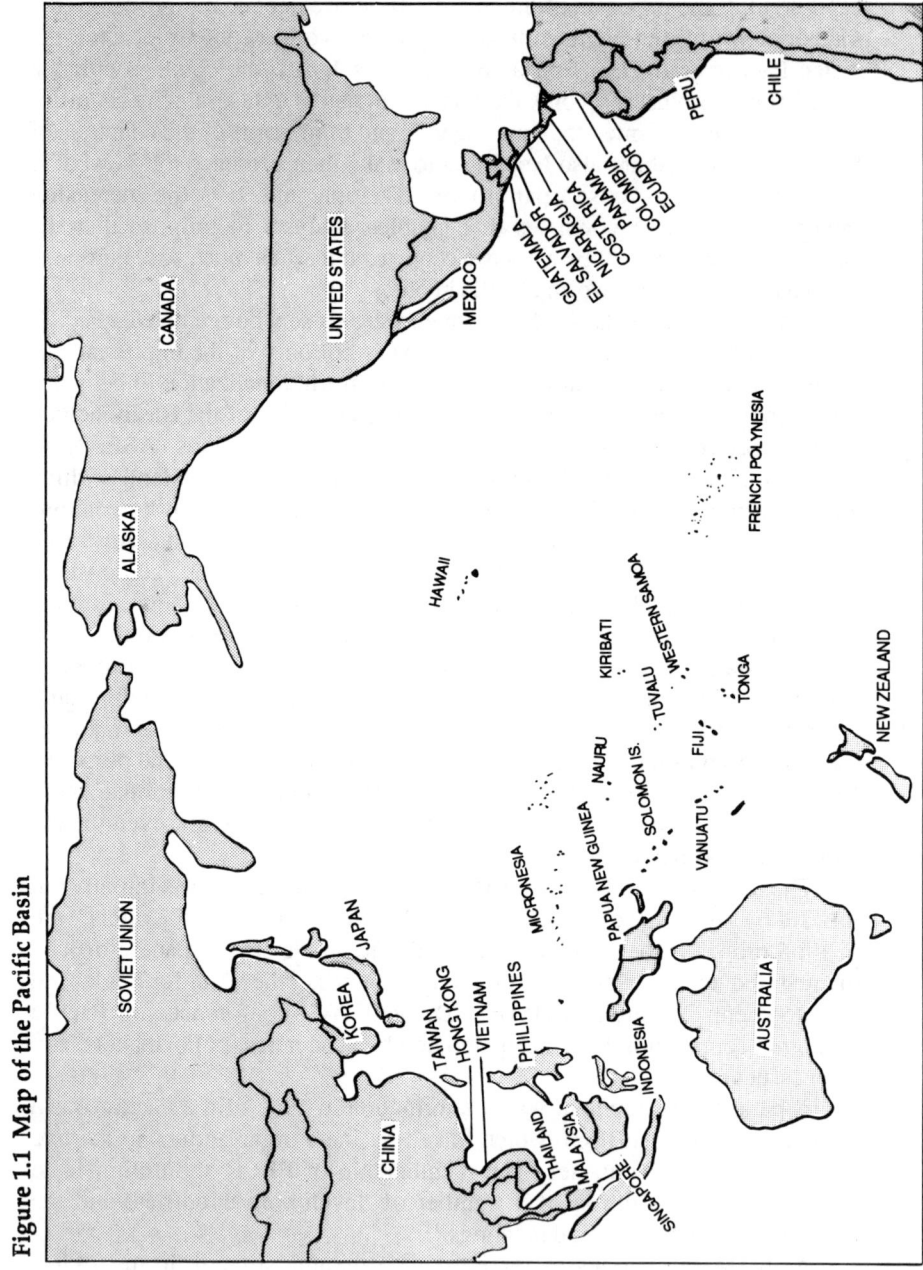

(OPTAD), similar to the Organization for Economic Cooperation and Development (OECD).[12] However, an unofficial U.S. mission sent to Southeast Asia in that year concluded that it would be premature to consider forming a new organization at that time.[13] Meanwhile, Japan's Prime Minister Masayoshi Ohira expressed keen support for Pacific cooperation and set up a task force to study the subject. The task force report strongly endorsed the idea of increased cooperation.[14] In 1980, Australian Prime Minister Malcolm Fraser and Prime Minister Ohira cosponsored a conference in Canberra on Pacific economic cooperation. However, ASEAN delegates at the conference expressed concern that Pacific cooperation would have an adverse impact on ASEAN and would be dominated by Japan and the United States. This reluctance on the part of the developing Asian countries eased in the 1980s as the region grew economically.[15]

In the 1980s, U.S. interest in the Pacific increased for economic and security reasons. President Ronald Reagan remarked in Japan in 1983 that the Basin was "the most exciting region of economic growth in the world today."[16] In 1988, Secretary of State George Shultz suggested in a speech in Jakarta that there should be "some kind of Pacific forum where like-minded countries could compare experiences, discuss ideas and prepare analyses on subjects that are of interest to most countries in the region." He went on to suggest a couple of models for the forum: the economic summit of the Group of Seven industrialized democracies, and the OECD.[17] Japan's Prime Minister Yasuhiro Nakasone approved the idea, as did the Australian and Thai governments. (Thailand and Indonesia have been the ASEAN countries most hospitable to the idea of Pacific cooperation.) However, the concept remained theoretical. When the administration of George Bush came to power, it chose to emphasize the U.S. strategic and economic interest in the Pacific region by sending Vice President Dan Quayle there on one of his first trips abroad. Later in the year (1989), Secretary of State James Baker revived the proposal for the creation of "a new mechanism for multilateral cooperation among the nations of the Pacific Rim," a Pan-Pacific "entity" that would encourage the flow of goods, services, capital, technology, and ideas. The entity might resemble the OECD and would "help, not hinder" other regional groups.[18] In November 1989, twelve Pacific Rim nations, including the United States, met in Australia to move toward launching an economic and trade organization dedicated to improving relations among the free-market economies of the region.

The impetus for the formation of the Asia Pacific Economic Cooperation forum (APEC), which now has thirteen members, was the approaching integration of Europe (1992). In the early 1990s, the Asian states themselves turned their focus to strengthening intraregional integration to counterbalance the creation of Western European and North American megablocs. (The creation of an ASEAN free-trade area was announced in January 1992.) A proposal for the creation of an East Asian trading bloc has been mooted—to the displeasure of the United States, which would be excluded—but remained on the drawing board in early to mid 1992. Historical experience has left the Asian states wary of Japan's dominance, and ASEAN and the NICs want to preserve their competitive edges. It is instructive that ASEAN states, at a 1991 meeting of the new APEC, declared their commitment to further talks on economic integration but also emphasized that they did not want to institutionalize this too quickly.[19]

Cooperation within the broader Basin has its obstacles. The diversity of the region, the reluctance of many Asian states, and the indifference of many Latin American states have in the past militated against institutionalization. However, the United States, Japan, Australia, Canada, Thailand, Indonesia, Colombia, Chile, and Mexico remain enthusiastic about some level of formal Pan-Pacific cooperation. In the new era of the "end" of ideology, the membership of China and the Commonwealth of Independent States in a Pacific body can also be envisaged. Given the rise of economic and social issues on the global agenda, bilateral and multilateral cooperation among Pacific Basin states is likely to be deepened in the 1990s and beyond.

Apart from APEC, a major avenue of Pan-Pacific cooperation has been the nongovernmental Pacific Economic Cooperation Conference (PECC). The PECC grew out of the 1980 Canberra conference mentioned earlier. The name and structure were formalized at the second conference held in Bangkok in June 1982 and later in Vancouver in 1986. PECC has held general meetings about every eighteen months since 1980. The PECC brings together representatives from government, academia, and business. Its membership includes the five Pacific industrialized countries; the six members of ASEAN; South Korea, China, Taiwan (admitted separately as the Chinese Taipei Member Committee); and the Pacific island nations represented by the South Pacific Bureau for Economic Cooperation, an organ of the South Pacific Forum. The Pacific South American nations and the (former) Soviet Union have attended as observers or guests. The PECC's highest decisionmaking body, the Standing Committee, includes representatives from the PBEC and PAFTAD described earlier. Task forces on trade policy, investment, minerals and energy, fisheries, livestock and grains, and a study group are active. It is likely that PECC will continue to institutionalize its activities and perhaps develop over the course of time into a strong regional institution.[20]

Whether or not Pacific Basin cooperation (or just Asian-Pacific cooperation) becomes more institutionalized, the region still promises to be of great global economic significance well into the twenty-first century. Countries bordering the Pacific account for more than 40 percent of the world's output of goods and services, measured by gross national product. The main trading links are between the Japan/NICs/ASEAN group and the United States and among Japan, the NICs, and ASEAN (see Table 1.1). On trans-Pacific linkages, U.S. Secretary of State Baker noted in 1989 that in 1988, U.S.

Table 1.1 Intra-Pacific Exports of Major Pacific Basin Countries/Groups, 1988
($ U.S. billion)

Exporter	U.S.A.	Japan	NICs[a]	ASEAN[b]	Aust./N.Z.	Pacific[c]
U.S.A.	—	37.7[d]	34.9[d]	7.1	7.9	0.3
Japan	90.2[e]	—	26.8[e]	13.1	7.7	5.5
NICs	72.8	27.8	22.1	15.8	5.1	0.3
ASEAN	12.5	16.7	13.8	19.2[f]	1.3	0.06
Australia/ New Zealand	4.7	10.3	6.0	1.9	3.2	1.2
Pacific[g]	0.9	0.7	0.1	0.03	0.2	0.05

Source: International Monetary Fund (IMF), *Direction of Trade Statistics Yearbook 1989* (Washington, D.C.: IMF, 1989).

[a] Newly industrializing countries: Korea, Taiwan, Singapore, and Hong Kong. All data for Taiwan are from partner data (i.e., imports) because of the absence of individual country data in the source (IMF).

[b] Association of Southeast Asian Nations: Brunei, Indonesia, Malaysia, Philippines, and Thailand. Singapore is also a member of ASEAN but is included only in the figures for intra-ASEAN trade. Because it is also a NIC, it is excluded from NIC-ASEAN trade figures.

[c] Includes data on dependent recipient countries.

[d] Total U.S. exports in 1988 were $320.4 billion. Exports to Japan constituted 11.8% of the total, exports to Asian NICs 10.9%.

[e] Total Japanese exports in 1988 were $265 billion. Exports to the United States constituted 34.1% of the total, exports to the Asian NICs 10%.

[f] Includes $9.3 billion in Singapore-ASEAN trade. The figure included for Singapore-Malaysia trade is from import partner data because no export data were recorded in the source.

[g] Export data recorded only for Fiji, New Caledonia, Papua New Guinea, Solomon Islands, Tonga, Vanuatu, and Western Samoa.

trans-Pacific trade "totaled $271 billion. U.S. trade with East Asia has more than doubled since 1982. Eight of our top 20 export markets are now in the Pacific. U.S. investment there, exceeding $33 billion, accounts for 23 percent of all overseas profits earned by U.S. corporations."[21] The figures had increased two years later, but the significance is the same: U.S. economic relations with East Asia are primary. The United States imports more from Japan alone than from the combined EC market.

The strong flow of trade between the Asians and the United States is by no means a balanced one. The United States has since the 1970s been experiencing large deficits in its trade with Japan and the NICs. By the late 1980s, estimates were that the United States would need a $200 billion improvement in trade by the early 1990s to restore balance to its external accounts. Of that amount, $100 billion would come from Japan, $70 billion from West Germany (now unified Germany), and $30 billion from the four Asian NICs.[22] Now that the 1990s are here, the picture is hardly brighter: The U.S. deficit with Japan had been leveling off (it declined in 1990 for the first time in eight years), but in 1991 the trade gap increased 3.7 percent to $43.4 billion or three-quarters of the total U.S. trade deficit.[23] The trade gap between the United States and the NICs also continues to widen. The situation has alarmed the United States, which has turned to pressuring the Asian countries to remove perceived trade and financial barriers that keep U.S. products out of their markets and to reorient their economies toward production for the domestic market. Japan, with the greatest trade surplus, has been pushed to play a more responsible role in the global economy by substantially increasing its aid. Although, as a result of a downturn in the Japanese economy in 1991-1992, Japan's investments abroad shifted out of long-term assets, the imbalance in the flow of Japanese investment has also been the source of U.S. alarm. Japanese direct investment in the United States (1951-1989) amounted to $104.4 billion; U.S. investment in Japan was only $7.9 billion.[24] In part, this disparity is simply attributable to market factors: Most U.S. investment has long been targeted to Europe and Latin America, and Japan is a high-priced market. Also, there is a psychological factor built into the high visibility of Japanese investment in U.S. banking, real estate, and the entertainment industry. But there is also a perception that the Japanese are doing little to remove statutory and other barriers to foreign direct investment.

The focus of the Pacific century, then, is not just on the potential power of a harmonious trans-Pacific community, but more directly on dealing with the problems and opportunities posed by the economic dominance of Japan and the advanced developing countries of Asia. How can countries rectify imbalances with these countries? More to the point, how can countries *profit* from relations with these countries? The response differs depending on whether the country is developed or developing. For the United States and Western Europe, the goal is to restrain imports and control (even while welcoming) investment from Asia and at the same time to attempt to penetrate Asian markets. For developing countries, market penetration is also a goal, but there is less concern about the volume of imports from Asia: Rather, there are benefits perceived to be derived in terms of quality and price of Asian products vis-à-vis other industrial-country imports, and above all, linkages with Asia Pacific are sought as a means of diversifying traditional trading ties. Likewise, Asian aid and investment are desired by capital-poor developing countries, especially because such aid is generally unencumbered by political considerations. Japan is the major target of pleas for economic assistance, and Japanese assistance, traditionally given mainly to Asia, is increasing in significance to other developing regions as the end of the Cold War reduces the assistance available from the United States and the former Soviet Union. In sum, the economic strength of the Asian-Pacific countries has the potential to provide some important opportunities and benefits to developing nations elsewhere.

Overall, then, the importance of the Pacific region in the 1990s and beyond lies in the following considerations: (1) the economic strength and increased global involvement of Japan; (2) the continued economic aggressiveness of the East Asian NICs and the emergence of the ASEAN countries; (3) the dominance of United States–Asia Pacific trade in the world economy; and (4) the future possibilities raised by the prospects of deeper and wider (Asia) Pacific cooperation, especially in a world of megablocs. At the extreme, the creation of a recognizable Pan-Pacific bloc, formalized or not, that embraces a diverse group of countries, including many industrialized and advanced developing countries, would have enormous significance for the global economy.

To these four reasons, it is possible to add a fifth consideration: the political and strategic importance of Pacific Basin countries. One superpower (the United States), a former superpower with residual strategic interests (the Commonwealth of Independent States, formerly the Soviet Union), one economic superpower (Japan) that is increasingly assuming a political role, and a potential superpower (China) all border on the Pacific and have vital security interests in the region. Asia Pacific has been a prime arena of strategic interest and remains politically important even in the post–Cold War environment. Although military-security issues per se are beyond the scope of this book, how Asia Pacific defines and redefines its security options is a matter of some interest here, given the fact that economic dynamism cannot be sustained without adequate security guarantees and a stable, secure environment.

This book explores the implications of the rise of the Asian-Pacific region for policymakers in the Caribbean. At first glance, there may appear to be few links between the Caribbean and Asia Pacific. The Caribbean is geographically distant from Asia Pacific, and there are few historical or cultural ties between the regions, other than those stemming from the presence of a small number of Chinese scattered throughout the Caribbean. But geographical distance has not prevented the development of trade and diplomatic links between the regions. Given the Caribbean countries' need to diversify their economies and exploit varied sources of aid and investment, the relationship between the two regions carries the potential for growth in the 1990s and beyond. Two policy-oriented issues are dealt with here: (1) the advisability of strengthening Caribbean-Pacific links and (2) what the Caribbean can learn from the experience of the Asia Pacific countries. Although the focus of the book is naturally on the dynamic Asian-Pacific region, Part Three includes a comparison of the smaller Caribbean islands with their Pacific counterparts and suggests ways they might work together to prevent their marginalization within the rapidly changing world economic and political environment.

Notes

1. Nicholas X. Rizopoulos, ed., *Sea Changes: American Policy in a World Transformed* (New York: Council on Foreign Relations Press, 1990), p. 1. The

cartoon was drawn by James Borgman.

2. Thomas L. Friedman, "As Ideology Receded, the U.S. Rearranges Its Global Struggles," *New York Times,* December 31, 1989, p. E2.

3. Robert Gilpin, "International Politics in the Pacific Rim Era," in *Annals of the American Academy of Political and Social Science,* special issue "The Pacific Region: Challenges to Policy and Theory," September 1989, p. 57.

4. Bernard K. Gordon, "Wanted: A New Pacific Policy," in Ronald A. Morse, Michael Oksenberg, Bernard K. Gordon, and Mark Borthwick, eds., *Pacific Basin: Concept and Challenge* (Washington, D.C.: Center for National Policy, July 1986), p. 38.

5. The enhancement of the role of the Pacific through economic globalization is discussed by Gilpin, "International Politics," p. 65.

6. See, for example, "Japanese-U.S. Relations Undergoing a Redesign," *New York Times,* June 4, 1990, p. A2; "New Pride Changes Japan's View of U.S.," *New York Times,* June 30, 1988, pp. A1, A9; and "U.S. Asks Japan to Take a Broader Role," *New York Times,* June 27, 1989, pp. D1, D6; "Baker Asks Japan to Broaden Role," *New York Times,* November 12, 1991, pp. A1, A12.

7. *New York Times,* December 31, 1989, p. E2.

8. Jerry F. Hough, "Gorbachev's Agenda for the 90s," *New York Times,* December 3, 1989, p. E11.

9. According to Takashi Inoguchi:

The well-known phrase "flying-goose formation" was invented by Kaname Akamatsu to characterize the development pattern of East and Southeast Asia. Like flying geese forming a triangular pattern headed by their leader, Pacific Asian development is spearheaded by Japan, which is followed by the Asian newly industrializing countries (NICs) . . . and now is followed increasingly by some other countries of the Association of Southeast Asian Nations (ASEAN), and, to a far lesser degree, China, Vietnam, North Korea, and the Soviet Union.

Inoguchi notes that the pattern of development is export-led and that the open market of the United States is indispensable to this pattern of development. Moreover, there are two other mechanisms of this development pattern: "(1) the success of the early starters in Pacific Asia has been emulated selectively to accelerate the late-comers' catch-up process; and (2) the gradually lost competitiveness of the early starters in some sectors enables latecomers to rise through the former's shift of production site from home to the latter." See Inoguchi, "Shaping and Sharing Pacific Dynamism," in *Annals of the American Academy of Political and Social Science,* September 1989, p. 48.

10. Michael West Oborne and Nicolas Fourt, *Pacific Basin Economic Cooperation* (Paris: Development Centre of the Organization for Economic Cooperation and Development [OECD], 1983), pp. 7–8; also Kumao Kaneko, "A New Pacific Initiative: Strengthening the PECC Process," *Japan Review of International Affairs* 2, 1 (Spring/Summer 1988): 69.

11. Kaneko, "New Pacific Initiative," p. 71.

12. Hugh Patrick and Peter Drysdale for the Congressional Research Service, Library of Congress, *An Asian-Pacific Regional Economic Organization: An Exploratory Concept Paper,* prepared for the Subcommittee on East Asian and Pacific Affairs of the Committee on Foreign Relations, U.S. Senate. (Washington, D.C.: Government Printing Office, 1979).

13. Oborne and Fourt, *Pacific Basin,* p. 10.

14. Ibid., p. 11.

15. Kaneko, "New Pacific Initiative," pp. 71–72.
16. Ibid., p. 72.
17. *Japan Times*, July 18, 1988, p. 17.
18. *New York Times*, June 27, 1989, pp. D1, D6.
19. *New York Times*, February 16, 1990, p. D2; July 25, 1991, p. A14.
20. Kaneko, "New Pacific Initiative," p. 84; see pp. 67–90 for details of PECC's activities.
21. *New York Times*, June 27, 1989; p. D6.
22. *New York Times*, November 27, 1987, p. D3. However, I hasten to point out that the benefits of trade and investment flows are not as one-sided as many perceive them to be. See, for example, Gordon, "Wanted: A New Pacific Policy," pp. 38–39.
23. *New York Times*, January 22, 1992, p. D4; July 9, 1992: D13.
24. Japan External Trade Organization (JETRO), *Nippon: Business Facts and Figures 1991* (Tokyo: JETRO, 1991), pp. 76, 108. Figures for U.S. investment in Japan are for 1950–1989.

2

Asia Pacific: Intraregional Relations

Jacqueline A. Braveboy-Wagner

The two primary geographical foci of this book are, on the one hand, the fast-growing Asian-Pacific region and, on the other, the English-speaking Caribbean. However, for reasons elaborated in the next chapter, a broader concept of the Caribbean is employed in the first part of the book, and in Part Three, the analysis turns to the smaller Pacific island nations, which share certain national attributes with the small Caribbean nations. Here it bears repeating the two questions addressed in the book—questions that, we hope, are policy-relevant: How can the Caribbean strengthen ties with the Asian-Pacific region in such a way as to reap some benefits from Asian dynamism? And second, can the Caribbean learn anything from the development experiences of the Asian-Pacific countries? Before considering these issues, we make the assumption that Caribbean-region specialists, whether scholars or policymakers, would be relatively unfamiliar with Asia Pacific (see Table 2.1 for basic data), and that Asian-Pacific specialists might have an interest but lack enough information about the geographically distant Caribbean region. Therefore, this chapter and the next are devoted to brief descriptions of the countries and regions under study and their interrelations.

The Asian-Pacific Region

As discussed in the previous chapter, the dynamism of the Pacific Rim comes primarily from the increased economic strength of first, Japan, then the newly industrializing countries, or NICs, and, as development expands outward in the flying-goose pattern with Japan as leader, the growing strength of the ASEAN countries (except Brunei, which is, as will be seen, in a very different position.) The concentration on Japan, East Asia,

Table 2.1 Basic Data, Independent Asian-Pacific Countries

Country	Area (thousands of square km.)	Population (millions, 1990 est.)	GNP per capita ($ U.S. 1988)
Japan	378	123.5	21,020
East Asian NICs			
Korea, Rep. of	99	42.8	3,600
Hong Kong	1	5.9	9,220
Singapore	.58	2.7	9,070
Taiwan	36	20.4	6,280
ASEAN members			
Indonesia	1,905	184.3	440
Brunei	6	.241	15,390
Malaysia	330	17.9	1,940
Philippines	300	62.4	630
Thailand	513	55.7	1,000

Sources: World Bank, *World Development Report 1990* (New York: Oxford University Press, 1990), pp. 178–179, 243; United Nations Development Program (UNDP), *Human Development Report 1991* (New York: Oxford University Press, 1991), pp. 152, 160–161; "Taiwan," *Financial Times Survey,* October 10, 1989, p. 1; Keizai Koho Center, *Japan: An International Comparison 1990* (Tokyo: Japan Institute for Social and Economic Affairs, 1990), p. 16.

and Southeast Asia in this analysis of the Pacific Rim in no way is intended to downplay the importance of North America, Australia, and New Zealand within the region. China, Vietnam, Cambodia, Laos, and Russia each can also claim to play important roles in Asia and the Pacific. But up to this point, their roles have been primarily in the security arena, within a Cold War context that is now being redefined. Nevertheless, it is generally accepted that the growth of East and Southeast Asia has had a tremendous impact on the global economy and that the Pacific Rim has become prominent precisely because of the major role that trans-Pacific and intra-Pacific trade plays in the world economy.

Japan

Japan has become the central player in the Pacific region, the world's premier economic player, and one of the seven main actors in global economic affairs. This archipelagic state comprises 3,922 islands, including four main inhabited ones. Its total land mass is 378,000 square kilometers (about 145,000 square miles) and its population an estimated 123.5 million (1990). Its per capita gross national product (GNP) as of 1988 was $21,020, higher than in all the industrial countries except Switzerland and Luxembourg.[1]

Japan was closed to the world until 1853 when the American Commodore Matthew Perry arrived in his Black Ships and forced the country to trade with the West.² From the middle of the seventeenth century, the Tokugawa clan had presided over a feudal society and prohibited international intercourse under pain of death. In 1868, rebellious southern clans "restored" the emperor (Meiji) and ushered in an era of rapid modernization: commercialization, industrialization, and Westernization. But the prevailing theme of *fukoku kyohei* (rich nation, strong army) led to various military adventures in Asia: annexation of Okinawa; conquest of Formosa, Korea, Manchuria, and Southeast Asia; and eventually World War II.³ After the war, the United States helped to rebuild Japan, prohibiting it from reestablishing an army, instituting political democracy in the form of a British-style government with U.S.-style legislative committees, and promoting social and economic democracy through educational reforms, land reform, and breakup of the business monopolies (*zaibatsu*). The Japanese concentrated on reviving and improving their industrial structure, primarily using capital generated from within the country. A finely tuned cooperation, dating from Meiji times, emerged among government (in the form of the Liberal Democratic Party, which has ruled continuously since 1948 despite being at the center of various scandals), big business (which supported the government in return for favors), and bureaucrats who managed the economy. In particular, the Ministry of Trade and Industry (MITI) gave "administrative guidance" to industries and enterprises, protecting and promoting them by tariffs, cheap bank loans, and tax exemptions.⁴ In view of this cooperative structure, which by all indicators is less obvious today, Japan has often been dubbed "Japan, Inc.," a term suggesting that the country can be viewed as one giant corporation.⁵

The Japanese economy has flourished as an export economy that has profited especially from the postwar U.S. Open Door policies. The strategy the Japanese used was to buy technology from abroad, copy and adapt it, and then produce their own highly price-competitive goods. The steel, auto, and electronic industries became particularly important. Large trading companies (*soga shosha*) controlled much of the economy and also expanded abroad. Moreover, the *keiretsu* system facilitated long-term relationships between Japanese companies and their suppliers.

Japanese economic growth averaged about 10 percent a year up to the 1970s, but the oil crisis of 1973, along with market saturation, production fatigue, and protectionism in developed-country markets, slowed growth in the late 1970s and 1980s to 3–5 percent.⁶ The real growth rate averaged 4.5 percent for the period 1984–1988; the growth rates for 1988, 1989, and 1990 were 6.2 percent, 4.7 percent, and 5.6 percent respectively.⁷ Japan's growth rate is well below the growth rates experienced by the Asian NICs. Whereas the postwar Japanese economy has traditionally been fueled by growth in both domestic and external demand, recent figures show negative growth in external demand. Nevertheless, the decline in the value of the dollar and the proportional appreciation of the yen have made Japan the strongest economy (and second largest) in the world today. Unprecedented surpluses were experienced in current accounts in the period 1986–1988 ($86 billion, $87 billion, and $79.6 billion respectively), and there was increased international pressure on Japan to reduce these by freeing trade. Helped by a boom in overseas travel and efforts to increase imports, these surpluses were reduced in the next few years to a surplus of $35.8 billion in 1990. The trend, however, was reversed in 1991 and 1992: In 1991 declining imports, increased exports to Europe and Asia, and reduced travel stemming from the Gulf crisis helped push up the current account surplus once again. The surplus with the United States alone was $40 billion, up 6.3 percent from 1990, and with the European Community $25 billion, quadruple the 1990 figure. The balance-of-trade surplus rose 60 percent to a record $103 billion in 1991 and was expected to be more than $135 billion in 1992.[8] Notably, a Japan Finance Ministry advisory group report in 1990 advised the ministry that surpluses not be reduced but maintained at a moderate level and used to attract private investment to developing countries and Eastern Europe.[9]

The rise in international pressure on Japan to reduce and recycle its surpluses has led Japan to take steps to liberalize its economy and increase the quantity and quality of its official development assistance (ODA), as discussed in more detail in Chapter 4. As a result of increases in aid, Japan became the world's largest donor in 1990, but the United States regained first position in 1991. (Japan experienced an economic decline as oil prices rose at the end of 1990.) Nevertheless, the country remains the world's largest donor, when private and non-ODA official flows are taken into account.

The Asian NICs

The world has been surprised by the resilience and dynamism of the economies of the four East Asian newly industrializing countries of South Korea, Taiwan, Singapore, and Hong Kong—indeed, so that these four are now commonly termed the East Asian "tigers" or "dragons." These countries experienced growth rates of 8–10 percent in the 1960s and 1970s and even now are growing at a rate faster than Japan: The average annual GDP growth rate (real) for the period 1984–1988 was 4.5 percent for Japan, but it was 10.5 percent for South Korea, 8.4 percent for Hong Kong, 8.9 percent for Taiwan, and 5.0 percent for Singapore.[10] Although exports grew by 14.6 percent for Japan between 1987 and 1988, they grew by 28.3 percent for Korea, 30.3 percent for Hong Kong, and 37 percent for Singapore in the same period. Taiwan registered a lower growth rate (13 percent), but at the same time also registered a trade surplus of nearly $20 billion, the third largest after Japan and West Germany.[11] (In the 1988–1990 period, Japan's export growth rate declined to below 5 percent, Korea's stabilized, Taiwan's grew only slightly, and the other NICs reduced their growth rates by half.)[12]

The Asian NICs have in common an export orientation and an industrial structure that began as import-substitution industrialization (ISI). Except for Hong Kong, they have successfully moved into heavy industry and electronics. The agricultural nations, Korea and Taiwan, like Japan, adopted land reform programs and subsidized agriculture. The NICs, however, have differed in terms of the openness of their economies and the level of involvement of the state in the economy. Specific current aspects of their development model are elaborated in Chapter 5, but a brief overview of their economic history is warranted here.[13]

Korea. Forty years ago, South Korea (Korea) was overwhelmingly agricultural and per capita income was $350. Today Korea's GNP per capita is $3,600 (1988) and agriculture contributes only 11 percent to GDP.[14]

Korea was a feudal society with strong Confucian traditions, and although the object of invasions from China and Japan, the society remained isolated into the nineteenth century. As happened in Japan and China, the Western powers forced the opening up of Korea and vied for influence there. However, Japan established its domination of Korea by first defeating the Chinese in 1894 and then the Russians in 1905. Japan then established a protectorate over Korea and annexed that country in 1910. Japanese colonization continued through to World War II when Korea came under Soviet and U.S. occupation. The Korean War of 1950 led to the formalization of the division between North and South Korea.

South Korea entered the 1950s as a largely rice-producing country. Its land mass was now condensed to 99,000 square kilometers (38,000 square miles), and its population was 20 million. (In 1990, it was 42.8 million.) Reunification with Korea was the primary goal in the 1950s, but in the 1960s the government of Park Chung Hee embarked on an ambitious economic program. The state played a large role in planning and supporting industrial growth and entrepreneurship even while increasing social expenditures despite the need to maintain a high military budget. Foreign investment was restricted and directed mainly to economic processing zones (EPZs), but foreign aid was welcomed.

South Korea industrialized through use of ISI, which led later to export promotion. Industrialization took place first in light manufacturing and then such heavy industries as shipbuilding, iron and steel, and automotive and electronics manufacturing.

The success of South Korea has usually been attributed to careful planning and state involvement (though state intervention did not always produce efficient outcomes)[15] and the willingness of Western, particularly U.S., markets at that time to absorb Asian exports. State control was facilitated by the authoritarian political structure, but presidential control was eased during the Chun Doo-Hwan administration, and some liberalization of the economy is occurring in the early 1990s in line with the limited liberalization of the polity.

Taiwan. Portuguese explorers called this island Formosa (meaning "beautiful") in 1590. The underdeveloped island became a trading center under the Dutch, was incorporated into China in 1683, and was finally ceded to the Japanese in 1895. The Japanese introduced sugar and rice cultivation and improved the infrastructure, but this regime was typical colonial government with little native participation and an economy geared only toward the needs of the colonial power. Japan withdrew after the Pacific war, and Taiwan became the home of the Nationalist Chinese government, which was defeated by the communists in 1949.

Taiwan has an area of 36,000 square kilometers (about 13,900 square miles) and a population of 20 million. Its per capita income has risen rapidly from slightly less that $5,000 in 1987 to $6,280 in 1988, $7,500 in the late 1980s, and more than $8,000 in the early 1990s.[16] Just as Korea was truncated by ideology, Taiwan—which until recently could be viewed as a "colonized" nation—became part of a battle between communists and anticommunists that forced it to maintain a high military budget. In the 1950s, security was a prime concern, and U.S. economic and military assistance was crucial. During this period, planning was introduced and agriculture was used to subsidize industrialization. Later, the economy flourished through encouragement of entrepreneurship small and large (native Taiwanese as well as Chinese, especially overseas Chinese); government efforts to attract foreign investment, especially through creation of EPZs (although foreign loans have been kept to a minimum); protection of infant industries in the import-substitution phase; land reform and changes in agricultural production to induce self-sufficiency; and adoption of export promotion as the official policy in the early 1960s. As one writer notes, the top exports throughout the period were just an extension of earlier import substitutes: textiles, garments, footwear, toys, and so on. "Only electrical apparatus showed a striking transformation as electronics were added and gave it a momentum that would eventually make the sector the second biggest export earner."[17] Eventually, the government also targeted some heavy industrial sectors: steel, shipbuilding, petrochemicals, and automobiles. These efforts have met with varying degrees of success. More recently, Taiwan has been trying to shift to high-technology products because of increased competition and higher wages in the traditionally low-technology areas.[18]

Among the NICs, Taiwan has been the most aggressive trader, posting a $19 billion trade surplus in 1987. With practically no debt, Taiwan has accumulated reserves that are second only to Japan's, more than $75 billion by 1989.[19] This situation has made Taiwan the target of complaints and pressure from Western countries, in particular the United States, which complains that Taiwan and the other NICs are gaining unusual trade advantages by holding down the value of their currencies.[20]

There has been some liberalization of Taiwan's political system because most of the life members of the legislature—those who came over from mainland China—have died, leaving room for elected members. The death of President Chiang Ching-kuo (Chiang Kai-shek's son) in 1988 paved the way for the election of a native Taiwanese president, Lee Teng-hui. In 1991, the first open elections were held to choose members of the legislature, who are expected to draft a new constitution in 1992. This constitution will replace the old one that endorses Taiwan's sovereignty over all of China. In December 1992, the liberalization process will be completed by the holding of elections for the full legislature. Meanwhile, relations with mainland China improved in the 1980s, but were set back by China's repression of its democracy movement in June 1989.

Singapore. Singapore and Hong Kong differ from the other NICs by virtue of their small size, entrepôt status, lack of an agricultural base, and more limited government role in the economy (amounting to laissez-faire in the case of Hong Kong).

After 1814, the British-Dutch rivalry in the East Indies was resolved by British acquisition of the Malay peninsula and North Borneo. Singapore, which was relatively uninhabited, was occupied in 1819 and quickly became a successful trading post, port of call, and the center of government of the British Straits settlement, which included Malacca, Penang, and a strip of territory in the Malay peninsula called Province Wellesley.[21]

Singapore's growth was stymied by the Japanese occupation of 1942–1945, and although the British returned after the war, they were preoccupied with communist and nationalist activity in Malaya. The Malayan Federation gained its independence in 1957. Singapore joined the federation in 1963, but was ejected two years later because of Malayan fears of Chinese domination. Singapore's population had been augmented in the nineteenth century by large numbers of immigrants from southeast China seeking commercial opportunities. In 1965, Singapore became an independent city-state.

Singapore has an area of 580 square kilometers (about 224 square miles) and a 1990 population of 2.7 million. (Some sources attribute to Singapore a land area of 618 square kilometers.) Its per capita GNP in 1988 was $9,070, according to World Bank figures. Among the NICs, Singapore is the most dependent on foreign trade: On an index of dependency measured by dividing trade values by GNP, Singapore was 139.3 percent dependent on exports and 158.1 percent dependent on imports in 1987/1988; comparable export/import dependency figures for Korea were 39.9 percent and 34.6 percent; for Hong Kong, 51.1 percent and 117.2 percent; for Taiwan, 55.3 percent and 35.7 percent.[22]

According to Jon Woronoff, Singapore's lack of an agricultural hinterland impelled it toward manufacturing from the start. And given a limited local market and expulsion from the ISI-oriented market of the Federation of Malaysia, Singapore had little choice but to turn to export promotion.[23] Because of the large population (for its size), manufacturing was initially labor-intensive, and infant industries were protected. But the economy was liberalized as Singapore entered the export-promotion phase. Singapore's entrepreneurs were primarily oriented toward trade and not manufactures, and foreign entrepreneurship thus took on an important role. Of the four NICs, Singapore made the most effort to attract multinational investment.[24] However, foreign aid was deliberately limited.

State planning was important in Singapore (as it was in Taiwan and South Korea), but was directed more toward improving the infrastructure and attracting investors and less toward forceful economic intervention. In the 1970s, Singapore moved into capital-intensive industry and eventually into high-tech production, which is now being vigorously promoted. Singapore's industries came to include a wide range: shipbuilding, petroleum refining, electronics, construction, tourism, and financial and business services.

Singapore's political system, dominated since preindependence days by the People's Action Party (PAP), became increasingly rigid in the 1980s. In earlier days (1960s), there was internal dissension between left-wing and moderate segments of the PAP, but the left-wing threat has long since dissipated. Some external threat is perceived from China and Vietnam, but the security apparatus has in the main been mobilized to keep the government (and the Chinese majority) in absolute control. Until 1990, PAP was headed by Lee Kuan Yew, prime minister since independence. Lee voluntarily stepped down in late 1990, paving the way for his handpicked successor, Goh Chok Tong, but Lee has maintained a strong voice in government. The PAP dominates parliament.

Hong Kong. Hong Kong Island was acquired by the British after the first Opium War. The Chinese ceded the island in perpetuity to Britain. In 1860 after the second Opium War, Kowloon Peninsula and Stonecutters Island were added, and in 1898 the New Territories, including the 235 outlying islands, were leased to Britain for 99 years. This lease expires in 1997, and Britain has agreed to transfer the entire territory to China. Hong Kong has an area of just over 1,000 square kilometers (about 380 square miles) and a population of 5.9 million (1990). Its per capita GNP was $9,220 in the latest year available, 1988.[25]

Like Singapore, Hong Kong Island was relatively uninhabited in 1841. The British transformed it into an important entrepôt, and the population grew rapidly by the turn of the century. Successive waves of Chinese immigrants further augmented the population between 1911 and 1950. When the entrepôt trade, geared toward China, declined after the communist takeover in China, resourceless Hong Kong turned to manufacturing. Given the large population, manufacturing was labor-intensive light industry. Entrepreneurs, the vase majority of them small-scale, came not only from local sources but from the refugee pool and, later, from Europe, the United States, or the Chinese diaspora. Later, U.S., European, and Japanese multinationals, attracted by Hong Kong's cheap labor and low taxes, set up offshore facilities.[26] Foreign investment and loans, however, have been limited.

Basically, Hong Kong has retained its focus on light industry. Its factories produce everything from textiles and garments to toys. Electronics became important in the 1970s, tourism has also been a strong income earner, and there is some heavy industry (shipbuilding, cement, and plastics).[27]

As a colony of Britain, Hong Kong is distinguished from the other NICs by the low level of government intervention in the economy. In fact, the government's role has been simply to provide the infrastructure for development. The biggest problem for Hong Kong at the moment is insecurity about its political future. Although China has guaranteed that there will be few economic changes for a least fifty years after 1997, Hong Kong residents are somewhat skeptical, and they are emigrating at the rate of 1,000 people a week, leaving for Canada, Australia, New Zealand, and the United States.[28]

ASEAN

The Association of Southeast Asian Nations (ASEAN) was formed in 1967 at a time of political transition and tension in the region. A change in government had brought an end to Indonesia's policy of "confrontation" with neighboring Malaysia (perceived as a threat by President Sukarno), but war was raging in Vietnam, and there were fears, at least in Indonesia and Malaysia, of destabilization by insurgents backed by China. ASEAN was intended to promote regional economic and social self-reliance but most of all, political coordination in the face of security threats.[29]

Over the years, especially after the U.S. withdrawal from Vietnam, ASEAN has become an important and vibrant political grouping, but it has been far less successful in economic integration: Regionalism has taken a backseat to strong national economic policies, although changes in the global economy in the 1990s have created an impetus toward stronger integration. In any event, ASEAN has created a climate of stability and cooperation that has allowed its members to enjoy high economic growth rates.[30] Member states have also benefited from the successes of Japan and the East Asian NICs.

The six members of ASEAN are Indonesia, Malaysia, Singapore, Thailand, Philippines, and Brunei (since 1984). Singapore, one of the four East Asian dragons has already been profiled. Brief descriptions of the other members follow:

Indonesia, the largest country in the group, has an area of 1,905,000 square kilometers (about 735,500 square miles) and a population (1990) of 184.3 million. By virtue of its size and historical prestige, as the Dutch East Indies, Indonesia has played a major role in the Asian region. Like Japan, it is an archipelagic state, with five main islands—Java, Sumatra, Borneo, Celebes, and Irian Jaya (Western New Guinea)—and about 13,600 smaller islands. The heart of the Dutch empire in the East Indies, Indonesia was taken over in 1942 by the Japanese. The Dutch tried to return to the islands after World War II, and the resulting civil war lasted four years. In 1949, the Dutch finally recognized Indonesia but retained a weak link under the Netherlands Indonesian Union until 1954. The first two decades of Indonesian independence were troubled ones: Communal (religious, ethnic, and regional) and ideological rivalries led to great internal instability in the 1950s. In the 1960s, the growing influence of the communists and the alienation of Islamic nationalists created further civil unrest. Moreover, in response to the creation of the Federation of Malaysia, Indonesia launched the *konfrontasi,* a policy of confrontation that led to armed conflict with Malaysia and Indonesia's announced withdrawal from the United Nations. All of this ended when the army gained the upper hand in Indonesia after an attempted coup in 1965 in which, interestingly, President Sukarno may have had a hand. The army (and Moslem elements) brutally purged the communists, and Sukarno's powers were whittled away until General Suharto took over the presidency in 1967.

Economic growth was hardly possible for Indonesia, or indeed for the region, during this turbulent time. Indonesia was primarily an agricultural country, although manufacturing, begun before World War II, by the 1960s included shipping, textiles, paper, construction, and rubber and chemical industries. But the Indonesian economy came to revolve around petroleum, which now accounts for the bulk of exports. Indonesia benefited handsomely from the increases in oil prices of the 1970s and, with the decline in these, has moved strongly into natural gas production. Nevertheless, with its huge population, most of it still concentrated (despite government efforts) on Java,[31] its reduced but still relatively high level of rural poverty,[32] and the lack of adequate infrastructure, Indonesia is the poorest ASEAN country with a per capita income of only $440 in 1988. With the growth of manufacturing and services, the economy continues to expand, but the decline in oil prices in the 1980s reduced the real growth rate from 8 percent in the 1970s to about 5 percent in the 1980s.[33] Still, Indonesia is attracting large-scale Japanese investment and integrating its economy with the other more dynamic economies of the region.

Indonesia's neighbor Malaysia is much smaller (330,000 square kilometers, or about 127,000 square miles, and 17.9 million people) and wealthier (per capita income $1,940 in 1988.) A federation of former British colonies—the Malay States, the Straits Settlements except Singapore, and the Bornean territories of Sarawak and Sabah—Malaysia, like the other Southeast Asian states, was occupied by Japan during World War II but was quickly returned to the British after the war. It gained its independence in 1957 as the Federation of Malaya before expanding to become Malaysia with the addition of the Bornean states in 1963. (Singapore also joined the federation at that time but was forced to leave in 1965.) Malaysia is the world's largest exporter of natural rubber, palm oil, and tin, and in the last two decades has experienced rapid growth in the manufacturing sector and in services. Like its neighbor Thailand, Malaysia has been one of the main beneficiaries of Japan/East Asian successes as advanced countries shift production to Malaysia and Thailand where labor costs are lower. Both countries are therefore moving into high-tech areas while also developing their own industry, notably the auto industry in Malaysia. In terms of exports, however, Malaysia remains dependent on a few primary products.

Thailand, in contrast, exports a more diversified range of products. The only Southeast Asian country to escape Western colonial control, Thailand also escaped Japanese occupation by collaborating with the Japanese and then cutting off ties just as Japan began to suffer losses. With a population of 55.7 million and an area of 513,000 square kilometers (about 199,000 square miles), Thailand has been experiencing an economic boom. Its economy grew by 8.4 percent in the 1960s, 7.1 percent in the 1970s, and 6 percent between 1980 and 1988.[34] The growth rate was particularly high in the late 1980s—11 percent for 1988 and estimated double-digit growth for 1989 and 1990, although the increase in oil prices in late 1990 had an adverse effect on growth that year.[35] Per capita income for 1988, the latest year available, was $1,000. As in the other ASEAN countries, agriculture, once the dominant contributor to GDP, now accounts for only 17 percent, whereas industry has climbed to a 35 percent share and services to 48 percent.[36] Thailand is the world's largest rice exporter, but its exports also include industrial raw materials, textiles, and a range of manufactures that, with increasing Japanese investment, are moving upscale into the more advanced technological areas. Computer chips are now the fourth largest manufactured export.[37]

The only stagnant economy among the ASEAN countries has been that of the Philippines. This economy has always been the weakest among ASEAN members, growing by 5.1 percent in the 1960s and 6 percent in the 1970s before experiencing negative or little growth in the 1980s. (The 1980–1988 growth rate, according to the World Bank, was 0.1 percent.)[38] The economic decline can be traced to political instability and to the decline in world prices for the country's traditional exports (sugar, copra, and bananas). The Philippines, a former U.S. colony that was occupied by the Japanese and was then given its independence in 1946, covers an area of 300,000 square kilometers (about 115,800 square miles) stretched across 7,000 islands. Its population of 62.4 million exceeds Thailand's, but its per capita income is only $630 (1988). The Philippines is the most industrialized ASEAN country after Singapore (in terms of the share of manufacturing in GDP), with manufactures ranging from light industry, including garments, to electronics. However, manufacturing exports have not made up for the loss of revenues from agricultural exports, and the Philippines has become heavily dependent on foreign loans, particularly from the United States. As noted, a major problem for the Philippines in recent times has been political instability: Large-scale civil unrest preceded the removal of the dictator Ferdinand Marcos; his successor, Corazon Aquino, survived six coup attempts during her tenure, and her administration was viewed as indecisive and ineffective, and even corrupt.[39] Under Aquino, the Philippines increased its dependence on U.S. military and economic assistance, itself a source of criticism of the regime. A successor to Aquino, Fidel Ramos, was elected in free elections held in 1992. Nevertheless, given the country's continuing economic and social problems, and also the unresolved Muslim and communist insurgencies in some regions, little economic growth was predicted for the early to mid-1990s.

The political picture in Indonesia, Malaysia, and Thailand is rosier but there are problems. Indonesia's General Suharto and Malaysia's Mahathir Mohammed have been dealing harshly with political opponents and are particularly wary of the rise of Islamic fundamentalism. Thailand has faced external security threats from Kampuchea (Cambodia) and from Muslim separatists within the country. The traditionally military-dominated country—which has had seventeen coups since the end of the absolute monarchy in 1932—has been democratizing, and an elected prime minister took office in 1989 for the first time in twelve years. However, the coalition government rested on relatively precarious foundations and was crisis-prone: At the end of 1990, the prime minister resigned after the military accused his government of corruption, only to return a day later to form a new coalition government. In February 1991, the government was overthrown once again by the Thai military. A year later general elections brought to power a coalition of pro-military parties that put in power the unpopular supreme commander of the military. Violent pro-democracy protests then paved the way for an interim administration committed to redefining the role of the military in Thai politics, and new elections in 1992 brought a nonmilitary coalition to power.

All ASEAN countries, and Thailand in particular, are also suffering the social costs of rapid development: urbanization, environmental degradation, and health problems, among others. (As elaborated in Chapter 5, the NICs have also experienced similar problems.) Governments are only just beginning to recognize and tackle these issues.

The sixth member of ASEAN, Brunei, is quite different from the others. It is a sultanate that became a British protectorate in 1888 after losing much of its territory to British interests. Brunei gained its independence on January 1, 1984, and joined ASEAN one week later. (The country had held observer status in the organization since 1981.) Brunei is small (6,000 square kilometers, or 2,227 square miles, and 241,000 people) and wealthy (per capita income $15,390 in 1988), and its economy is dominated by production and export of oil and natural gas, with some diversification into silica exploitation.[40]

Japan, the NICs, and ASEAN

Although there is no formal integration movement encompassing all the countries described, there is an informal relationship of community, and the level of interaction, both political and economic, is relatively high and increasing.

Southeast Asia is Japan's second most important trade focus after the United States; in fact, imports from the region have traditionally exceeded imports from the United States. In 1990, Japan's exports to the United States were valued at $90.3 billion and imports at $52.3 billion; the corresponding figures for Southeast Asian trade were $88.8 billion and $66.6 billion respectively.[41] It should also be noted that Japan's exports to Southeast Asia were on a par in value with those to the United States in the 1970s, although the gap has grown considerably since 1985. Recent evidence indicates that Japan is making up for slower export growth in the United States by expanding its trade with Asia as well as Europe.[42]

A breakdown of figures available for 1990 shows that of the $89.8 billion in exports to Southeast Asia in that year, Japan exported $56.7 billion to the Asian NICs, and of the $66.6 billion in imports from Southeast Asia, $25.9 billion came from the NICs.[43]

Investment and aid figures are also instructive as a way to emphasize the close ties between Japan and certain countries in Asia. The United States is by far the largest recipient of investment from Japan (42.9 percent of total investment 1951–1989), and Asia's share has been declining over the years. Asia accounts for 15.9 percent of total Japanese investment (compare Europe, 17.1 percent; Latin America, 14.5 percent). But of the Asian investment, 11 percent is in Indonesia, Hong Kong, Singapore, and Korea combined. The countries are listed in descending order of investment importance, with Indonesia the largest recipient (4.1 percent). Other Asian countries listed as recipients of aid through 1989 are Thailand, China, Malaysia, Taiwan, and the Philippines.[44]

Finally, Asia as a whole and Southeast Asia in particular have traditionally been the major recipients of Japanese Official Development Assistance (ODA). Aid began in the postwar period as reparations, generally paid as capital goods, and was stepped up in the 1960s and 1970s. Initially, over 90 percent of ODA went to Asia, and half of that to Southeast Asia, but in the 1970s there was a sharp increase in aid to the Middle East that reduced the share for Asia to 60 percent. The share for 1988 was 62.8 percent, for Southeast Asia 34.2 percent, and for ASEAN 29.9 percent; (put another way, 54.5 percent of Asian aid went to Southeast Asia, and 87.4 percent of that to ASEAN).[45] Indonesia, China, Philippines, and Thailand have been the major recipients of Japanese aid in the last few years. At the multilateral level, Japan is a major contributor to the Asian Development Bank and as the second largest contributor to the World Bank, is influencing that agency's decisions with respect to Asia.

Available data show that in 1988 Japan was the major trading partner (exports and imports) for Indonesia and the second major partner for China and the Philippines. Hong Kong, Korea, Singapore, and Malaysia also ranked Japan in their top three partners for both exports and imports.[46] The economic relationship between Japan and industrializing Asia is no longer based on the exploitation of natural resources and cheap labor. As one analyst notes, the Japanese "are moving to a new level of sophistication by transforming the region into a manufacturing base with the flexibility to switch among different plants and to alter products quickly to meet shifts in consumer demand. In doing so, the companies are also cultivating budding markets for advanced goods."[47] In essence, Japan is turning strongly to joint investment in high-tech fields in the low-cost labor countries of Asia in order to establish a presence in these fast-growing markets. For the Asians, Japanese investment is welcome as a means to acquire advanced technology: Japan once guarded its technological advantage closely, but is now somewhat more willing to transfer technology in order to preserve its investment edge.

From the 1970s into the 1990s, the industrializing Asians have, in fact, become more appreciative of Japan. The prevailing postwar sentiment was one of distrust of the power that forced on them a "Greater Asian Co-Prosperity Sphere" and brutally established its domination during the Pacific war. Later, in the 1970s, resentment of the growing Japanese economic presence led to riots during the visit of Prime Minister Kakuei Tanaka in 1974. But when Prime Minister Takeo Fukuda launched a new era of "heart-to-heart" diplomacy in the late 1970s that was accompanied by extensive aid commitments, he was well received in Southeast Asia. In the 1980s and 1990s, despite lingering wariness, the Asians have adopted a conscious policy of "looking East," a policy inaugurated by Lee Kuan Yew and elaborated by Malaysia's prime minister as follows:

> In the past we looked to the West to get new knowledge, to learn about technology, about the methods of production, even systems. This was what we looked at because at that time the West was very successful . . . so successful they conquered the whole world. Naturally, one wants to copy the successful example. Now the situation has changed somewhat whether people like it or not, we see a competition between the Japanese method and the Western method. And, in the contest, we see

the Japanese have made headway while the West has not only not made headway, but appears to be regressing. So, in order for Malaysia to progress, we have to learn from the better example, and the better example is the Japanese example. That is why we now want to look East where before we were looking West.[48]

The economic community that has been formed in Asia Pacific includes not only ties between Japan and Asia but also increasing ties among the other countries. ASEAN/NIC neighbors rank in the top four as trading partners for Asian-Pacific states. For example, Hong Kong trades heavily with Korea, Philippines, and Singapore; Singapore and Malaysia have long been major trading partners; Singapore also has a significant amount of trade with Thailand and Indonesia; and there are strong patterns of trade among Korea, Hong Kong, Philippines, Indonesia, and Malaysia.[49] Moreover, the NICs, in particular Korea and Taiwan, have been investing and giving aid and technical assistance to other Asian developing countries.

Politically, ties are strong within ASEAN. Most residual postcolonial feuds over borders and Indonesia's confrontation politics toward Malaysia are conflicts of the past. ASEAN united to deal with the communist takeover in Indochina and the repercussions that are still reflected in the Cambodian situation today.[50] Even though ASEAN states are friendly toward the United States—Thailand once was a U.S. military partner before asking U.S. troops to leave in 1975, and the Philippines remains strongly linked militarily to the United States—ASEAN members no longer look to the United States to solve regional problems. Rather, as detailed in a later chapter, they have united to form an effective force in themselves within a policy of "regional resilience."[51] In the rest of Asia Pacific, Taiwan and South Korea depend heavily on U.S. security assistance, but have actively promoted ties to ASEAN.[52] Most Asian-Pacific states have shared common concerns about China, but relations with that country improved in the 1980s. Finally, along with its economic ties, Japan has strengthened its diplomatic and political relations with the countries it once dominated. Japan has begun to assert itself politically in Asia, in particular by involving itself, with ASEAN, in attempts to resolve the conflict in Cambodia.

Notes

1. Unless otherwise indicated, the sources for the basic statistical information given in this chapter for area and GNP per capita are World Bank, *World Development Report 1990*, pp. 178–179, and for estimated population 1990, United Nations Development Program (UNDP), *Human Development Report 1991*, pp. 160–161, 180. Both reports, as well as editions for other years, are published in New York by Oxford University Press. (These annual editions are cited hereafter as *World Development Report 19xx* and *Human Development*

Report 19xx.) Note that the conversion of land area from square meters to square miles is approximate due to rounding.

2. Some of the following discussion is reproduced (by permission) from Jacqueline A. Braveboy-Wagner "Japan and the Caribbean: Linkages and Possibilities," *Caribbean Affairs* 2, 4 (October–December 1989) (special issue "The Caribbean and the World"): 109–122.

3. The history of Japan is complex and fascinating. For details, see, among others, W. G. Beasley, *The Modern History of Japan* (New York: Praeger, 1963); Richard Storry, *A History of Modern Japan* (Baltimore, Md.: Penguin, 1960); and Edwin O. Reischauer, *Japan: The Story of a Nation* (New York: Alfred A. Knopf, 1974).

4. Chalmers Johnson, *MITI and the Japanese Miracle* (Stanford, Calif.: Stanford University Press, 1982).

5. See Jon Woronoff, *Inside Japan, Inc.* (Tokyo: Lotus, 1982). The Japanese themselves do not share this view. For example, Kenichi Ohmae, a leading management consultant, notes that "Japan, Inc." is an American invention promoted by U.S. scholarship. "We know," he says, "how little the Ministry of International Trade and Industry [MITI] influences the decisions of Japanese management. But outside Japan MITI was portrayed as the mastermind behind Japan's economic miracle." See Ohmae, *Beyond National Borders: Reflections on Japan and the World* (Tokyo and New York: Kodansha International, 1988). See also "Mighty MITI Loses Its Grip," *New York Times,* July 9, 1989, pp. F1, F9.

6. Jon Woronoff, *Asia's "Miracle" Economies* (Tokyo: Lotus, 1986), p. 59. For a view of GDP growth rates in the mid-1970s to the late 1980s, see Keizai Koho Center (KKC) (Japan Institute for Social and Economic Affairs, Tokyo), *Japan: An International Comparison 1988, 1989, 1990,* p. 12, and p. 14 respectively. (These annual reports are cited hereafter as KKC, *Japan 19xx.*) Except for GNP per capita, figures given in this chapter are GDP- rather than GNP -based, unless otherwise indicated.

7. KKC, *Japan 1990,* p. 12; and Japan External Trade Organization (JETRO), *Nippon: Business Facts and Figures 1991* (Tokyo: JETRO, 1991), p. 16. (The JETRO annual reports are cited hereafter as JETRO, *Nippon 19xx.*) These are GNP growth rates.

8. For trends in the current balance since 1982, see JETRO, *Nippon 1991,* pp. 54–55, 74–75. The 1991 figures on trade are cited from *New York Times,* July 1, 1992, pp. 1, 33 and July 9, 1992, p. D13.

9. *New York Times,* June 4, 1990, pp. A1, D4.

10. KKC, *Japan 1990,* pp. 12, 16. The figures given for the NICs in this source are listed sometimes under GNP but are GDP-based. NIC figures are for 1983–1987. For comparison, Japan's GDP growth rate for that period was 3.96 percent (calculated).

11. Calculated from International Monetary Fund (IMF), *Direction of Trade Statistics Yearbook 1991* (Washington, D.C.: IMF, 1991), pp. 3, 5. (The annual IMF reports are cited hereafter as IMF, *Yearbook 19xx.*)

12. Ibid. Growth rates for 1984–1990 are calculated.

13. The following discussion of the NICs draws largely from Woronoff, *"Miracle" Economies.*

14. *World Development Report 1990,* pp. 179, 183.

15. See, for example, Chung-in Moon, "Beyond Statism: Rethinking the Political Economy of Growth in South Korea," *International Studies Notes* 15, 1 (Winter 1990): 24–28.

16. For the 1987 Taiwan figure, see KKC, *Japan 1990,* p. 12. Later figures

are from "How Taiwan Wins Friends and Miffs Beijing," *New York Times,* December 3, 1989, p. 6; "Taiwan," *Financial Times Survey,* October 10, 1989, p. 1; Republic of China, "Today's Taiwan," *New York Times,* August 26, 1991, p. A19.

17. Woronoff, *"Miracle" Economies,* p. 83.
18. "Taiwanese Trying a Shift to High-Tech Niches," *New York Times,* November 26, 1990, pp. D1, D7.
19. *New York Times,* November 27, 1987, pp. D1–3; and December 3, 1989, p. 6.
20. *New York Times,* November 27, 1987, pp. D1, D3.
21. John Bastin and Harry J. Benda, *A History of Modern Southeast Asia* (Englewood Cliffs, N.J.: Prentice-Hall, 1968), p. 36.
22. KKC, *Japan 1990,* p. 31 (table 4–1). Figures for Taiwan have been calculated separately from trade data in IMF, *Yearbook 1991,* pp. 3, 5; and from GDP information provided in KKC, *Japan 1990,* p. 12. Figures for Taiwan, Korea, and Singapore are for 1987, for Hong Kong and Taiwan 1988. All data the latest available at the time of writing. Singapore's land area is from the KKC report, p. 16. Woronoff, *"Miracle" Economies,* p. 122, uses the 618 figure.
23. Woronoff, *"Miracle" Economies,* pp. 124, 135.
24. Ibid., p. 131.
25. Figure is GDP-based.
26. Woronoff, *"Miracle" Economies,* pp. 148, 153–154.
27. Ibid., p. 156.
28. See, for example, *New York Times,* July 11, 1990, p. A6.
29. On ASEAN, see, among others, Chan Heng Chee, "ASEAN: Subregional Resilience," in James W. Morley, ed., *Security Interdependence in the Asia Pacific Region* (Lexington, Mass.: D.C. Heath, 1986), pp. 111–144; and chs. 3 and 7 of Masahide Shibusawa, *Japan and the Asian Pacific Region* (New York: St. Martin's, 1984). Also see Chapter 6 of this book.
30. Chan Heng Chee, "ASEAN," p. 136.
31. See *World Development Report 1984,* p. 99, for a description of Indonesia's transmigration program.
32. Poverty as a whole has been reduced in Indonesia from 60 percent to 20 percent in the last few decades.
33. The GDP growth vote for 1960 to 1970 was 3.9 percent; for 1970 to 1980 7.6 percent; for 1980 to 1988 5.1 percent. See *World Bank Report 1990,* p. 1. See *World Development Report 1984,* p. 220; and *World Development Report 1990,* p. 180.
34. Ibid., for sources.
35. KKC, *Japan 1990,* p. 12. See also Editorial Notebook, "Thailand, the Next Tiger," *New York Times,* August 6, 1990, p. A12.
36. *World Development Report 1990,* p. 182.
37. "Economic Developments During 1989, Newly Industrialized Economies: Asia," in Caribbean Development Bank, *Annual Report 1989* (St. Michael, Barbados, 1990), p. 19.
38. *World Development Report 1984,* p. 220; *World Development Report 1990,* p. 180.
39. Steven Erlanger, "With Time and Influence Evaporating, Aquino Finds Rivals All Around Her," *New York Times,* July 15, 1990, p. 10.
40. General information on Brunei is from Arthur S. Banks, ed., *Political Handbook of the World 1990* (Binghamton: State University of New York, 1990), pp. 81–82. Banks's 1990 population estimate is 256,000, which may be somewhat high. The figure here is for 1988 from *World Development Report*

1990, p. 243. The per capita income figure is from *Human Development Report 1991*, p. 122.

41. KKC, *Japan 1990*, pp. 36–37. See also Table 1.1, Chapter 1 of this book.

42. *New York Times*, January 22, 1992, p. D2.

43. JETRO, *Nippon 1989*, p. 58. In later years, figures for the specific Southeast Asian region are not given.

44. JETRO, *Nippon 1991*, p. 76; and KKC, *Japan 1990*, p. 56.

45. Japan Ministry of Foreign Affairs (MFA), *Japan's Official Development Assistance, ODA, 1989 Report* (Tokyo: 1990), pp. 59–60.

46. KKC, *Japan 1990*, p. 39 (table 4–10).

47. "Japan Builds Marketing Links in East Asia," *New York Times*, May 8, 1990, pp. D1, D18.

48. Quoted in Woronoff, *"Miracle" Economies*, pp. 352–353 from *Far East Economic Review*, June 11, 1982, p. 38.

49. KKC, *Japan 1989* and *1990*, p. 39. The source lists trading partner ranks for Thailand in 1987, and for the other countries in 1988.

50. See Chung Heng Chee, "ASEAN," pp. 111–143 for details.

51. Ibid.; and see Chapter 6 of this book.

52. See Byung-joon Ahn, "South Korea and Taiwan: Local Deterrence," in Morley, *Security Interdependence*, pp. 93–110.

3
The Caribbean: Intraregional Relations

Jacqueline A. Braveboy-Wagner

Although the focus of this book is on Asian-Pacific relations with the English-speaking subgroup of Caribbean nations—chosen for their historical, political, and economic commonalities—a slightly broader approach proves useful in analyzing current and future linkages between the two regions. The broader concept of the Caribbean Basin is employed in this section for two reasons: First, from the perspective of the Asian-Pacific states, all the Caribbean nations tend to be subsumed within the rubric of "Latin America" or "South and Central America," and economic policies are formulated by private and official entities based on that conception. At the very least, therefore, we need to discuss Asian-Pacific relations with "Latin" Caribbean states before focusing specifically on the small English-speaking region. Second, it is the larger Caribbean and circum-Caribbean nations that currently have the strongest links with the Asian-Pacific countries; the pattern of these linkages should reveal possibilities for the newer and smaller Caribbean nations that are only now seeking deeper ties to Asia Pacific.

The Basin conception of the Caribbean is primarily a geopolitical construct (see Fig. 3.1). It encompasses the Central American States (technically excluding El Salvador, which does not have a Caribbean coast, but programmatically including it), the Caribbean South American states, and the multicultural island Caribbean. Basic data for these countries are provided in Table 3.1.

Central America

The Central American countries (except Belize) that border the Caribbean share commonalities that distinguish them from the rest of the Caribbean. They do not have a primary interest in the core Caribbean region, which we can define as the island nations. Their historical focus has been the United States, and the community of interest between Central America and the

Figure 3.1 Map of the Caribbean Basin

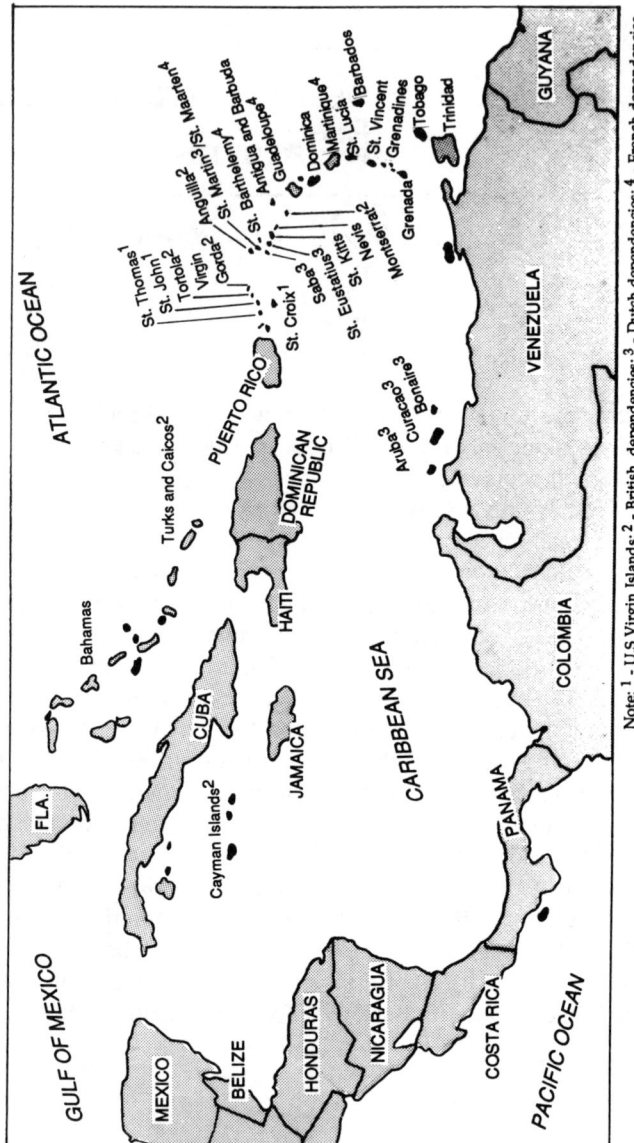

Note: [1] - U.S Virgin Islands; [2] - British dependencies; [3] - Dutch dependencies; [4] - French dependencies.

Table 3.1 Basic Data, Caribbean Basin States

Country	Area (thousands of square km.)	Population (millions, 1990 est.)	GNP per capita ($ U.S. 1988)
CORE CARIBBEAN COUNTRIES			
Spanish-speaking countries/Haiti			
Cuba	115	10.6	2,000
Dominican Republic	49	7.2	720
Haiti	28	6.5	380
English-speaking countries[a]			
Antigua and Barbuda	.440	.83	3,690
Bahamas	14	.249	10,700
Barbados	.431	.256	6,010
Belize	23	.183	1,500
Dominica	.750	.082	1,680
Grenada	.345	.100	1,720
Guyana	215	.755	420
Jamaica	11	2.5	1,070
St. Kitts/Nevis	.269	.043	2,630
St. Lucia	.616	.148	1,540
St. Vincent	.388	.115	1,200
Trinidad and Tobago	5	1.3	3,350
CIRCUM-CARIBBEAN COUNTRIES			
Central American region[b]			
Costa Rica	51	3.0	1,690
Guatemala	109	9.2	900
Honduras	112	5.1	860
Nicaragua	130	3.9	830
Panama	77	2.4	2,120
Mexico	1,958	88.6	1,760
South America			
Colombia	1,139	33.3	1,180
Suriname	163	.427[c]	2,460
Venezuela	912	19.7	3,250

Sources: World Bank, *World Development Report 1990* (New York: Oxford University Press, 1990), pp. 178–179, 243; United Nations Development Program (UNDP), *Human Development Report 1991* (New York: Oxford University Press, 1991), pp. 152, 160–161; Caribbean Development Bank, *Annual Report 1990* (St. Michael, Barbados: CDB, 1991), p. 15.
[a] Population figures for countries of less than 1 million people are for 1989.
[b] Excluding El Salvador, which does not have a Caribbean coast.
[c] 1988 figures.

Caribbean has been a strategic artifact created primarily by U.S. policymakers. Nevertheless, because key U.S. economic programs, including a recent free-trade initiative, have grouped Central America and the Caribbean together, the regions have become linked by circumstances and thus recently have begun to initiate stronger contacts: For example, foreign ministers of both regions have begun to meet to coordinate policy (the first such talks were in Honduras early in 1992), and representatives to the United Nations are also working more closely together. Moreover, Belize, the only English-speaking nation in Central America and one with traditionally strong ties to the rest of the English-speaking Caribbean, represents a bridge between the two cultural regions: It has close economic links to Central American nations, and now that a troublesome territorial dispute with Guatemala is being played down by that country, Belize is beginning to participate in various Central American policy forums.[1]

The five Spanish-speaking Central American nations—Costa Rica, (non-Caribbean) El Salvador, Guatemala, Honduras, and Nicaragua—were historically controlled from Guatemala as part of the Spanish viceroyalty of New Spain (Mexico). They declared their independence as one unit, the United Provinces of Central America, in 1823, but later disbanded into five separate territories. Guatemala is the largest country in terms of population (an estimated 9.2 million in 1990), followed by El Salvador (5.3 million), Honduras (5.1 million), Nicaragua (3.9 million), and Costa Rica (3.0 million). Land area ranges from Nicaragua's 130,000 square kilometers (about 150,200 square miles) to El Salvador's 21,000 square kilometers (about 8,000 square miles).[2]

The Central American republics have shared a difficult political and social history. Colonialism left a highly skewed pattern of land tenure, later aggravated by the development of export agriculture and hierarchical, authoritarian societies that engendered conservative, military-supported government. Only in Costa Rica did a democratic system of government emerge, and that was accomplished only after a decisive civil war in 1948. Various other experiments in political and social democracy did not survive.

Geographical proximity to the United States also led to U.S. interventions, initially primarily for economic reasons, later as part of the U.S. crusade against communism. Meanwhile, social inequities resulted, particularly in the 1970s and 1980s, in violent conflict between haves and have-nots and between left-wing insurgents and conservative regimes, with extremists emerging on both sides.[3] In Nicaragua the civil war between the haves and have-nots eventually led to emergence of a socialist government in 1979, but it faced a counterrevolutionary movement for the next eleven years as well as external pressure from the United States and the other regional states. Beset by economic problems, the leaders bowed to general elections and were voted out in 1990.

The Central American economies were, and have remained, basically plantation economies, dependent on primary products, especially coffee and bananas. Until the political crisis of the 1970s, Central America experienced economic growth, accelerated by the formation of the Central American Common Market (CACM) in 1960. Trade among Central American countries rose from 6.9 percent of the total in 1961 to 26.1 percent in 1970. Although the process of integration was slowed somewhat by war between El Salvador and Honduras in 1969, intraregional trade grew to $1 billion in 1980 from $33 million in 1960. In fact, there was a spurt in extraregional trade as well during this period.[4] All this ended in the 1980s.

The post–World War II period was also a period of industrialization based on import-substitution. Guatemala in particular became the most industrialized country, exporting chemical products, textiles, processed foods, and glass products. El Salvador and Costa Rica also produced similar manufactures,[5] but Honduras remained relatively underdeveloped in this regard.

Guerrilla war and regional turmoil caused negative growth rates in the 1980s for El Salvador, Guatemala, and Nicaragua. Honduras and Costa Rica also felt the effects of Nicaragua's civil war, but economic growth was primarily hurt by the fall in international commodity prices in the late 1970s and 1980s and the rise in oil prices in the late 1970s. Costa Rica incurred a high foreign debt that added to its problems. Lower oil prices, more stable prices for commodities, and the end of the war in Nicaragua were expected to improve economic conditions in these countries in the 1990s, but prospects for improvement remained very dim in the early 1990s.

The World Bank lists all the Central American countries as lower-middle-income states. Per capita incomes in 1988 were Honduras, $860; El Salvador, $940; Guatemala, $900; Costa Rica, $1,690; and Nicaragua, $830.[6]

Venezuela, Colombia, Mexico, and Panama

These circum-Caribbean territories have a stronger interest in the Caribbean core than the Central American nations have. Panama, which was joined with Colombia until a U.S.-supported revolt led to independence in 1903,[7] attracted large numbers of migrants from the British West Indies during the building of the Panama Canal and afterward. Nevertheless, its Caribbean linkages are today quite concentrated geographically: Relatively strong trade and diplomatic (consular) links exist only with Jamaica, Bahamas, and Belize. Until the U.S. intervention of 1989, Cuba and Panama also maintained quite close relations. But Panama is a small country—2.4 million people, though they are dispersed in a relatively large 77,000 square kilometers (about 29,700 square miles)—and it has historically looked toward the United States rather than the Caribbean or the South. Until the United States imposed economic sanctions on Panama in order to induce its leader Manuel Noriega to resign, Panama was an upper-middle-income country with a per capita income of $2,120 (1988) and an economy that depended primarily on services, including offshore banking and shipping. Exports consist mainly of primary products such as bananas. Panama was seriously hurt by U.S. sanctions and later by the U.S. invasion that removed Noriega from power. Reconstruction is expected to be a long process.

Colombia has a Caribbean coast and in the 1970s began to exhibit a strong interest in the Caribbean region, partly to offset growing Venezuelan influence. Bilateral initiatives toward Cuba and the English-speaking Caribbean were accompanied by membership (as a contributor but not borrower) in the Caribbean Development Bank (CDB), which lends to the English-speaking Caribbean nations. In the early 1990s, with an eye on hemispheric integration and the global trend toward economic blocs, Colombia has been courting Barbados as a trading gateway to other Caribbean countries and the Northern Hemisphere.[8] A lower-middle-income country (1988 per capita income $1,180), Colombia is a middle power in the region with a population of 33 million in a relatively large area of 1,139,000 square kilometers (about 440,000 square miles). Some 50 percent of Colombia's exports are primary commodities, mainly coffee, and fuel and mineral exports account for another quarter.

Venezuela and Mexico are regional powers that have in some ways competed for influence in the Caribbean and in the Third World. Both are important oil producers that accumulated vast wealth in the 1970s, but were forced in the late 1980s to undergo a painful period of structural adjustment as a result of the fall in oil prices and the need to restructure the high debt incurred during the period of expansion. Mexico is the larger country, with 88.6 million people and an area of 1,958,000 square kilometers (756,000 square miles). Because of its size and other social characteristics, its per capita income is lower than Venezuela's, at $1,760 in 1988. Venezuela has a population of 19.7 million in an area about half the size of Mexico (912,000 square kilometers, or about 352,000 square miles). Its per capita income ($3,250), considerably reduced these days, is still almost twice that of Mexico. Both Mexico and Venezuela can be considered NICs, having invested heavily not only in light manufacturing but also in heavy industry. Both countries have industrialized with the help of sizable amounts of foreign direct investment, and although they have in the past imposed fairly rigid controls on this investment, they began liberalizing this economic policy in the late 1980s and 1990s. Mexico's *maquiladora* (EPZ) sector is one of the Third World's most attractive areas for foreign investors, including Asian-Pacific investors.

Mexico and Venezuela both became noticeably more Third World–oriented in the 1970s and at the same time more interested in a Caribbean identity. In fact, they joined forces at that time to provide oil to the Caribbean and Central American countries on concessionary terms.[9] Much of this interest was also intended to serve as a counterpoint to increased Cuban activity in the region in the 1970s.

Of the two countries, however, Venezuela has exhibited by far the most sustained interest in the Caribbean. Mexico's initiatives, focused on economic, technical, and cultural cooperation, were concentrated in multilateral agencies such as the Economic Commission for Latin America and the Caribbean (ECLAC), the Latin American Energy Organization

(OLADE), and the Latin American Economic System (SELA); Mexico targeted its bilateral efforts mainly toward Central America (including neighboring Belize) and Jamaica. Despite concerns about growing Cuban influence in the 1970s, Mexico has been the Latin American state with the strongest links to Cuba and was the only country to maintain diplomatic relations with it during the embargo years of the 1960s and early 1970s. Mexico's links to the southern Caribbean have been much more limited, and since the late 1970s, Mexico has moved away from the avowedly Third World–oriented policy of the earlier period in order to concentrate more on its relationship with the United States. By 1992, the United States and Mexico were moving toward finalizing arrangements for a free-trade zone.

In contrast, Venezuela's interest in the Caribbean has been defined in geopolitical and strategic terms: The Caribbean islands, often considered as being in the backyard of the United States, are perceived to be in Venezuela's front yard. Venezuela therefore invested a great deal of effort in promoting economic, financial, and cultural initiatives in the geographically proximate English-speaking Caribbean islands. It became a major contributing member of the CDB and established a trust fund for development projects. Relations with neighboring English-speaking Guyana, marred since the 1960s by Venezuela's territorial claim to five-eighths of Guyana,[10] improved in the 1980s. With the decline in its petrodollar reserves, Venezuela began to focus more on investment and trade with the Caribbean than on official projects. However, preserving its Caribbean identity and activity remains an important aspect of Venezuela's foreign policy. Recent overtures to the English-speaking region include an offer of a one-way free-trade arrangement and application to join that subregion's integration movement.

The Caribbean Islands, Belize, and Guyana

The island region is the core Caribbean region and is usually subdivided by language. Along with the Commonwealth of Puerto Rico, Cuba and the Dominican Republic comprise the Spanish-speaking Caribbean. Haiti is the only independent French Caribbean territory. By contrast, the English-speaking region encompasses ten independent islands: Antigua and Barbuda, Bahamas, Barbados, Dominica, Grenada, Jamaica, St. Christopher (Kitts)/Nevis, St. Lucia, St. Vincent and the Grenadines, and Trinidad and Tobago. By history, culture, and institutional development, two mainland countries, Belize (in Central America) and Guyana (in South America) also belong to the English-speaking Caribbean.

The linkages between the different linguistic areas are not strong. In this respect, the most important institutional development has been the creation of the Caribbean Community and Common Market (Caricom) by the

English-speaking Caribbean. The Dominican Republic and Haiti (as well as the Netherlands Antilles and Suriname) enjoy observer status in various committees of Caricom and, in the long term, could probably be admitted as full members.

Cuba's relations with the rest of the Caribbean have been occasionally warm but more often cold. In the period after the 1959 revolution, Cuba engaged in hostile activities against Venezuela, Panama, the Dominican Republic, Nicaragua, and Haiti and was excluded from participation in the inter-American system or Organization of American States (OAS) in 1962. After sanctions were voted by the OAS in 1963, only Mexico retained diplomatic ties with Cuba. Cuba remained isolated from its Caribbean neighbors until the early 1970s, when relations warmed with socialist Guyana and with a new modernizing military regime in Panama led by Omar Torrijos. Subsequently, Jamaica, Trinidad and Tobago, Barbados, and Guyana collectively established diplomatic relations with Cuba. The latter's relations with Latin America as a whole improved by the mid-1970s when OAS sanctions were repealed. There followed a period of heightened Cuban influence in the Caribbean as the country sought to assist the revolutionary and nationalist regimes that coincidentally emerged at this time in Jamaica, in Grenada, and in Nicaragua. This boom period for Cuba ended with the U.S. intervention in Grenada in 1983, and Cuban influence declined further with the electoral defeat of the Nicaraguan government in 1990.

For many Caribbean countries, Cuba has been attractive because of its relative social development and technological advancement. Economically, however, as a result of the liberalization of the Eastern bloc in the early 1990s, Cuba has been cut off from its primary sources of aid and trade and has been plunged into an economic crisis, which has, among other things, led it to seek closer economic and functional links with the English-speaking Caribbean. Most of its export revenue continues to come from exports of primary products, particularly sugar, but Cuba early on developed light industries, particularly agroindustry, and some heavy industry. Cuba is the largest Caribbean island, with over 10.6 million people and an area of 115,000 square kilometers (44,400 square miles).

The Dominican Republic is the only other independent Spanish-speaking island in the Caribbean. It has 7.2 million people in an area of 49,000 square kilometers (roughly 18,900 square miles); the per capita income was $720 in 1988. Its relations with the rest of the Caribbean are relatively weak because its traditional external focus has been the United States. However, links have grown somewhat over the years: The country became a member, with Jamaica, Guyana, Haiti, and Suriname and other non-Caribbean countries, of the International Bauxite Association (IBA), a cartel formed in 1974. It also has observer status in some committees of Caricom. The Dominican Republic depends mainly on primary products for its export revenue, particularly sugar, though this product competes with sugar coming from the rest of the Caribbean. Within the Caribbean Basin, Venezuela and Mexico are the Dominican Republic's major (oil) import partners. Panama and Colombia have also been relatively important import partners, and geography has generated moderately strong links with Haiti.[11]

Haiti, the oldest Latin American republic, shares the island of Hispaniola with the Dominican Republic but is considerably poorer, in large measure because of its long political history of dictatorship and instability. Haiti has the dubious distinction of being the poorest country in the hemisphere, with a per capita income of $380 in 1988. Its population, 6.5 million in a land area of 28,000 square kilometers (10,800 square miles), engages primarily in agriculture, and along with agricultural products, Haiti produces some bauxite. Industry remains primarily cottage industry. Apart from Haiti's historical links to the Dominican Republic, there are moderately strong links with Jamaica, Bahamas, Barbados, Trinidad and Tobago, and the Netherlands Antilles. In fact, Haiti has applied for membership in Caricom but its political problems have precluded its admission and limited its participation as an observer. Haiti has experienced almost continuous political turmoil since the dictator Jean-Claude Duvalier was overthrown in 1986. A brief period of political promise in 1991 under elected president Jean-Bertrand Aristide was interrupted by a military coup. As of mid-1992, concerted attempts by the Organization of American States to reach an agreement that would allow the return of President Aristide to power have been frustrated.

The English-speaking Caribbean is usually subdivided into the more developed countries, or MDCs (the larger countries, Jamaica, Trinidad and Tobago, Guyana, and Barbados) and the smaller countries of the eastern Caribbean. Belize, on the Central American mainland, and Bahamas to the north occupy special positions, somewhat remote from the core area, but Bahamas ranks also as an MDC. Along with two dependent countries, Montserrat and Anguilla, these countries comprise the integrated community Caricom, but the eastern Caribbean countries have their own common market and regional organization, the Organization of Eastern Caribbean States (OECS).

As can be seen in Table 3.1, the independent English-speaking countries range in size of population from Jamaica (2.5 million) to St. Kitts/Nevis (43,000)[12] and in land area from Guyana (214,970 square kilometers, or 830,000 square miles) to St. Kitts (269 square kilometers, or 104 square miles). These small nations are middle-income countries that until the 1970s were generally considered to be some of the most socially developed as well as democratically stable countries in the Third World. Since the 1970s, however, they have experienced economic and social dislocations that have been matched in some instances—notably in Jamaica, Grenada, and Trinidad and Tobago—by political instability.

Despite an economic downturn in the last few years, the Bahamas has remained the most economically healthy, with a per capita GNP in 1988 of

$10,700 and in 1989 a little over $10,000[13] derived from tourism, manufacturing, and the country's role in financial services. Overall, the smaller islands of the eastern Caribbean, as well as mainland Belize, have experienced moderate rates of economic growth based on their export of traditional products (bananas, spices, citrus, sugar) and on variable income from tourism. The most troubled economies, however, have been the larger ones: Over the years, declines in commodity prices have adversely affected bauxite-producing Jamaica and oil-dependent Trinidad and Tobago; Barbados, until recently relatively immune from problems, began experiencing economic difficulties in the early 1990s as a result of the downturn in sugar, tourism, and manufacturing engendered by recession in the United States; the other MDC, Guyana, has been in economic decline since the 1970s, a condition attributable to both international factors and internal economic and political mismanagement. With a per capita income of $420 in 1988 and only $337 in 1989, it was one of the poorest countries of the hemisphere.

As detailed in Chapters 6 and 7, the level of institutional development of the English-speaking Caribbean region is quite high. The two institutions for regional integration in the area, Caricom and the OECS, focus on a range of cooperative spheres: economic integration, functional cooperation, and some foreign policy coordination. The OECS is a more closely knit community and has been more successful in fostering economic and political cooperation. Caricom's performance has been hampered, inter alia, by problems stemming from its members' differing levels of development and by ideological and political differences.

Suriname

Somewhat isolated among the Caribbean states is Suriname, formerly Dutch Guiana. The country gained its independence in 1975 and for much of the 1980s was embroiled in political turmoil that began with a military takeover in 1980. After a short period of civilian rule, another military coup occurred late in 1990; general elections followed in 1991. Suriname has traditionally looked toward the Netherlands, but is associated with Caricom as an observer on various committees. Suriname has a population of 427,000 people in an area of 163,000 square kilometers.

The Caribbean and Asia Pacific: Potential Ties

As seen by the descriptions in this chapter, the Caribbean, like the Pacific Basin, is an extremely diverse region in terms of size, levels of development, culture, and politics. As in the Pacific Basin (or indeed in the Asian-Pacific subregion), the only institutional mechanism that links all these countries is the Organization of American States (OAS), but it has an even broader hemispheric scope. The Basin has been more of a strategic concept, perceived in terms of U.S. security interests, than one that reflects concrete forms of cooperation. Yet there are moderate intralinkages throughout, and certainly the future promises greater integration, formal and informal. Currently, the Caribbean has more integrative mechanisms than can be found in the Asian-Pacific region: CACM in Central America, Caricom for the English-speaking Caribbean, and OECS for the eastern Caribbean states.

Geopolitical and historical considerations have inclined the Caribbean states toward strong relationships with the hemispheric power and global superpower, the United States. History (specifically, colonialism) has also locked these countries into close economic ties with Europe—Spain, Britain, Holland, France. But the Caribbean is linked to the Pacific by the fact that the countries to the west, from Colombia to Mexico, share both Caribbean and Pacific coasts. It would seem only natural, therefore, that as the Asian-Pacific nations rise to prominence, at least these Caribbean nations should be poised to interact and to diversify their relations in the direction of the Pacific as a counterpoint to their Atlantic and North American emphasis. The other states that do not share a Pacific coastline are bound to be attracted as well by the economic strength of the Asian-Pacific countries. Although current relations between the Asian-Pacific countries and the Caribbean are relatively underdeveloped and focused on a select group of nations, there is increasing official interest in intensifying relations with the fast-growing Asian-Pacific region. In the next chapter, we continue to take a broad view in an effort to identify the patterns of linkages that exist between the two regions and to make some proposals for future linkages, particularly as they may pertain to the smaller and newer nations that have only recently begun to be attracted to the East.

Notes

1. For details on the Guatemala-Belize territorial dispute, see L. M. Bloomfield, *The British Honduras–Guatemala Dispute* (Toronto: Carswell, 1953); D.A.G. Waddell, "Developments in the Belize Question," *American Journal of International Law* 55, 2 (April 1961): 459–469; and O. Nigel Bolland, *Belize: A New Nation in Central America* (Boulder, Colo.: Westview, 1986), pp. 128–136.

2. Area and per capita figures here and for all later references are from World Bank, *World Development Report 1990* (New York: Oxford University Press, 1990), pp. 178–179, unless otherwise indicated. Population figures are the 1990 estimate given in United Nations Development Program (UNDP), *Human Development Report 1991* (New York: Oxford University Press, 1991), pp. 160–

161. The conversion of square meters to square miles is approximate due to rounding.

3. There was an outpouring of literature on Central America in the 1980s. Among the many books available are Thomas W. Walker, *Nicaragua: The Land of Sandino* (Boulder, Colo.: Westview, 1981); Tommie Sue Montgomery, *Revolution in El Salvador: Origins and Evolution* (Boulder, Colo.: Westview, 1982); Patricia Taylor Edmisten, *Nicaragua Divided: LA PRENSA and the Chamorro Legacy* (Pensacola: University of West Florida, 1990); Mark Falcoff and Robert Royal, eds., *Crisis and Opportunity: U.S. Policy in Central America and the Caribbean* (Washington, D.C.: Ethics and Public Policy Center, 1984); and Nora Hamilton, Jeffrey A. Frieden, Linda Fuller, and Manuel Pastor, Jr., eds., *Crisis in Central America: Regional Dynamics and U.S. Policy in the 1990s* (Boulder, Colo.: Westview, 1988).

4. See, for example, Edelberto Torres Rivas, "The Central American Crisis and the Common Market," in Hamilton et al., *Crisis in Central America*, p. 141; and *Report of the National Bipartisan Commission on Central America* (Washington, D.C., January 1984), p. 23.

5. Rivas, "Central American Crisis," pp. 143–144.

6. GNP per capita for Nicaragua is not listed in the usual source (*World Development Report 1990*) and is taken instead from *Human Development Report 1991*, p. 122.

7. The United States helped engineer the revolt because it was interested in building a transoceanic canal. See, among other works, Frederico G. Gil, *Latin American–United States Relations* (New York: Harcourt Brace Jovanovich, 1971), pp. 121–140.

8. Caribbean News Agency report in *Trinidad Express*, January 16, 1992, p. 19.

9. The arrangement to provide oil was done under the San José accord. For a text, see Jack Hopkins, ed., *Latin America and Caribbean Contemporary Record*, vol. 1, 1981–1982 (New York: Holmes and Meier, 1983), pp. 651–652.

10. See my (Jacqueline A. Braveboy-Wagner) *Venezuela-Guyana Border Dispute: Britain's Colonial Legacy in Latin America* (Boulder, Colo.: Westview, 1984).

11. For trade data, see International Monetary Fund, *Direction of Trade Statistics Yearbook 1991* (Washington, D.C.: IMF, 1991), pp. 159–160.

12. Population figure is for 1989. All data on the English-speaking Caribbean are from Caribbean Development Bank, *Annual Report 1990* (Barbados, 1991), p. 15. This source gives more complete data on the small states than the World Bank source.

13. Ibid. 1989 figures for the English-speaking Caribbean nations are GDP-based.

4

Japan, East Asia, and the Caribbean: Economic Linkages

Jacqueline A. Braveboy-Wagner

Caribbean Relations with East Asia

The increased economic significance of the Asian-Pacific region has generated much Caribbean interest and growing trade, investment, and aid relationships. Although these relationships remain very weak compared with the Caribbean's relationships with the Atlantic countries, they are much stronger today than twenty—or even ten—years ago. In 1976, well-respected analyst Miguel S. Wionczek noted that for Latin America, the commercial exchange across the Pacific was of "marginal importance to all parties concerned." He continued:

> Trade between Latin America and the rest of the Pacific region over the past decade has consisted of the following flows: Latin America exported primary industrial commodities—minerals from Chile and Peru, mainly to Japan, oil from Venezuela [and bauxite and alumina from the Caribbean to Canada]—and tropical agricultural products, including coffee and cotton from Brazil, Central America, and Mexico, principally to Japan [and Canada]. Moreover, some products of temperate zone agriculture, such as grains and meat, were exported to Japan and smaller Far Eastern countries.
>   In the opposite direction, there have been imports of wool and tin from Australia and Malaysia, respectively; of capital goods by major Latin American countries from Japan [and Canada]; and of consumer durables and nondurables by the less developing [sic] Latin American republics, particularly Central America, Panama, and Venezuela, from Japan and, in negligible quantities, from Hong Kong. As one might have expected, Latin American trade with New Zealand, the Far East, and Southeast Asian developing countries, such as South Korea, Taiwan, the Philippines, Indonesia, and Thailand . . . has been practically nonexistent.[1]

As the 1990s began, trade and investment flows across the Pacific were already intensifying, not only because of the fast growth of the Asian-Pacific region but also because many Latin American countries themselves—Venezuela, Mexico, Brazil—were experiencing spurts in economic growth. Nevertheless, the quote is instructive: As will be seen, relations between the two regions remain somewhat concentrated but have improved modestly. While the composition and even the percentage of exports from Latin America to Asia Pacific have remained stable, there has been remarkable growth in imports from the region, and there has also been a diversification of trade to include not only Japan but also other Asian nations, in particular, South Korea, Taiwan, and Hong Kong. Still, Japan remains the major focus of trans-Pacific trade. For Caribbean Basin countries, Japan ranks as second or third (industrial) import partner for a majority of countries. While nowhere near the premier partner, the United States, it competes favorably with the United Kingdom and Canada, and usually places in the top five export markets as well. Because of the predominance of Japan, most of this chapter will be devoted to analyzing the relations between the Caribbean Basin and Japan. However, a brief preliminary discussion of Caribbean relations with other areas of Asia Pacific is also necessary.

The patterns of trade uncovered by Wionczek for Latin America hold true as well for the non-Hispanic Caribbean, which as previously mentioned is usually subsumed under Latin America in the perception of Asian policymakers. For example, in the English-speaking Caribbean, trade with Asia has traditionally been minimal and centered on imports from Japan and Hong Kong. The persistent trickle of trade with Hong Kong reflected the British legacy as well as the presence throughout the Caribbean of small but significant numbers of ethnic Chinese (nowhere in the region are they more than 1 percent of the population today). These Chinese came as indentured laborers after emancipation. Some 18,000 immigrated to Jamaica, Trinidad, and Guyana (then British Guiana), coming primarily from Canton, Hong Kong's neighboring province. (A larger number of Chinese immigrants, 125,000, went to Cuba.)[2]

By the late 1980s, English-speaking Caribbean countries had joined the rest of Latin America in actively seeking to diversify their economic relations in the direction of the Far East. Most of the effort focused on Japan, but Korea and Taiwan also became relatively important sources of imports. Hong Kong has been courted as a source of investment funds, especially in view of the recent Caribbean (and Latin American) push to establish economic processing/free-trade zones in order to attract investors. The English-speaking Caribbean has, in fact, been so eager to attract investment and aid from Korea and Taiwan that most of these states receive resident diplomatic missions from Korea (but none send missions there)—although Barbados, Jamaica, St. Vincent, and St. Lucia also maintain links with North Korea[3]—and there seems to be a growing movement to recognize the Republic of China (Taiwan). Among those that have established relations with Taiwan are Dominica, St. Vincent, St. Kitts, Bahamas, Grenada, and Belize. In the case of the last two countries, diplomatic relations had previously been established with Beijing (People's Republic of China). Although Taiwan in recent years has pursued a flexible policy of allowing dual recognition of both China and Taiwan by third countries, Beijing has not moved away from its "one China" policy, and it suspended relations with Grenada and Belize after they recognized Taiwan.[4] Belize is the only country of the English-speaking Caribbean to have resident diplomatic representation in Taiwan.

The English-speaking Caribbean countries are not the only Basin countries to have diplomatic links with Taiwan. Costa Rica, Dominican

Table 4.1 Trade of Caribbean Basin Countries with Developing Asia, 1990, as percent of total trade[a]

Country	Exports to Asia (as % of total)	Imports from Asia (as % of total)
CORE CARIBBEAN COUNTRIES		
Spanish-speaking countries/Haiti		
Cuba	20.6	10.3
Dominican Republic	4.3	2.9
Haiti	0.1	7.3
English-speaking countries[b]		
Bahamas	0.2	1.6
Barbados[c]	—	3.3
Belize	0.5	3.9
Dominica	12.5	38.8
Grenada	0.8	10.3
Guyana[c]	—	2.9
Jamaica	0.1	4.1
St. Vincent	2.8	8.7
Trinidad and Tobago	3.1	1.9
CIRCUM-CARIBBEAN COUNTRIES		
Central American region		
Costa Rica	1.3	5.4
Guatemala	2.4	5.9
Honduras	1.6	6.7
Nicaragua	0.9	1.5
Panama	0.2	4.6
Mexico	1.4	2.7
South America		
Colombia	1.1	1.3
Suriname	0.2	3.6
Venezuela	1.0	2.1

Source: International Monetary Fund, *Direction of Trade Statistics Yearbook 1991* (Washington, D.C.: IMF, 1991).
[a] Excludes Japan but includes People's Republic of China.
[b] No data are reported for Antigua and Barbuda, St. Kitts/Nevis, and St. Lucia.
[c] Negligible amount of exports/imports.

Table 4.2 Trade Between Caribbean Basin Countries and Asian-Pacific Countries, 1990 ($ U.S. million)

Country (Exports to / Imports from)	Asian NICs				ASEAN Countries[a]			
	Korea	Taiwan	Singapore	Hong Kong	Indonesia	Thailand	Malaysia	Philippines
CORE CARIBBEAN COUNTRIES								
Spanish-speaking countries/Haiti								
Cuba	...	...	—	0.2	0.1	—	17.1[c]	...
	...	...		0.4	—	35.2	0.2[c]	...
Dominican Republic	9.8	22.9	0.3	0.1	0.1	1.6	1.8	0.1
	—	—	—	18.7	0.1	—	0.3	—
Haiti	9.3	15.5	0.3	0.1	—	0.4	—	0.3
				10.8			17.3	
English-speaking countries[b]								
Bahamas	—	0.5	0.8	0.5[c]	0.2	0.2	—	0.3
	1.9	2.1	35.1	5.2	—	0.7	0.3	0.4
Barbados	8.7	7.8	0.6	—	0.2	0.1	0.2	—
	—	—	—	2.4	—	—	1.5	0.1
Belize	1.4	4.0	0.2	1.9	—	—	—	—
	3.0	—	—	—	—	0.9	4.5	0.1
Dominica	36.9	25.1	0.1[c]	0.7[c]	—	0.2	0.6	[c]
				0.1			1.3	
Grenada	—	—	...	8.3	...	0.3	—	...
	0.5	0.5	...		...	—	—	...
Guyana	1.8	2.0	—	1.6	0.2	0.4	—	—
	—	—	0.2	0.5	—	—	0.1	0.4
Jamaica	13.3	18.9	3.7	19.2	0.7	3.3	5.8	—
St. Vincent	—	0.2	2.7	...	...	...	—	...
	0.4	0.8	9.3	...	3.1	—	—	...
Trinidad and Tobago	0.1[c]	3.5	0.3[c]	0.1	0.4	1.3	1.0	0.8
	7.8	16.6	2.7	3.6				

Table 4.2 continued

Country (Exports to / Imports from)	Asian NICs				ASEAN Countries[a]			
	Korea	Taiwan	Singapore	Hong Kong	Indonesia	Thailand	Malaysia	Philippines
CIRCUM-CARIBBEAN COUNTRIES								
Central American region								
Costa Rica	5.4	4.5[c]	1.0	1.5	0.1	2.5	2.3	0.4
	39.0	53.9	2.0	11.4	0.3	0.5	1.4	0.2[c]
Guatemala	5.4	9.6	10.6	0.6	—	0.4	2.7	0.1
	26.3	39.6	1.1	19.4	0.5	0.5	4.7	1.0
Honduras	12.2	—	2.2	4.3	0.1	0.3	—	—[d]
	22.6	12.5	11.0	15.6	0.3	0.5	0.8	0.1
Nicaragua	—	1.0	—	—	0.2	0.2	—	0.3[c]
	13.2	1.8	—	—	—[c]	—	—	—[c]
Panama	0.3[c]	—	1.2[d]	0.5	0.1	1.4	0.5	0.1[c]
	27.0	23.0	0.4	15.7	34.0	40.0	9.0	0.3
Mexico	51.0	19.0	31.0	69.0				11.0
	186.0	71.0	56.0	236.0	32.0	26.0	39.0	12.0
South America								
Colombia	14.5	3.1	2.3	25.0	4.2	7.2	2.8	0.1
	15.3	20.2	14.7	9.4	3.9	1.4	2.1	0.1
Suriname	—	—	—	0.3	0.8	0.1[c]	0.1	—
	2.7	5.1	0.4[d]	5.0	0.3	1.3	0.5	1.3[c]
Venezuela	6.0	26.0	44.0	26.0	6.0	40.0	—	1.0
	25.0	5.2	6.0	29.0	4.0	1.0	5.0	—

Sources: International Monetary Fund, *Direction of Trade Statistics Yearbook 1991* (Washington, D.C.: IMF, 1991).
[a] Singapore is also a member of the Association of Southeast Asian Nations. Brunei is omitted because its only recorded Caribbean Basin partner was Colombia, which registered $0.1 million in imports from Brunei in 1990.
[b] No trade figures are available for Antigua and Barbuda, St. Kitts/Nevis, and St. Lucia.
[c] 1989.
[d] 1988.

Note: The symbol — represents negligible trade values; the symbol . . . indicates no trade recorded.

Republic, Guatemala, Honduras, Haiti, and Panama also do. Countries that do not maintain formal links with Taiwan nevertheless are generally hosts to trade and interests sections or are in other ways involved in trading relationships with Taiwan. In other words, Taiwan's policy of "buying hearts" is paying off in the Caribbean Basin. As a country with vast foreign reserves, Taiwan offers friendly nations the prospect of technical and economic aid, particularly from a new Overseas Economic Cooperation Fund that amounted to $1.2 billion in 1989.[5]

Although South Korea also seeks to "score points" vis-à-vis North Korea by its economic success and relatively extensive diplomatic ties, it does not suffer like Taiwan from an urgent need to break out of diplomatic isolation. Nevertheless, it welcomes global attention and needs to expand its trading markets. The Central American "Basin" countries—Dominican Republic, Haiti, Panama, Mexico, Venezuela, and Colombia—all have established resident diplomatic representation in Korea, a presence that points to the importance of the economic relationship with that country. Although figures are not readily available on aid and investment, anecdotal evidence suggests that the Caribbean Basin linkage with Korea and Taiwan has been reflected in aid and investment flows, some relatively small-scale (for example, the donation of Hyundai cars to Grenada and other eastern Caribbean governments), some larger development assistance and technical cooperation in agriculture and engineering, and the rest in joint investment ventures in fishing, manufacturing, construction, and industry.

Trade figures are much more accessible. Shown in Table 4.1 are percentages for trade with "developing Asia" (as the term is defined by the International Monetary Fund, IMF), which consists primarily, though not exclusively, of the region under study and China. Table 4.2 follows this up with figures for trade between the Caribbean Basin and the Asian-Pacific region (except Japan) for 1990, the latest year for which relatively complete figures were available at the time of writing (early 1992). (A note of caution is in order: IMF figures for the "latest" year available at any given time are often substantially revised a year or two later.) As can be seen, the percentage of trade between the Caribbean and Asia and the Pacific remains low, except for the small island of Dominica, which has relatively large imports from Korea and Taiwan. Cuba's relatively large percentage of exports to Asia (20.6 percent) reflects primarily its exports to China, which amount to 88 percent of its Asian exports. For the rest of the countries, however, we can see some modest levels of trade, especially imports from Taiwan in the case of Central American states (except Nicaragua), Panama, Colombia, Dominican Republic, Haiti, Dominica, Jamaica, and Trinidad and Tobago, and from Korea in the case of Dominica, all the Central American states, Panama, Mexico, Colombia, Venezuela, and (proportionally) Barbados. Mexico has the strongest trade with all the NICs but especially Hong Kong. The Dominican Republic,

Haiti, Jamaica, Guatemala, Honduras, Panama, and, less so, Costa Rica and Grenada have moderate levels of imports from Hong Kong. Singapore's imports are of growing significance to Bahamas, Colombia, Honduras, and St. Vincent.

Trade with ASEAN nations other than Singapore is considerably less vibrant. Mexico is the only country with moderate amounts of trade (imports and exports) with ASEAN, but its trade with the Philippines is small. Thailand has moderate exports to Cuba and imports from Venezuela; Malaysia has some trade with Cuba and Haiti. Although the amount is small in absolute terms, Dominica's exports to Malaysia are its highest to any developing Asian nation, and Jamaica also imports a small but significant amount from Malaysia. And despite the low levels of 1990 trade, the Bahamas traded heavily with Indonesia between 1984 and 1987 ($493.5 million in imports in 1986) and with Malaysia in the mid-1980s ($57.5 million in imports in 1984). An important trade-related footnote may be made here: Although no trade with Indonesia is noted for Grenada, the two countries control the world's market for spices such as nutmeg and mace, and they cooperate in pricing despite the breakdown of the last price agreement in 1989.[6] Overall, trade trends show an improvement in Caribbean-Asian trade compared with a decade or two ago, but it is clear that in general the improvement relates to the growth of the East Asian NICs rather than a wider phenomenon of, say, conscious expansion of South-South linkages. Nevertheless, larger countries like Mexico appear to be interested in both dimensions: profiting from the growth of the NICs and diversifying their relations. As one official noted not long ago: "[Americans] resent the fact that Mexico is trying to establish links with Pacific Rim countries like, mainly, Japan and Korea.... We have to diversify. If you U.S. investors are not coming then we have to get some resources from others and we know that Mexico is an attractive area, not only because we represent an interesting market but also because we are next to the U.S."[7] With the United States spreading its economic resources thinly in the post–Cold War era, diversification will become more imperative for the Caribbean. The creation of free-trade megablocs in the Western Hemisphere and in Asia may make diversification more difficult but no less important.

The trade patterns for "developing Asia" (Table 4.1) in no way match the pattern for trade with Japan, which always has been the focal point of the Caribbean's Asian trade. The relationship with Japan has grown so remarkably over the years that it ranks among the top four import partners for almost all the Caribbean countries (see Table 4.3). The rest of this chapter therefore focuses on the "Japan link" and includes some suggestions as to how the Caribbean might exploit this link in the future.

Table 4.3 Trade Between Caribbean Basin Countries and Japan, 1990, ($ U.S. million) and Ranking of Japan as a Trade Partner[a]

Country	Exports to Japan	Partner Rank	Imports From Japan	Partner Rank
CORE CARIBBEAN COUNTRIES				
Spanish-speaking countries/Haiti				
Cuba	86.7	2	80.3	4
Dominican Republic	35.0	3	201.5	2
Haiti	0.8	*	24.6	3
English-speaking countries[a]				
Bahamas	13.6	*	471.1	2
Barbados	0.8	5	35.7	5
Belize	0.7	5	8.9	3
Dominica	1.9	4	5.9	3
Grenada	1.3	5	4.3	3
Guyana	14.5	4	14.1	3
Jamaica	11.1	*	82.9	4
St. Vincent	2.6	4	10.5	3
Trinidad and Tobago	16.1	*	44.3	4
CIRCUM-CARIBBEAN COUNTRIES				
Central American region				
Costa Rica	15.3	*	170.0	2
Guatemala	27.9	5	88.5	3
Honduras	78.2	3	66.1	2
Nicaragua	16.4	3	30.3	2
Panama	2.0	*	74.8	2
Mexico	1,610.0	2	1,682.0	2
South America				
Colombia	260.7	4	508.9	2
Suriname	16.0	*	12.4	5
Venezuela	550.0	3	315.0	4

Source: International Monetary Fund, *Direction of Trade Statistics Yearbook 1991* (Washington, D.C.: IMF, 1991).
[a] Japan's rank among industrial countries.
* denotes a ranking lower than fifth.

Caribbean Relations with Japan

The Japanese have long been interested in Latin America both for economic and cultural reasons, but have had only a marginal interest in the poorer economies of the Caribbean.[8] Nevertheless, the figures show that Japan's exports to these countries have been growing steadily over the years and that the Caribbean has been caught up in the tail wind of the Japanese thrust toward intensive foreign investment in both the United States and key countries of Latin America. Thus, the Caribbean has become increasingly linked to Japan through various economic and financial ties.

Background on Japan

Japan's postwar foreign policy has understandably been geared toward economic goals and, until recently, was relatively devoid of political content. In fact, the tendency for Japan to subordinate global political interest to economic security and expansion has long been criticized by some of Japan's own intellectuals and politicians. For example, Shintaro Ishihara, a former Liberal Democratic Party (LDP) member of the Diet, wrote in 1976:

> Our national values have never had the backing of any distinct, definable morality. This is important in that the lack of morality in politics, economics, foreign relations, even in domestic affairs, is going to affect our future. In the frantic scramble to modernize, no time was left to think about the need for a clear moral law behind politics and diplomacy. . . . The motives that govern diplomatic behavior were bluntly revealed in the much-criticized, rough way that Sino-Japanese relations were normalized. Japan's inconsistent handling of the oil problem is another instance of the same glaring self-interest that comes through its Middle Eastern diplomacy as well. . . . Morality and consistency govern relations between states, but they do not exist in Japanese diplomacy, since no metaphysical quality can be governed by rational efficiency.[9]

Japanese diplomatic self-interest has moderated in recent times for several reasons: First, the external economic environment has become increasingly harsh for Japan. One White Paper of the Ministry of Foreign Affairs concluded that

> Given the harsh and constantly changing international climate, Japan has an especially important role to play in the international community. To date, Japan has developed rather smoothly in a favorable international environment centered on the free-trade system, yet it is not impossible to maintain that international order without coordination and untiring efforts on the part of all countries. It is thus important that Japan, taking the long-term perspective and respecting international coordination, work to contribute positively to world peace and prosperity through playing an important and responsible role as a standard-bearer sustaining the international order. Japan is truly at a major turning point in its history, and never before has the Japanese posture been watched so closely as it is today.[10]

Second, and related to the rise in "Japan bashing," Japan's increased wealth has made the country more assertive, more ready to play a world role, both economically and politically, in accord with its status as a global great power. Japan now sees itself as the global partner of the United States in what is being termed "pax consortis." Recent Foreign Ministry reports stress certain "tasks" for Japanese foreign policy: (1) efforts for world peace and stability (in areas such as East-West disarmament and regional conflicts); (2) contribution to the sound development of the world economy (through transforming its economy into one driven not by exports but by domestic demand and by coordinating policy with the Western powers); and (3) cooperation for the developing countries; stability and development.[11] Overall, Japanese foreign policy is still driven by economic imperatives, but Japan is seeking a bigger role now in global peacekeeping efforts through stepped-up financial aid to the United Nations peacekeeping unit and also, for the first time, contributions of personnel to monitor the peace in Afghanistan and Cambodia and, earlier, Namibia. Japan also made large financial and nonmilitary contributions, with U.S. approval and urging, to the allied effort against Iraq in 1991, though the government's offer to send some nonmilitary personnel ran into substantial popular opposition. Japan is prohibited constitutionally from engaging in military activities abroad and the public is very wary of any commitment of troops, even to U.N. peacekeeping operations. This stance has, however, reduced Japan's ability to exert global influence. In June 1992, the Japanese Diet reluctantly passed a bill allowing for the country's participation in global peacekeeping but not in any activities or situations that may lead to combat. Because Japan's efforts to be more assertive politically are focused more on Asia than anywhere else, its first troop involvement has, not unexpectedly, been in Cambodia.[12]

Japan's relations with the developing world have traditionally centered on Asia. Because Japan is a resource-poor nation, its early interest in Asia hinged on its need for raw materials. Military adventures in the region, undertaken in the name of a "Greater Asian Co-Prosperity Sphere," gave way after World War II to economic investment and trade. The importance of Asia to Japan was revealed in the trade figures (see Chapter 2) and is also confirmed in Table 4.4. In 1990, 30.9 percent of Japan's exports (78.4 percent of exports to developing countries) went to Asia; 28.4 percent of Japan's imports (60.3 percent of Japan's imports from developing countries) came from Asia. (An additional 2.1 percent of exports and 5.1 percent of imports constituted trade with China.)

In terms of investments, 15.9 percent of Japanese direct investment is in Asia (Table 4.5). Japan's trade and investment in Asia have been accompanied by financial assistance of various kinds. As previously noted, aid to Asia began as postwar reparations, and Asia received over 90 percent—and sometimes nearly 100 percent—of Japan's bilateral official development assistance (ODA) in the 1960s and 1970s. This has now leveled off to about 60–69 percent. Half of this aid to Asia (about 30 percent of all ODA) goes to the countries of ASEAN. Aid to the Southwest Asian nations has increased considerably, and China, which was the largest recipient of bilateral ODA between 1982 and 1986, now ranks second after Indonesia.[13] Table 4.6

Table 4.4 Japan's Trade by Region and Country, 1990 ($ U.S. million)

	Exports	%	Imports	%
Total[a]	286,965	100.0	234,565	100.0
Advanced countries	169,948	59.2	111,185	50.8
U.S.A.	90,315	31.5	52,287	22.3
EC	53,510	18.6	35,063	14.9
Australia	6,903	2.4	12,320	5.3
Developing areas	113,280	39.5	110,448	47.1
Latin America	10,283	3.6	9,826	4.2
Asia	88,814	30.9	66,586	28.4
Asian NICs[b]	56,664	19.7	25,936	11.1
Middle East[c]	9,919	3.5	31,335	13.4
Africa[c]	3,409	1.2	1,875	0.8
Other countries	9,864	3.4	16,945	7.2
Commonwealth of Independent States	2,564	0.9	3,354	1.4
China	6,128	2.1	12,018	5.1

Source: Japan External Trade Organization (JETRO), *Nippon, Business Facts and Figures, 1991,* p. 56.
[a] Due to technical differences in accounting, totals are not equal to the sum of the individual figures and percentages.
[b] Korea, Taiwan, Hong Kong, and Singapore.
[c] Libya, Egypt, Sudan, Ethiopia, and Somalia and included in the Middle East, not in Africa.

highlights the importance of Asia in the geographical distribution of Japan's ODA.

Up to the late 1970s, most of Japan's foreign lending was primarily in the form of loans and was tied to exports or the procurement of goods and services. By the mid-1970s, Japan was the only country falling below the Development Assistance Committee (DAC)'s recommended target of an 84 percent grant element in ODA. However, since the late 1970s, Japan has been pressured by the international community to accept the global responsibility that comes with economic wealth. In response to this pressure, and increasingly conscious of the importance of foreign aid, Japan announced in 1977 that it would double its ODA in the next three years. The goal was quickly attained and a new goal was set for 1981–1985 to double the ODA volume achieved in 1976–1980. This second goal was almost achieved, and new targets were set for 1986 to 1992 aimed at increasing ODA to $40 billion (increased to more than $50 billion in 1988) and improving the ODA/GNP ratio, which reached .32 percent in 1988 compared with the United Nations target of 0.7 percent.

In 1988, Japan's net ODA disbursements amounted to $9.13 billion, almost as much as that of the United States ($9.78 billion). The overall grant

Table 4.5 Japanese Direct Investment Abroad by Region ($ U.S. million)

	Fiscal Year 1989 Value	Fiscal Years 1951–1989	
		Value	%
North America	33,902	108,993	42.9
U.S.A.	32,540	104,400	41.1
Latin America	5,238	36,855	14.5
Panama	2,044	14,902	5.9
Cayman Islands	1,658	6,743	2.7
Brazil	349	5,945	2.3
Bahamas	620	3,338	1.3
Asia	8,238	40,465	15.9
Indonesia	631	10,435	4.1
Hong Kong	1,898	8,065	3.2
Singapore	1,902	5,714	2.3
Korea	606	3,854	1.5
Thailand	1,276	3,268	1.3
Middle East	66	3,404	1.3
U.A.E.	6	441	0.2
Europe	14,808	44,972	17.7
U.K.	5,239	15,793	6.2
Netherlands	4,547	10,072	4.0
Luxembourg	654	5,383	2.1
Germany, F.R.	409	2,364	1.3
Africa	671	5,275	2.1
Liberia	643	4,301	1.7
Oceania	4,618	13,933	5.5
Australia	4,256	12,393	4.9
Total	67,540	253,896	100.0

Source: Japan External Trade Organization (JETRO), *Nippon, Business Facts and Figures, 1991* (Tokyo: JETRO, 1991), p. 76.
Note: Columns may not total exactly due to rounding.

element increased from 69.9 percent in 1976 to 75.4 percent in 1987, but this was still the lowest percentage among DAC countries. Untied aid increased to 72.1 percent of commitments in 1987, only a little behind Norway, Sweden, and Denmark and far ahead of most of the other donors.[14]

In 1987, Japan announced that it would recycle in the next three years over $30 billion in official and private funds to developing countries on a completely untied basis. By July 1989, over 90 percent of the target had

Table 4.6 Geographical Distribution of Bilateral ODA, Net Disbursements
($ U.S. million and percent)

	1987	1988
Asia	3,416 (65.1)	4,034 (62.8)
Northeast Asia	577 (11.0)	725 (11.3)
Southeast Asia	1,866 (35.6)	2,197 (34.2)
ASEAN	1,680 (32.0)	1,920 (29.9)
Southwest Asia	970 (18.5)	1,109 (17.3)
Unspecified	3 (0.1)	4 (0.1)
Middle East	526 (10.0)	583 (9.1)
Africa	516 (9.8)	884 (13.8)
Central and South America	418 (8.0)	399 (6.2)
Oceania	68 (1.3)	93 (1.4)
Europe	2 (0.0)	4 (0.1)
Unallocated	302 (5.8)	425 (6.6)
Total bilateral ODA	5,248 (100)	3,846 (100)

Source: Ministry of Foreign Affairs, *Japan's Official Development Assistance (ODA), 1989 Annual Report* (Tokyo, March 1990), p. 59.

already been achieved, and that year Japan expanded the original program to at least $65 billion over five years, including the original three-year period.[15]

In sum, in the 1980s and 1990s, Japan has not only established itself as the world's strongest economic power but also is beginning to redefine its world role—to move away from a strictly passive, even amoral policy of economic self-interest toward greater concern for global cooperation and development.

Japan and Latin America

Because the Caribbean is viewed by Japanese policymakers as a subregion of Latin America, a word is in order about Japan's relations with the larger region. Japan's growth as an economic power has been accompanied by a broadening of its interests to include the developing world beyond the Asian region. Japanese businesses have long been attracted to Latin America, partly because of the sizable Japanese presence in the largest Latin American country, Brazil, and partly because the region is more advanced economically and socially than other Third World regions.[16] In the 1970s, the Japanese government's view was that the Latin American economies were "mid-developing," and government policy was that "economic cooperation in mid-developing countries should be extended through private resources rather than on an official basis." Thus, Latin America received more foreign private long-term capital than Africa or Asia.[17] As Table 4.5 indicates, Panama and Brazil have been major recipients of Japanese foreign direct investment in Latin America. Although Mexico does not appear in that particular table, it consistently appeared on Japanese lists until edged out by the Cayman Islands tax haven in 1987 and by the Bahamas as well in 1988. Japanese overseas investment in Latin America and the Caribbean represented 5.1 percent of all its investment in 1970, but rose to over 20 percent in the 1970s and 1980s. A decline began in the late 1980s, mainly attributable to the decline in Brazilian investments and to increased investment in the United States and Europe.[18] In contrast to the relatively rosy picture for investments, Japan's ODA to Latin America has been rather stable: from 5.6 percent of all ODA in 1975 to a peak of 0.9 percent in 1983 and 6.2 percent in 1988.[19] The recent decline, according to the Japanese foreign ministry, results from the fact that "income levels are generally high in those countries compared with other developing regions, with the result that few countries qualify for financial assistance." Also, "many of the countries that are eligible for repayable financial assistance cannot be provided with ODA loans due to their massive accumulated debt and involvement in debt rescheduling."[20] Note that the emphasis is on loans rather than on grants for Latin America.

In trade, the volume of exports to Latin America rose dramatically from $1.2 billion in 1970 to a peak of $10.5 billion in 1981 and $10.3 billion in 1990; likewise, the volume of imports increased from $1.4 billion in 1970 to $7.2 billion in 1984 and a peak of $9.8 billion in 1989.[21] But in reality, the percentage share of trade with Latin America in Japan's total trade has not changed much over the years. In 1970, 6.1 percent of Japan's exports went to Latin America; the figure was only 6.9 percent in the peak 1981 year. Imports from Latin America represented 7.3 percent of Japan's imports in 1970 and only 4.2 percent in the peak year (to date) 1989. Brazil and Mexico are the dominant trading partners for Japan.

A Japanese businessman and writer with much international experience notes:

> Japan's classification of the world's countries is the natural outcome of its own self-image. Just mention Brazil and China and eyes light up, but talk about India and Argentina and you will elicit only shrugs. The Japanese divide the world into two types: resource-rich countries that promise to alleviate Japan's natural poverty, and consumer countries that provide markets for manufactured goods.[22]

Japan has long been interested in certain resource-rich Latin American countries. It has imported sugar and iron from Brazil, cotton from Nicaragua, coffee from Colombia, cocoa from Ecuador, and foodstuffs from Panama.[23] It has been even more interested in the export markets and joint investment possibilities in the NICs of Latin America, in particular Brazil, Mexico, and Venezuela. But Japan's relations with Latin America have been highly selective, concentrated (in terms of a range of economic activities) on Brazil in particular. Poor countries that do not promise much by way of markets or a good return on investments do not hold the interest of a country that has traditionally had no political underpinnings to its economic foreign policy. Moreover, once economic deterioration sets in, as in Brazil and most of Latin America in the 1980s, Japan loses interest.[24]

Nevertheless, because Japanese commercial banks have held a large number of outstanding loans to Latin America (15 percent of Latin America's total foreign debt),[25] Japan has shown increasing interest in cooperating in international financial assistance to debt-ridden countries, especially Mexico and Brazil. In 1987, it was the second largest ODA contributor to Brazil (after Germany) and the third largest to Mexico (after the United States and France).[26] It has contributed substantially to international structural adjustment lending, and in June 1988, at the annual summit meeting of leaders of the industrialized democracies, Japan proposed that a trustee fund be set up, administered by the International Monetary Fund, to guarantee bonds that debtor nations could swap at a substantial discount for the loans owed to commercial banks. Although this plan was not approved, Japan later announced that it was prepared to support the structural adjustment efforts of debtor nations by providing untied financial help in cooperation with the IMF. The U.S. Brady Plan (termed "Strengthened Debt Strategy") announced in March 1989 incorporated some of the Japanese recommendations. Japan then announced that it would strive to contribute about $10 billion from the enhanced capital-recycling program specifically to countries to which the Strengthened Debt Strategy would be applied.[27] Because the Latin American countries feature prominently among the highly indebted, it was not surprising that Mexico was the first country to reach an agreement under the Brady Plan in 1989. Other Latin American nations have worked out arrangements under somewhat less favorable terms. In addition, Latin American countries such as Brazil have been seeking more bilateral project loans from Japan and have in general received Japanese assurance of support.[28] An interesting development in 1990 was the election of a Japanese Peruvian to the presidency of Peru. The campaign and election raised expectations of a large influx of aid from Japan. These expectations were not borne out, but Japan has marginally increased its aid to Peru.

Japan and the Caribbean Basin

Tables 4.3 (earlier in the chapter) and 4.7 provide basic information about the relationship between Japan and the wider Caribbean. The most important or interesting relationships are highlighted in the sections that follow.

Central America and Panama. All the Central American countries, including Nicaragua, have benefited from some measure of official assistance from Japan, primarily in the form of grants and technical assistance. The

Table 4.7 Japan's Bilateral ODA to Caribbean Basin Countries, 1988

Country	Net Bilateral ODA ($ U.S. million)	% of Total Bilateral ODA	Type[a]
CORE CARIBBEAN COUNTRIES			
Spanish-speaking countries/Haiti			
Cuba	0.48	0.0	G, T, L
Dominican Republic[b]	22.88	0.4	G, T, L
Haiti	15.00	0.2	G, T
English-speaking countries			
Antigua and Barbuda	0.01	0.0	T
Bahamas	0.02	0.0	T
Barbados	0.05	0.0	T
Belize	0.05	0.0	T
Dominica	0.24	0.0	T
Grenada	0.18	0.0	T
Guyana	2.00	0.0	G, T, L
Jamaica	5.62	0.1	G, T, L
St. Kitts/Nevis	0.10	0.0	T
St. Lucia	1.07	0.0	G, T
St. Vincent	1.36	0.0	G, T
Trinidad and Tobago	0.30	0.0	T
CIRCUM-CARIBBEAN COUNTRIES			
Central American region			
Costa Rica	6.32	0.1	G, T, L
Guatemala	4.36	0.1	G, T
Honduras[b]	48.10	0.8	G, T, L
Nicaragua	0.41	0.0	T
Panama[b]	4.52	0.1	G, T
Mexico[c]	38.83	0.6	G, T, L
South America			
Colombia	6.69	0.1	G, T, L
Suriname	−0.37[d]	—	T
Venezuela[e]	3.19	0.1	G, T, L

Source: Ministry of Foreign Affairs, *Japan's Official Development Assistance (ODA), Annual Report 1989* (Tokyo, March 1990), pp. 230–256.
[a] G=grant aid; T=technical cooperation; L=loan aid. Both grant aid and technical cooperation fall under the ODA grant element.
[b] Japan was the second largest DAC aid donor to this country in 1987.
[c] Japan was the third largest DAC aid donor to this country in 1987.
[d] Negative figure reflects outflows on loan aid.
[e] Japan was the fourth largest DAC aid donor to this country in 1987.

biggest recipient of ODA in recent years has been Honduras (Table 4.7), for which Japan was the second largest donor in 1987. Not exactly coincidentally, Honduras also is (with Cuba) the largest Caribbean nonoil exporter to Japan (see Table 4.3). Trade between Central America and Japan has traditionally been in the form of exchange of cotton, coffee, bananas, and products for Japan's industrial output. The volume of trade is still relatively small, except for Japan's exports to Panama. Panama is (on paper) Japan's largest export partner in Latin America. Marine exports have traditionally accounted for the bulk of this trade because Panama is a major purchaser of ships used by third countries to sail under its flag.[29] It is significant that Japanese export figures to Panama are forty times higher than Panama's reported imports from Japan, a discrepancy that suggests differences in accounting attributable to third-country routing and/or exports.[30] Panama is also the recipient of some 40 percent of Japanese direct investment in Latin America, and Japan was second only to the United States in 1987 aid to Panama. (See Tables 4.3, 4.5, and 4.7 for trade, investment, and aid figures.)

The formalization of Pacific cooperation (the history of which has been discussed in Chapter 1) has the potential to benefit Central American countries. Although the establishment of an official integration movement involving the entire Pacific Basin is a long way off, given the fears of the ASEAN states and other obstacles, Central American states can be a part of other unofficial or semiofficial cooperative efforts. The most viable of these are the newly formed Asia Pacific Economic Cooperation Forum and the semiofficial Pacific Economic Cooperation Conference (PECC), formed in 1980. PECC, the more institutionally advanced of the two, already has a broad membership, including Japan, the United States, Canada, Australia, and New Zealand; the six members of ASEAN; South Korea, China, Taiwan, and the Pacific island nations as a group. Attending meetings as observers have been the former Soviet Union, the Pacific Latin American nations, and Guatemala (alone among Central American states). The conference aim is to promote economic cooperation in the Pacific Basin, specifically "free and open economic exchanges." The membership may be expanded to include Latin America; if this occurs, Central Americans may find it in their interest to join.[31]

Finally, Central America is likely to continue to benefit from Japanese efforts to play a useful role in a region of political import to the United States. Before the settlement of the Nicaraguan issue, the Japanese Ministry of Foreign Affairs noted: "Japan has firmly supported Contadora Group and other efforts for peaceful solution of Central American disputes and has cooperated in economic and social development of the Central American and Caribbean region."[32] At the urging of the United States, Japan increased its economic assistance to the region. According to Juichi Inada writing in 1988:

> The U.S. government has feared that its diplomatic strategy will be

undermined by Congressional budget cuts in aid for areas of conflict, like Central America and the Middle East. . . . This is the background against which the Americans have been seeking a greater Japanese contribution in aid, particularly to regions that are of special strategic significance to the United States.[33]

Despite the democratic transition in Nicaragua, Central America remains a region beset by economic and political problems, and for the time being, the U.S.-Japanese collaboration in assistance to the region is likely to hold firm. However, the diversion of assistance to Eastern Europe and the Commonwealth of Independent States has already reduced the levels of assistance by both the United States and Japan to Central America.

Venezuela. Venezuela views itself as a major Caribbean nation and therefore a brief consideration of Japan's relationship with that country is useful. Japan's trade with Venezuela increased in the 1970s, with 90 percent of Japan's imports being mineral fuels,[34] and the country remains today a backup supplier of oil to Japan (Japan's leading suppliers in 1990 were Saudi Arabia, Indonesia, Iran, China, and Mexico).[35] In the late 1980s, it ranked behind only Panama, Mexico, and Brazil in terms of the Latin American market for Japan's industrial exports, but the level of its imports has declined markedly, to fall below those of Chile and Colombia.

Venezuela is one of the few Latin American countries that seems to be poised for an influx of Japanese investment and trade. Japanese interest in Venezuela has been heightened by new investment incentives, by Venezuela's drive in the late 1980s to seek private partners in state-controlled enterprises, and by its relative economic and political stability compared with other countries, not withstanding sporadic social and political turmoil in the early 1990s.[36] Japan is Venezuela's fifth largest foreign investor with $74 million invested in Venezuela in 1988. However, this amount represented only 4 percent of total Venezuelan investment.[37] In the 1960s and 1970s, Venezuela's relatively high income drew Japanese investors in consumer-goods manufacturing and in the aluminum industry. New Venezuelan incentives announced in 1988 (including debt-equity conversions) have attracted Japanese joint ventures in petrochemicals, steel, hydroelectricity, and communications industries. Venezuela has been receiving increasingly larger amounts of ODA from Japan, primarily technical assistance but also, more recently, grant aid. In 1987, the latest year for which data are available, Japan was the fourth largest aid donor to Venezuela, after Germany, France, and Italy. Venezuela has received major untied loans for various projects as part of Japan's commitment to recycle its trade surplus to developing countries.[38]

Cuba. As shown in Table 4.3, there is a relatively high level of trade between Japan and Cuba—more than $80 million in both exports and imports—compared with that of other Caribbean countries. Through the 1970s,

Cuba was one of Japan's main Latin American trading partners. In 1975, Cuba imported more than $400 million in textiles and agricultural machinery (among other products) from Japan and exported about $343 million in commodities, primarily sugar, to Japan.[39] In fact, Cuba that year was Japan's third largest Latin American partner, behind the perennial leaders Panama and Brazil, and its second largest import partner, behind Brazil. Since that peak, Cuba's position has been taken over by a number of other countries. In 1990, Cuba's trade with Japan was only a fifth of what it was in 1975; however, Cuba remains Japan's major market for sugar imports. In the 1990s, Cuba may be expected to increase its trade with Japan and the East Asians as it aggressively seeks new markets to meet the economic crisis caused by the loss of its traditional socialist markets and continuing U.S. sanctions. Despite Japan's collaborative relationship with the United States, it has not shown any inclination to conform to U.S.-imposed sanctions in Panama, Peru, or Cuba. Finally, Cuba continues to receive a small amount of ODA from Japan in the form of technical cooperation assistance (see Table 4.7).

The English-speaking Caribbean. This subregion has had minimal importance to Japan because of its small size and relative poverty, but from the point of view of the English-speaking Caribbean countries, relations with Japan have grown considerably. An overview of the region's trade and aid performance[40] shows that since the middle to late 1970s, Japanese imports have increased in importance for all countries. The volume of imports from Japan is largest by far for Bahamas, with a moderate volume for Jamaica, Trinidad and Tobago, and Barbados. As indicated in the last chapter, these countries are all considered to be the more developed countries (MDCs) of the subregion. However, exports of the English-speaking Caribbean to Japan are generally very limited. Again, the larger countries—Trinidad and Tobago, Guyana, Bahamas, and Jamaica—have the highest levels of exports.

As far as official and private aid is concerned, an overview of net disbursements shows that Japan surpassed the United States, the United Kingdom, and Canada in aid to Barbados in the mid-1980s and that in the 1980s, its aid to Jamaica, Trinidad and Tobago, and the Bahamas increased in importance.[41] This aid began in the 1970s. By the mid-1970s, a small amount of bilateral aid had been disbursed to bauxite-rich Jamaica and Guyana ($15 million), and Japan was involved in investment and joint ventures in the auto and steel industries in Trinidad and fishing in Guyana and Trinidad.[42] Financial investments were made primarily in the Bahamas, which today ranks fourth as host to Japanese investment in Latin America. Another English-speaking tax-free haven, the Cayman Islands, in the last few years has received such large inflows of Japanese investment that in 1990 it surpassed Brazil to become the number two host of Japanese foreign investment in Latin America.[43] Because of Trinidad's oil boom, the country became the focus of Japanese technical assistance in such areas as petroleum, health, and dam construction.

From 1981 to 1983, Jamaica received a relatively large injection of Japanese official aid—loans, grants, and technical assistance—which was apparently "strategic aid" sought by the United States to boost the position of the pro-U.S. Edward Seaga administration that had just come to power.[44] The aid (measured by notes exchanged and therefore not comparable to the disbursements given in Table 4.7) amounted to about $14.5 million in 1981 and $108.3 million in 1983 (calculating US$1 at 150 yen in those years). Aid has since declined to about $1–2 million a year.

Details of official development assistance flows to other English-speaking Caribbean countries are given in Table 4.7. As can be seen, the largest recipient of Japanese aid after Jamaica is Guyana, which has received primarily grant aid and technical assistance. The other islands have received technical assistance grants, especially for fisheries projects. Finally, the low figures for Bahamas may be a bit deceiving. Japan ranks among the top five aid donors to that country, according to DAC figures for the late 1980s.

The Caribbean and Japan: Potential Ties

Japan will never be as important to the Caribbean Basin as is the United States and other traditional targets of Caribbean foreign policy. However, there is widespread recognition of the importance of Japan as an economic superpower, and the country can therefore be useful to the Caribbean if certain rules are borne in mind.

Japan's foreign policy remains guided by economics rather than politics. The Japanese call this *seikei bunri,* the separation of business from politics.[45] Japan does not pursue ideological interests. One report contrasts the Japanese position in the Panama crisis of 1989, for example, with that of the United States: Japan refused to participate in the U.S. preinvasion campaign of economic and political pressure against the regime of Manuel Noriega. The same report noted that the Japanese are interested in secure export markets and new locations for downstream manufacturing. They are wary of making investments in unstable environments and seek to minimize and spread the risk among companies and/or government agencies. They are amenable to joint ventures, but "if an investment becomes problematic, a Japanese firm may move quickly to close down operation—even at a substantial loss."[46]

Given these considerations, we can say that, as the larger Caribbean Basin countries have discovered, the Japanese can be relatively ideal partners for Caribbean business on the basis of their nonpolitical stance. It should be added that the Japanese also have reasonably accommodating attitudes toward two important issues in developing countries: technology transfer and local participation. Technology transfer was not always in the vocabulary of the Japanese, and Asians still complain about the problems they encounter in getting the Japanese to transfer skills. But in recent times, the Japanese have become more accommodating in the interest of preserving their investments. Japan now officially views technology transfer as a major part of it technical cooperation. Japanese industries view technology transfer as the inevitable cost of doing business, even at the expense of creating competitive Koreas, Taiwans, and Singapores. Some forward-minded Japanese even maintain that the transference of certain industries to lower-cost areas can be helpful to Japan if used as a way to "power the transition toward higher-value-added industries."[47] Similar considerations hold in the related area of localization of industries, a Third World aim that has been softened today in the general thrust toward less state control. Nevertheless, the participation of local private capital in investment ventures is still considered important. Japanese businesses in Asia, unlike U.S. firms in Latin America, did not fight strongly against state-mandated localization because of a pragmatic perception that it is better to have half of the pie (or less) than none at all. As for private capital, the Japanese are relatively happy to be minority partners in joint ventures with local firms, especially in unfamiliar regions such as the Caribbean.

The problem for Caribbean countries is, however, that most of them (excluding the NICs of the wider Basin and the tax havens like the Bahamas) are not particularly attractive for Japanese investment. Many of these countries are poor, though not necessarily resource-poor, and lack the necessary infrastructure for investment or the sizable market for Japanese goods. (Most, however, have consumers who are highly attracted to Japanese products. The Japanese have adapted many of their products to meet the needs and pockets of developing Asia and are also selling these products to Caribbean countries.) In the case of those countries that are relatively developed, such as Jamaica, Trinidad and Tobago, or Dominican Republic, not only has the atmosphere sometimes been one of political and economic instability, but also prospective investors face the problems of high labor costs, communications and transportation difficulties, and insufficient incentives to overcome these uncertainties. In the declining economic climate prevalent throughout the region today, the wary Japanese or other desirable East Asian investors are unlikely to be interested in investment without receiving special incentives from governments. Here the Venezuelan example of the enactment of a range of incentives, as cited earlier, is instructive.

International pressure on Japan to open its markets has led the Japanese to seek to produce abroad goods for sale at home, the major trend to date being in the beef industry. If this trend continues, the Japanese may find the Caribbean Basin area more attractive, for example, for investment in citrus production. In the shorter term, Caribbean countries can push harder to export their primary products to resource-poor Japan and to Asia as a whole. They can also profit from the international pressure on Japan to import more by more vigorously marketing their ethnic food and specialty products in Japan. In the manufacturing area, many Caribbean countries are seeking to encourage investment through the creation of economic processing zones, EPZs (free-trade zones). The problem is that there are so many competing zones in developing countries and in Latin America and the Caribbean that the "buyer's market" is unlikely to favor the smaller Caribbean countries. For example, Japan's prime interest in the late 1980s and early 1990s has been in Mexico's *maquiladora* zones near the borders with the United States. Here U.S. interests are fueling Japanese investment. Ironically, then, Caribbean countries may have a better chance to attract Japanese investment through arrangements with the United States than direct deals with Japan. Failing the ability to get U.S. attention, Caribbean countries can "spin their wheels" in individual competition for EPZ investment—a competition that necessarily favors Mexico, Venezuela, Colombia, and a few others[48]—or adopt a regional/subregional approach to investment and trade. Harmonization of fiscal incentives and coordination of national economic strategies can occur within Caricom and the Central American Common Market and be followed up by Caricom-CACM cooperation. Fortunately, this type of cooperation is being initiated in the 1990s in view of the U.S. offer of hemispheric integration—what U.S. President Bush called his "Enterprise for the Americas."

Consideration of U.S. interest also drives some aspects of Japanese aid. Japanese assistance is given in pursuit of the following goals: (1) to cooperate in countries' economic development as a means of strengthening bilateral relations with them; (2) to foster international economic stability and thereby promote Japan's own economic stability and well-being; and (3) to fulfill a part of Japan's international responsibilities by indirectly contributing to the political stability of the countries receiving aid.[49]

The third goal needs some explanation: Japan is prevented by a 1978 parliamentary Foreign Affairs Committee resolution from giving external economic assistance "of a sort that will be applied toward military use or that will promote international conflict."[50] Yet some of Japan's aid, dating from the 1960s, has been "political" or "strategic" in the sense that the maintenance of world peace and stability is viewed as important to Japan's economic interests. Most of Japan's "political" concerns (hence economic assistance) have centered on Asia. However, a part of this political aid has been more fundamentally strategic, not in Japanese terms but in terms of the Japanese desire to help the United States achieve its strategic goals. Thus, Inada cites Japanese aid to Jamaica in the early 1980s as well as aid to Pakistan, Somalia, Sudan, and Turkey as assistance that resulted from U.S. urging.[51] Aid in the later 1980s to Central America and assistance in the 1990s to the former Soviet Union and Eastern Europe clearly also fall within that category.

The Caribbean countries could benefit from increased Japanese assistance through the United States provided they find an effective way to convince the latter of their urgent economic needs. Traditionally, U.S. interest in the region has been so tied to political considerations that in the absence of crisis, aid levels have fallen. Caribbean countries would need to engage in more effective lobbying if they are to receive more assistance from both the United States and its partner-in-aid Japan. This is a difficult task in view of the diversion of U.S. interest to other areas of the world, but Latin America and the Caribbean remain of strategic (albeit more restricted) and economic importance to the United States, a fact that seems to be understood in U.S. policy circles.

Japan could also be directly helpful to the Caribbean. Given its willingness to recycle its trade surplus to developing countries on less stringent terms than usual, Caribbean countries would do well to follow the examples of Brazil and Mexico and make a concerted effort to enlist Japanese help in debt relief and other forms of official aid. It may be noted that Japan is currently a large donor of aid in the environmental field, which in Japan's definition includes aid given to deal with "pollution, water supply and sewerage systems, urban hygiene, water resource development, forestry and forest conservation, and disaster prevention."[52] In this area and others, the Japanese are stepping up their technical cooperation to developing countries. Their programs include receiving trainees (17.5 percent of the total trainees received came from Central and South America in 1988); dispatching experts (22.6 percent of the total went to Central and South America in 1988); providing equipment and machinery to help the experts, as well as the trainees after they return from Japan; extending project-type technical cooperation (cooperation incorporating the three preceding elements); promoting development surveys; and dispatching Japan Overseas Cooperation Volunteers (the Japanese equivalent of the U.S. Peace Corps). An interesting element of the trainee program is the "third country" program, designed to provide the developing countries with trainees from neighboring countries that have similar natural, social, and cultural environments with financial and technical support from Japan.[53] In the 1990s, Japan has plans for further increases in its technical assistance to match the growing demand.

The Japanese Ministry of Foreign Affairs notes that requests for technical assistance from developing countries have changed contextually over the years:

> The majority of the requests in the past, in general, were in rather traditional areas such as vocational training, agricultural development, forestry development, urban transportation control, broadcasting technology and medical cooperation. In recent years, however, there have been increasing demands for specialized high technology, new energy development, computer technology, biotechnology, biogenetic

resources research, etc. There is also an increasing demand for the transfer of skills and software needed by administrations such as management control, improvement of productivity, measuring standards, quality control, and patented information.[54]

Many of these areas are of direct interest to Caribbean countries. Of course, the cultural groundwork has to be laid carefully if Japanese technical cooperation is to be encouraged. This would include provision of language assistance and wider dissemination by Caribbean governments of knowledge about Japan.[55] The Japanese government is aware of the cultural implications of expanding its technical assistance programs and is doing its part to make the process as effective as possible. Caribbean countries may wish to take advantage of Japan's new willingness to open itself to the world and its desire to improve its image through promoting its culture worldwide (for example, through tours by Kabuki troupes, sumo wrestlers, and Japanese drummers) and promoting student and youth exchanges and other activities.[56]

Finally, related to this issue, the Caribbean may find some value in promoting itself culturally in Japan. Japan has a relatively vibrant, though not economically significant, tourist industry that has traditionally relied more on internal than international traveling. But the Japanese, with their newly acquired wealth,[57] have themselves become a nation of travelers. The Japan External Trade Bureau notes: "The annual number of Japanese tourists traveling abroad broke through the 10 million mark for the first time in 1990. There has been an explosive increase in the number of Japanese spending year-end vacation periods overseas."[58] The Japanese have not changed their favorite tourist destinations noticeably over the years: The most popular destination remains the United States, followed by the Asian NICs and China; Thailand and the Philippines are also popular. Other than the United States, the only other non-Asian countries ranking in the top ten popular destinations are France, the United Kingdom, and Australia.[59] Nevertheless, there are signs that the Japanese are willing to expand their travel horizons beyond Europe, Asia, and the United States. If they employ rigorous packaging, Caribbean tourist destinations can be rewarded with brisk business from Japan in particular and from newly industrialized Asia in general.

Notes

1. Miguel S. Wionczek, "Latin America and the Pacific Region: Trade, Investment, and Technology Issues" in Roger W. Fontaine and James D. Theberge, eds., *Latin America's New Internationalism: The End of Hemispheric Isolation* (New York: Praeger, 1976), pp. 56–57.

2. An interesting though brief discussion of the Chinese experience is Christine Ho's "'Hold the Chow Mein, Gimme Soca': Creolization of the Chinese

in Guyana, Trinidad, and Jamaica," *Amerasia Journal* 15, 2 (1989) (special issue "Asians in the Americas"): 3–25. Figures are quoted from p. 4.

3. South Korea closed its embassy in Barbados in March 1990; North Korea was hoping to establish an embassy in early 1992.

4. See *New York Times*, December 3, 1989, p. 6. For details on the diplomatic relations of the English-speaking Caribbean countries, see Jacqueline A. Braveboy-Wagner, *Caribbean in World Affairs: The Foreign Policies of the English-speaking States* (Boulder, Colo.: Westview, 1989).

5. *New York Times*, December 3, 1989, p. 6.

6. Caribbean Development Bank, *Annual Report 1989* (St. Michael, Barbados, 1990), p. 30.

7. Noted by the Mexican ambassador to the United Nations, Jorge Montano, in an interview quoted in *The Diplomatic World Bulletin*, February 18–25, 1991, p. 1.

A noticeable feature of the analysis of trade patterns is the lack of other than negligible amounts of trade between the Caribbean and the Pacific islands. The small Pacific island states are agricultural, exporting commodities that are competitive with Caribbean products. This fact, combined with distance, reduces the possibility of any major trade relationships with this group. However, a major form of trade cooperation between the Pacific islands and the Caribbean countries was initiated in 1975 when the first Lomé Convention was signed. The entry of Britain into the European Community was the catalyst for one of the most successful efforts at South-South collaboration: Caribbean countries joined with African and Pacific countries to work to assure continued preferential access of their primary products to the British and expanded European market. The African-Caribbean-Pacific group (ACP), headquartered in Brussels, has collaborated on three more Lomé conventions since the first expired. Under the conventions, countries receive duty-free access for all their industrial and most of their agricultural products as well as development assistance and assistance under the European Community's export-stabilization scheme, Stabex. See Chapter 7 for more on Caribbean-Pacific cooperation.

8. The rest of the chapter is reproduced in large part from Jacqueline A. Braveboy-Wagner, "Japan and the Caribbean: Linkages and Possibilities," *Caribbean Affairs* 2, 4, (October–December 1989): 109–122. By permission of the publisher, Trinidad Express Newspapers Ltd./Inprint Caribbean Ltd.

9. Shintaro Ishihara, "A Nation Without Morality," in Japan Center for International Exchange, ed., *The Silent Power: Japan's Identity and World Role* (Tokyo: Simul, 1976), pp. 84–85.

10. Japan Institute for International Affairs (JIIA), *White Papers on Japan, Foreign Policy* (Tokyo: Ministry of Foreign Affairs, 1988), p. 20.

11. For example, ibid., pp. 20–21.

12. *New York Times*, June 21, 1992, p. E4; on Japan's new political visibility in Asia, see *New York Times*, September 6, 1988, p. A8.

13. Japan Ministry of Foreign Affairs (MFA), *Japan's Official Development Assistance, ODA, 1989 Report* (Tokyo: MFA, (March 1990), pp. 60–62. (These annual reports are cited hereafter as MFA, *ODA 19xx*.)

14. Ibid., pp. 7, 23, 24; and Jacqueline Braveboy-Wagner, "The Japanese in Trinidad: A Report on Japanese Behavior Beyond the Asian Region," *Asian Profile* 9, 1 (February 1981): 22.

15. MFA, *ODA 1989*, p. 7.

16. For a study of the attitudes of Japanese businesspeople toward the Third World, including Latin America, see my (Jacqueline A. Braveboy-Wagner) "Japan and the Third World: A Study of the Attitudes of Japanese Businessmen Toward

Developing Countries and Peoples," *Asian Profile* 8, 4 (August 1980): 329–348.

17. Hiroya Ichikawa, "Japan's Economic Relationship with Latin America," in Fontaine and Theberge, *Latin America's New Internationalism*, p. 74.

18. Ibid., p. 91; Japan External Trade Organization (JETRO), *Nippon: Business Facts and Figures 1988* (Tokyo: JETRO), p. 74; (The JETRO annual reports are cited hereafter as JETRO, *Nippon 19xx.*). See JETRO, *Nippon 1989*, p. 80, and *Nippon 1991*, p. 76. See also Keizai Koho Center (Japan Institute for Social and Economic Affairs), *Japan: An International Comparison 1990*, p. 56.

19. MFA *ODA 1987*, p. 55, and *ODA 1989*, p. 59.

20. MFA, *ODA 1989*, p. 62.

21. Japan Ministry of Trade and Industry (MITI), *White Paper on International Trade, Japan* (Tokyo: MITI, 1976), p. 211 (chart); JETRO, *Nippon 1991*, p. 56.

22. Kenichi Ohmae, *Beyond National Borders: Reflections on Japan and the World* (Tokyo and New York: Kodansha International, 1987), pp. 3–4.

23. MITI, *White Paper, Trade*, pp. 221–224.

24. See, for example, "Debt, Economy, and Politics Convince Japan to 'Take Five' on Brazilian Investments," *Business Latin America*, May 16, 1988, p. 153.

25. *Business Latin America*, March 28, 1988, p. 99.

26. MFA, *ODA 1989*, pp. 235, 247.

27. *New York Times*, September 26, 1988, p. D3; MFA, *ODA 1989*, pp. 42–43; and see pp. 37–43 for full details on structural lending.

28. See, for example, *Japan Times*, July 8, 1988, p. 10.

29. See *Business Latin America*, March 28, 1988, p. 99.

30. Japan reported exports to Panama amounting to $2.9 billion in 1990 (compare Panama's reported imports of $748 million) and imports from Panama at $113 million (compare Panama's $2.0 million). See International Monetary Fund (IMF), *Direction of Trade Statistics Yearbook 1991* (Washington, D.C.: IMF, 1991).

31. See Kumao Kaneko, "A New Pacific Initiative: Strengthening the PECC Process," *Japan Review of International Affairs* 2, 1 (Spring/Summer 1988): 67–90 for a detailed discussion of PECC's activities to 1988.

32. JIAA, *White Papers, Foreign Policy*, p. 29.

33. Juichi Inada, "Japan's Aid Diplomacy: Increasing Role for Global Security," *Japan Review of International Affairs* 2, 1 (Spring/Summer 1988): 96.

34. MITI, *White Paper, Trade*, p. 217.

35. JETRO, *Nippon 1991*, p. 62.

36. *Business Latin America*, May 23, 1988, p. 163.

37. Ibid.

38. Ibid., p. 184; and MFA, *ODA 1989* p. 256 (tables).

39. MITI, *White Paper, Trade*, p. 216.

40. Braveboy-Wagner, *Caribbean in World Affairs*, pp. 74–92.

41. Ibid., pp. 83–89.

42. Leslie Manigat, "The Year in Perspective from the Late 1950s to 1975: The Emergence of the Caribbean on the International Scene," in *Caribbean Yearbook of International Relations* (Trinidad and Tobago: Institute of International Relations; Leyden, Netherlands: A. W. Sijthoff, 1975), p. 3; Braveboy-Wagner, "The Japanese in Trinidad," p. 23.

43. JETRO, *Nippon 1991*, p. 76.

44. Inada, "Aid Diplomacy," p. 98.

45. *Business Latin America*, March 28, 1988, p. 97.

46. Ibid., pp. 97–98.

47. Ohmae, *Beyond National Borders*, p. 118.

48. Colombia, for example, recently launched some new duty-free zones to attract investors to marginal regions of the country and stimulate exports. Incentives for foreign capital include free repatriation of profits and exemption of sales to overseas markets from income tax, as well as the usual freedom from import duties. See *Times of the Americas* (Washington, D.C.), January 22, 1992, p. B4.

49. Inada, "Aid Diplomacy," p. 107.

50. Ibid., p. 96.

51. Ibid., pp. 97–98.

52. MFA, *ODA 1989*, p. 46.

53. Ibid., pp. 82–97, esp. pp. 82–88; and MFA, *ODA 1988*, pp. 105–111, esp. 105–106, 108.

54. MFA, *ODA 1988*, p. 106.

55. For a discussion of problems encountered by the Japanese in Trinidad, see Braveboy-Wagner, "The Japanese in Trinidad," pp. 19–32; and for a discussion of problems encountered by the Japanese in the developing world in general, see Braveboy-Wagner, "Japan and the Third World."

56. JIIA, *White Papers, Foreign Policy*, p. 23.

57. Although Japan as a country is rich, and many Japanese companies are rich, the Japanese people as a whole do not consider themselves to be affluent: The cost of living is extremely high, housing is at a premium, open space is limited, and only 34 percent of the population is provided with sewage services. See JETRO, *Nippon 1988*, pp. 140–158 for statistical details. For a sense of the Japanese lifestyle, see also statistics in JETRO, *Nippon 1989, 1990*, and *1991* pp. 140–158.

58. JETRO, *Nippon 1991*, p. 158.

59. Ibid.

PART 2

DEVELOPMENT: WHAT CAN THE ENGLISH-SPEAKING CARIBBEAN LEARN FROM ASIA PACIFIC?

5
Applying the East Asian Development Model to the English-Speaking Caribbean

Dennis J. Gayle

In the first part of this book, the question of linkages between the Caribbean Basin and the Asian-Pacific region was addressed. The focus in the next two chapters turns to the specific English-speaking Caribbean subregion and to this question: What, if anything, can this region learn from Asia Pacific? This chapter focuses specifically on the relevance of the East Asian model of development. Other authors have compared Latin America and East Asia in socioeconomic terms, as elaborated briefly later. However, hardly anyone has systematically done the same for the subset of "newer" Caribbean nations. This is the rationale for narrowing the focus in this chapter.

Naturally, no model of development, whether Western, socialist, or East Asian, can be successfully transferred without adaptation to countries with different histories, cultures, and polities. But this does not preclude the adoption of certain aspects of a model that might be useful, given the particular circumstances of the borrowing country. At first glance, any commonalities between East Asia and the Caribbean seem to be so obscured by cultural idiosyncrasies as to make any emulation of development policies impossible. Yet within the Caribbean, there are countries that can be described as newly industrializing (the NICs)—that are aggressively moving into more sophisticated areas of manufacturing and industry and adopting export-promotion strategies in the hopes of achieving the successes of the East Asians and the fast-growing ASEAN countries. In the circum-Caribbean, Mexico and Venezuela are already NICs. In the core region, the Puerto Rican industrialization-by-invitation (import-substitution) model was followed by many countries and later modified to suit individual circumstances. Of the countries that began by following the Puerto Rican model, Jamaica and Trinidad and Tobago are relatively advanced and, at least in the subregion, can be classified as "little NICs." In territorial size, these two countries are considerably larger than Singapore or Hong Kong. In population size, Jamaica compares favorably with Singapore. Trinidad is half their size but nevertheless comparable. Both are islands, like Hong Kong and Singapore, and they share with Hong Kong and Singapore a history of British colonialism.

Many comparisons, invariably unfavorable to Latin America, have been made between the East Asian NICs and the Latin American industrializing countries. In fact, a certain defensiveness tends to creep into the analysis of why Latin America has not succeeded as Asia has.[1] Some analysts emphasize the cultural differences: Confucian values of thrift and hard work versus Roman Catholicism and various Iberian traits. But Confucianism used to be considered an obstacle to growth in Asia because it emphasized factors such as deference to authority, resistance to change, and aversion to risk.[2] Perhaps the better approach is to look at policy differences and changes in the international economic environment: for example, the outward-looking policies of the East Asian countries versus the prolonged period of import-substitution industrialization (ISI) adopted by the Latin Americans; the role of government guidance and intervention; or the influence of authoritarian political systems.

Most analysts point out that the East Asian NICs were forced to look outward (after short periods of ISI) because of their artificial separation from the hinterland or truncation/division. Singapore was a city-state originally united with a Malaysian hinterland until forced out of the Malaysian Federation in 1965; Hong Kong was a British colony separated by politics from China; Taiwan and Korea were ideologically separated from China and industrial North Korea respectively. It is therefore true to say that "for national security, as much as for economic reasons, [these countries] were constrained to seek commercial outlets in distant . . . markets."[3] Moreover, because of geopolitical circumstances and a strong resource base, Latin American economies depended heavily on foreign investment, whereas the resource-poor East Asians imposed controls on investment. Foreign aid has not been as crucial to the Asian NICs as to Latin America; the result is that Latin American development has become hampered by debt and heavy debt-service burdens. Finally, the East Asians were clearly helped in their export thrust by the openness of the developed country markets. Latin Americans have turned their attention to export promotion only relatively recently—unfortunately, at a time when protectionist measures are being implemented by the developed countries and the market is saturated with Japanese and East Asian products. Japan and East Asia have in fact been compelled by international pressure to pull back and expand their domestic markets.[4]

Although a number of analysts have compared Latin American development with that of East Asia—and these comparisons are relevant to the circum-Caribbean countries—the English-speaking Caribbean subregion can provide a useful point of comparison. As noted, in size and colonial history, the "little NICs" of the Caribbean (Jamaica and Trinidad, in particular, but also Barbados) can be compared with Singapore or

Hong Kong. As in East Asia, education levels are high. Small size and island status combine with a history of colonial domination and plantation agriculture to produce an outward orientation, although no traumatic truncation has occurred. Industrialization by import substitution has been replaced, albeit belatedly, by export-promotion policies. Politically, governments have been somewhat authoritarian, though adhering to democratic norms, and state intervention and planning have been attempted. Trinidad and Tobago, in particular, has imposed some labor market controls on labor, as has been done in East Asia (except Hong Kong). But these Caribbean states are similar to Latin America in their reliance on foreign investment and aid. Rather than serve as catalysts of the economy, foreign investment and aid have generated dependence and often exploitative relationships between multinationals and hosts, and an intrusive rather than constructive presence on the part of the main donor, the United States. Moreover, Caribbean exports are still concentrated on a limited range of primary products and a few markets. In view of these similarities and differences, the rest of this chapter is devoted to a more specific comparison of the economic performance and strategies of the Caribbean and Asian-Pacific states; it concludes with a few suggestions for Caribbean countries.

Background

During the 1980s, average per capita income in the least developed countries (LDCs) of the world declined from $560 to $450, compared with an increase from $11,000 to $13,000 among the industrial market economies. Meanwhile, the most successful NICs remained Singapore, Hong Kong, South Korea, and Taiwan. By 1989, Hong Kong's gross domestic product (GDP) per person was $9,500, about the same as New Zealand's and more than Ireland's. Similarly, Singapore's 1989 GDP per capita of $9,158 exceeded Spain's and was not much less than Italy's. Whereas China's GDP per person totaled $300, Taiwan's amounted to $7,500. The comparable indicator for other rapidly growing Southeast Asian countries averaged $675, but South Korea generated an impressive GDP per capita of $4,500.[5]

Global financial markets have become increasingly integrated, even as international trading blocs, such as the European Community as well as the U.S.-Canada and Asian-Pacific regions, continue to evolve.[6] Such developments are driven by structural and technological changes in information processing, telecommunications, robotics, remote-sensing equipment, synthetic material applications, multinational corporate competition, and public-sector management. Taken together, the twelve largest economies of the Asian-Pacific region accounted for 24 percent of world output in 1988, or approximately the same amount as that produced by the United States, with a real gross domestic product (GDP) of $4.85 trillion. Capital goods were a major international trade component for the six most expansive regional economies: In 1987, aggregate export ($47 billion) and import ($57 billion) values rose sharply. In addition intraregional merchandise trade grew by 33 percent to a value of $259 billion in 1988, making the Asian-Pacific region the globe's fastest-growing trading area, with 9 percent of total world merchandise trade.[7]

Some analysts argue for the "Taiwanization" of the Caribbean, whereas others assert that the East Asian experience has only limited relevance for the region.[8] In this chapter, East Asian as well as Caribbean Basin models of growth and development are reappraised.

Given the public-policy concerns of this chapter, nonindependent territories are excluded—for example the U.S.-affiliated but self-governing Puerto Rico and the British and U.S. Virgin Islands. Even so, as pointed out in earlier chapters, there is substantial variance in scale, economic growth rates, and sociopolitical development levels within the Basin. In the light of such variance, it is most productive to probe the comparative economic growth and development models applied, as well as the outcomes observed, within a more coherent subsystem. The Caribbean Community and Common Market (Caricom) countries share a common institutional and political heritage, including an established commitment to pluralistic democracy.[9] Accordingly, this chapter focuses upon the four East Asian NICs of Singapore, Hong Kong, South Korea, and Taiwan on the one hand, and the four MDCs (more developed countries) of the English-speaking Caribbean—Barbados, Jamaica, Trinidad and Tobago, and Guyana—on the other.

As an initial step, it is essential to distinguish between economic growth and development. Economic growth connotes the constant creation of enhanced capacity to produce wealth. As Arthur Lewis argued, such growth gives people greater potential control over their environment and thereby increases their freedom.[10] Economic growth is easily measured, in terms of GDP levels and rates of increase. Such growth requires significant disparities in income and wealth that serve as performance incentives. In contrast, development emphasizes distribution: the widespread possession and use of resources.[11] The most basic criterion of development is productivity, or the creation over time of optimal capacity to challenge human abilities as well as to satisfy human needs and desires. In the sections that follow, I successively compare East-Asian NIC and Caricom economic growth and development models as well as the observed results to date. The conclusion explores the inferences that these experiences suggest, despite the difficulties of generalizing from sets of cases that remain diverse in some respects.

The East Asian Model

There is broad consensus as to the prime components of the East Asian model of economic growth. These include a Confucian political culture; extensive agricultural reform, where applicable; widespread emphasis upon education; continuity in ruling elite or party; strong and relatively authoritarian government; continuous industrial upgrading along the product cycle; and export-led economic growth. The four initial NICs have implemented essentially liberal international trade policies since the 1960s, in the sense that price distortions have been minimal and the market has allocated most resources. To be sure, protectionism has become increasingly evident in many international trading sectors. As a result, total world trade stagnated from 1976 until 1984, when volume began to expand at an annual rate of 8.7 percent.

Both trade volume and value have remained variable: international trade volume again declined to a growth rate of 2.9 percent in 1985; however, international trade value increased by 18 percent in 1987 and again by 15 percent in 1988, to yield a record total of $2.7 trillion.[12] NIC labor-intensive manufactures have ridden a surge in global manufacturing exports, which has essentially continued since 1950.[13] Multinational companies located in these NICs because of a ready supply of relatively low-cost skilled labor in the 1960s, domestic market opportunities in the 1970s, and sites to develop bases for regional operations in the 1980s. In partial consequence, the share of manufactured exports in the developing countries' nonfuel exports expanded from 10 percent in 1955 to 65 percent in 1986.[14]

The effective protection of domestic manufactures was reduced substantially, and significant export incentives put in place.[15] Exports enabled NICs to overcome the limitations of their domestic markets in exploiting economies of scale and ensuring full capacity utilization.[16] Well-organized bureaucratic authoritarian elites shaped economic policy.[17] In each case, the state's strategic economic direction was supported by complementary social norms and value orientations.[18] Because domestic income-distribution patterns were less unequal than those observed in other developing regions, such as Latin America and the Caribbean (or in the United States, for that matter), populist appeals were less potent. At the same time, Hong Kong, Singapore, and Taiwan have equaled and in some cases exceeded the life expectancy and infant mortality levels prevailing in Britain and the United States.[19] Within most NICs, prototypical urban preferences for food subsidies and cheap imports were countered by the characteristic concern of agricultural and manufacturing interest groups for competitive exchange rates that would promote exports.

One recurring argument used to explain NIC economic success is that the instilled Confucian political philosophy led to accepted cultural traditions, which permitted effective sociopolitical institutions to encourage entrepreneurial acumen and to attract foreign direct investment. Such traditions were associated with social coherence and individual achievement, driven by pervasive respect for high levels of formal education and savings.[20] Ironically, acquisitive materialism was practically unknown in Confucian societies until very recently. However, some analysts, such as James Riedel, have discounted the contribution of the Confucian ethic as an ex post facto rationalization, contending that in the 1950s, economic stagnation in Japan, Korea, and China was routinely attributed to their Confucian heritage.[21] Bela Balassa concurs, focusing instead upon the relationship between export expansion and economic growth, as demonstrated by regression analysis of a set of twelve developing countries observed between 1963 and 1984.[22] The principal contribution of government had been to create a modern infrastructure, provide a stable incentive system, and ensure that government bureaucracy would help rather than hinder exports.

Similarly, Ching-yuan Lin compares the economic performances of Taiwan and South Korea with those of several Latin American countries, primarily Chile and Argentina, from 1949 to 1985. After the 1973–1974 oil shock, most East Asian countries quickly restored domestic price stability and eliminated large external deficits. In contrast Latin American countries experienced extended difficulties in controlling inflation and relied upon expanded external borrowing rather than increased net exports.

Lin traces the causative factors to economic policy reforms implemented by the NICs during the 1950s in Taiwan and in 1964 in Korea. These reforms (e.g., protection of local industry and export incentives) were fully supported by successive policymakers and were not reversed. During the 1960s, Chile and Argentina also implemented a range of nontraditional export incentives. However, in 1970, effective protection remained as high as 47 percent in Argentina (probably higher in Chile), compared with 5 percent in Taiwan and 10 percent in South Korea.[23]

Commitment to policy reform fluctuated because of the lack of social consensus. For Taiwan and South Korea, impacted by intense population pressure and limited primary export potentials, the need to promote manufactured exports was substantially stronger than in Chile and Argentina, which had much lower population density and greater primary export potential. In Latin America, consistent reluctance to restrain domestic demand for fear of depressing output and employment growth led to a vicious circle: balance-of-payments crises, persistent inflation, constricted domestic savings, reliance upon external credit, and sluggish growth.

By contrast, Gary Hamilton and Nicole Biggart illuminate the success of NIC management and organization by distinguishing between growth and structure. Their initial premise, based on assessments of scholars such as Bruce Cummings, is that in countries such as Taiwan and South Korea, successful industrial development is partly a regional phenomenon, in the sense that the common factor of Confucianism helped to explain the importance of the family, high literacy rates, the desire to achieve, and the willingness to work hard.[24] However, cultural attributes could not explain many evident differences among these NICs. Although economic and cultural factors helped to account for market growth, domestic authority factors were much more helpful for understanding enterprise structure, which in turn influenced market structure and income distribution.[25]

Both Taiwan and South Korea possessed well-developed internal transportation and communication systems, together with growing internal markets. Both countries shared many cultural traits, partly because of conquest and colonization by Japan. In South Korea, fifty *chaebol* (dominant industrial conglomerates) controlled 552 firms, generating 45 percent of national GNP by 1985 in cooperation with a strong state.[26] The ten largest *chaebol* accounted for approximately one-third of all manufacturing sales. In Taiwan, however, the family firm and the business group were the prime organizational forms, especially in the export sector. In 1976, 67,058 small to medium firms employed some 60 percent of Taiwan's workers. This group of corporations accounted for 46 percent of the country's GNP and 65 percent of total exports.

South Korea

In 1988, South Korea had an overall trade surplus, which was expanding at the rate of $10 billion a year. Seoul remained Asia's largest debtor, with $37 billion in outstanding external loans. The country was also trade-dependent; exports equaled 40 percent of GNP. However, South Korea was highly competitive, producing basic consumer electronics and steel more cheaply than any other country in the world.[27] Less than 20 percent of import categories remain subject to quotas. The nation's average tariff declined from almost 40 percent in 1980 to about 24 percent in 1984.[28] During the same period, the ratio of net export subsidies to exports fell to zero.[29] At the same time, urban poverty and inner-city violence became serious problems. Rental housing for low-paid workers was in short supply. Care of the elderly was left to their families. Industrial fatalities were high—3 percent of all workers could expect to be injured on the job each year.[30]

South Korean *chaebol* such as Goldstar, Samsung, Hyundai, and Daewoo have expanded rapidly, given an environment in which the home market was protected from foreign competition, managed floating of the Korean currency (the won) favored exports, labor unions were banned, and government-guaranteed or direct loans facilitated access to credit. However, state intervention in the economy has not always had positive results, as evidenced by South Korea's chemical-industry drive in the 1970s and the government's efforts to promote construction exports to the Middle East in the mid-1980s.[31] After the inauguration of a democratic government led by President Roh Tae Woo in 1988, however, violent strikes disrupted production, and wages soared by 60 percent.[32] Between March 1988 and September 1989, the value of Korea's won increased by 14 percent against the U.S. dollar. In partial consequence, the profits of the twenty largest *chaebol* declined during the first half of 1989, and Korea's overall trade surplus plunged to $175 million from $5.3 billion during the period January–September 1989.[33] With economic growth slowing to a rate of 6.5 percent per year and unemployment increasing, the Economic Planning Board has been increasingly pressed to change its liberalization program.[34]

By the beginning of 1992, South Korea ranked twelfth in the world in trade volume, tenth in automobile assembly, sixth in electronics production, and second in shipbuilding. However, at that point, Korea (together with China) also had the world's highest per capita rate of deaths from tuberculosis as well as the highest per capita rate of fatal traffic accidents. Its hospitals and schools are among the most crowded in the world.[35]

Taiwan

Taiwan offered a similar combination of rapid economic growth with rather counterproductive development consequences. In 1952, the country's GNP per capita was only $48; in 1989, it amounted to $7,500 after the achievement of a 7.3 percent GNP growth rate during the year. As annual per capita income has grown, so has private consumption, but gross national savings has declined as a proportion of GNP, from a high of 38 percent in 1986 to an estimated 31 percent by 1989.[36] An explanation of such outcomes requires that land reform be taken into account. During the 1940s, the Kuomintang's "land-to-the-tiller" program extended lease tenure to a minimum of six years and reduced farm rentals to a maximum 37.5 percent of the average crop yield of the preceding three years.[37] Public land was also sold to tenant families at 2.5 times annual crop proceeds. One result was that only 6 percent of farming families were tenants by 1988.

In 1986, the Taiwanese government feared that Korea's giant *chaebol* would leave Taiwan far behind in semiconductor development, given substantial disparities in corporate size and willingness to invest in capital-intensive factories. In any event, soaring stock market prices enabled Taiwanese chipmakers to create four large-scale wafer fabrication facilities and to invest $1.2 billion in building six more installations.[38] Meanwhile, the Taiwanese state supervised internal moral order and managed foreign affairs, though it also encouraged the private sector to seize all available economic opportunities.

Unemployment and inflation levels remain minimal. Taipei's foreign exchange reserves were second only to Japan's by 1988, at $75 billion, while its 1987 trade surplus totaled $19 billion, compared with $1.8 billion in 1981. Between 1985 and 1989, the New Taiwan dollar appreciated by more than 50 percent against the U.S. dollar. One result was a surge in Taiwanese investment directed toward the United States; the amount expanded to $348.7 million in the period January–August 1989, a fourfold increase from the previous year.[39]

By 1992, Taiwan's Central Bank of China held $100 billion in foreign exchange reserves, the largest such holdings in the world. This was intended to contribute toward a $300 billion six-year development plan focused on infrastructure, industrial projects, and technology transfer.[40]

It was only in December 1989 and 1991 that Taiwan's 10 million voters had an opportunity to elect, in the first instance, 79 out of the 320 Legislative Yuan members and, in the second, the majority of legislators in a legal contest between the Kuomintang (KMT) and the opposition Democratic Progressive Party (DPP).[41] In both elections, the KMT won overwhelmingly, a result interpreted as a vote for the status quo of neither alienating nor embracing China.[42] A new democratic constitution is to be drafted by the end of 1992.

Meanwhile, during the past decade, the number of factories in Taiwan doubled to nearly 90,000. The industrial plants that multiplied most rapidly were those producing hazardous wastes, such as plastics, chemicals, leather tanning, and pesticides.[43] This growth was fueled by government export incentives, tax and customs-duty rebates, low-interest credits, the establishment of export processing zones, and undervalued exchange rates. In a notable example of state policy failure, Taiwan's auto industrial policy was unable to generate a comparative advantage in automobile production.[44] However, since 1980, the number of domestic cars and motorcycles has tripled to 10 million. Air quality in the Taipei industrial suburb of Sanchung has registered 188 on the Pollution Standard Index, compared with a historical maximum of 170 in Los Angeles.[45] At the same time, the average employee cannot earn enough in a lifetime to purchase a new two-bedroom apartment in residential Taipei.[46] Water contamination is widespread because less than 1 percent of sewage receives primary treatment. Household garbage continues to be dumped in open landfills. Among Taiwanese citizens, the three prime concerns are rising crime, traffic congestion, and environmental pollution.

Singapore

The cases of Singapore and Hong Kong demonstrate no substantial deviation from this pattern of rapid economic growth accompanied by perverse development outcomes. During the decade to 1988, Singapore maintained an average real GDP growth rate of 7.2 percent and an average 2.9 percent inflation rate. Singapore has achieved the highest national savings rate in the world, at 42 percent of GDP.[47] Unemployment is practically nonexistent: Since 1982, the city-state's government has imposed an employer levy that currently is $250 per month for each alien employee, and by 1990 there were some 150,000 foreign workers in residence.[48] Singapore was then the world's eighteenth largest exporter; in 1988, total external trade amounted to 350 percent of the country's GDP. Meanwhile, Singapore's International Monetary Exchange (SIMEX) expanded from zero to 20,000 daily futures contracts during the period 1985–1989, and all of its 550 seats were sold.

Yet Singapore's "rugged society" demonstrates both the costs and the benefits of NIC economic success with unusual clarity. Singapore is a model of political and monetary stability, managed by an effective set of sociopolitical institutions. Under former Prime Minister Lee Kuan Yew, who remained in power from 1960 to 1990, the Peoples' Action Party (PAP) consistently attempted to improve the nation's human capital stock, almost to the point of obsession. The paramount operational goals of the PAP government in post-1965 independent Singapore were rapid industrialization and internal security. An explicit cultural policy that promoted only those Asian and Western values compatible with rapid economic growth (such as hard work, capital accumulation, cooperative work habits, and willingness to innovate) was implemented.[49]

The government created a market socialist state, committing itself to provide a sound socioeconomic infrastructure, to create an attractive environment for foreign investment, and to participate directly in critical economic sectors that involved considerable uncertainty. Singapore is a technocratic authoritarian state,[50] and such states seek to create a policy environment characterized by predictability and strategic direction. For instance, under the 1963 Internal Security Act still in force in 1992, subversive elements may be detained indefinitely without charge or trial. Similarly, the 1968 Employment and Industrial Relations Act reduced wage levels as well as the political and economic power of organized labor. Production and export microincentives were repeatedly refined. For example, after Singapore's first recession in 1985, the government decreased the level of compulsory employee contributions to the Central Provident Fund from 25 percent to 23 percent of salary and selectively slashed corporate taxes. The social costs of Singapore's "directive development" model are evidenced by the level of net migration, some 16,000 in 1989—proportionally not much less than the number of people who emigrated from Hong Kong during that year.[51]

Hong Kong

In 1951, almost all exports of the British colony of Hong Kong consisted of entrepôt trade. By the early 1970s, domestic exports accounted for over four-fifths of total exports, as Hong Kong became the world's largest exporter of garments, toys, watches, and radios. The prime internal causes for this transformation included the intense will to achieve demonstrated by the incoming refugees from Mao Zedong's China during the late 1940s (40 percent of the territory's 5.73 million population) and Britain's relatively effective system of colonial public administration. After a brief recession in 1985, Hong Kong's real GDP grew by 12 percent in 1986 and 14 percent in 1987, then declined 7.5 percent in 1988 and an estimated 5 percent in 1989. In mid-1989, the colony's inflation level was 9.9 percent, and the seasonally adjusted unemployment rate was 1.3 percent.[52]

Traffic congestion and atmospheric pollution are pervasive, as exemplified by the difficulty of access to Kai Tak airport and the government's decision to ban the sale of all local seafood in early 1989. Hong Kong is similar to Taiwan in that large companies are the exception; it also parallels Singapore in that some 200,000 manufacturing, retailing, and financial services employment vacancies remained unfilled during 1988.[53] (This demand for labor was completely unaffected by the importation of some 42,600 Filipinos to work as domestic helpers.)

At the same time, Hong Kong continues to suffer human capital flight. Emigration amounted to 19,000 in 1986, just under 30,000 in 1987, and about 45,000 in 1988. About 1,000 people were emigrating a week in 1990 as the July 1, 1997, deadline for the agreed transfer of sovereignty from Britain to the People's Republic of China drew nearer. Meanwhile, political and economic interaction between Hong Kong and China is increasing. Up to 3 million workers in China's Guangdong province were employed by Hong Kong companies in 1988; at the same time, some 500 companies within the colony, such as the Bank of China and China Merchants Steam Navigation, represent approved Chinese investments having a total value of up to $10 billion.[54]

The Commonwealth Caribbean Model

The English-speaking Caribbean countries have applied several economic growth models that roughly correspond to the four decades since 1950, though with considerable overlap: the Puerto Rican "Bootstrap" formula, ironically described as "industrialization by invitation"; import substitution and regional economic integration; joint venture incentives and majority state shareholding; and attempted export-driven growth as well as variable degrees of domestic privatization and deregulation.[55]

Puerto Rico has became a model of dependent industrialization, specializing in the processing and export of goods for the U.S. market. In 1987, 88.9 percent of all such exports went to the United States, and 4.7 percent was directed to the Caribbean Basin, with the Dominican Republic, Haiti, and the Netherlands Antilles accounting for two-thirds of this latter amount. Puerto Rico's aggregate manufacturing wage costs are about 60 percent of comparable U.S. mainland costs but fourfold those of Singapore,

Hong Kong, South Korea, and Taiwan.[56] The island had a per capita income of $5,653 in 1989, about half that of Mississippi, the poorest U.S. state, and federal transfer payments make up 31 percent of an average resident's income.

Since 1984, the English-speaking Caribbean has enjoyed several sets of export preferences provided by the U.S. Caribbean Basin Economic Recovery Act (CBERA), first passed in August 1983; the European Community's third and fourth Lomé conventions, implemented in 1986 and 1989; and Canada's Caribbean-Canadian Trade Agreement (CARIBCAN), put in place during June 1986.[57] Although U.S. imports from CBERA beneficiary states fell from $9.0 billion in 1983 to $6.1 billion in 1988,[58] such countries became the most rapidly expanding exporters of clothing to the United States under the bilaterally negotiated Super 807 program. These exports quickly doubled in value, rising from $590 million to $1.97 billion between 1985 and 1987 alone.[59]

The English-speaking Caribbean is doubly institutionalized, as reflected in the inclusive Caribbean Community and Common Market (Caricom) and a subset constituting the eight island nations belonging to the Organization of Eastern Caribbean States (OECS). Caricom's population is about 5.6 million, with 42 percent in Jamaica, 22 percent in Trinidad and Tobago, 13 percent in Guyana, and 5 percent in Barbados. The remaining 18 percent reside within the OECS states. Across the subregion, production and trade remain highly concentrated; the islands of Jamaica, Trinidad and Tobago, and the Bahamas account for approximately 75 percent of both.

Most of the potential for employment, income, and foreign-exchange earnings within Caricom is provided by the tourism and sugar industries. (Banana rather than sugar production fulfills this role in the case of the Windward Islands.) The performance of these sectors has been variable. For instance, in the late 1980s, sugar production suffered annual declines down to a level of some 623,000 metric tons, a decline that was finally halted in 1990.[60] However, in the tourist industry, upon which some 326,000 workers depended, the number of stopover tourists increased during the same period before the adverse effects of the Persian Gulf crisis were felt. In turn, banana production expanded for most of the period but declined in 1989 because of adverse weather conditions. In 1990, regional banana exports rose 13 percent to about 365,000 metric tons. During the late 1980s, purchase prices fell in the major export market, Britain. The impact of the decline on Caribbean exports fluctuated with the appreciation/depreciation of sterling against the U.S. dollar.[61] This development clearly illustrated the structural dependence associated with such Anglophone Caribbean primary product exports.

In 1988, Caricom member-states spent more than $1.2 billion in imported food as well as agricultural-sector inputs, whereas primary export proceeds amounted to less than $600 million.[62] A 1989–1991 Caricom Program for Agricultural Development was implemented in an attempt to promote agricultural export diversification as well as import substitution. In the 1980s, the contribution of manufactures to GDP amounted to only 15.2 percent in Jamaica, 11.6 percent in Barbados, and 11.2 percent in Trinidad and Tobago.[63] The projected benefits of intra-regional trade have been elusive. By 1983, such trade had declined to 6.07 percent of imports, less than the level recorded when Caricom was established in 1973.[64] Intraregional trade levels continued to decline until 1987, when an expansion of just under 8 percent was achieved, followed by further growth of 14.6 percent in 1988, 24 percent in 1989, and about 10 percent in 1990.[65]

In contrast, total external indebtedness had mounted to $9 billion by 1988–1989, when the combined balance-of-payments deficit of the subregion averaged almost $2.0 billion, or about one-sixth of aggregate GDP.[66] At the same time, reported unemployment levels ranged from 15 percent in Belize to 20 percent in Trinidad and Tobago, and to 25 percent in Guyana. Table 5.1 compares selected 1965–1988 economic growth indicators for the NIC and Caricom country sets under consideration.

During the period 1965–1988, Caribbean countries registered low or negative growth rates in real per capita GNP. These rates compared unfavorably with those of over 6 percent for the East Asian NICs. For the shorter period 1980–1988, real per capita GNP declined by 7.3 percent in Trinidad and Tobago, 5.5 percent in Guyana, 2.1 percent in Jamaica, and 1.4 percent for Barbados; there was a moderate increase of 3.7 percent (average) in the OECS states.[67] By comparison, real per capita GNP grew by 8.8 percent in South Korea and 6.8 percent in both Singapore and Hong Kong.[68] These disparities did not change when average hourly wage costs for semiskilled production workers in export manufacturing industries rose to $1.98 in Hong Kong and $1.84 in Taiwan by 1987, compared with $0.63 in a Caricom country such as Jamaica.[69] The only Commonwealth Caribbean state to earn a balance-of-trade surplus in that year was Dominica.[70] Guyana, which best exemplifies the attempt to generate growth driven by public-sector expansion, had become the poorest country of the hemisphere by the end of the decade.[71]

Guyana

Guyana's authoritarian People's National Congress (PNC) government represents a deviant case within the Caribbean Community. The continued drift toward authoritarianism began with former Prime Minister Forbes Burnham's decision to restructure the civil service in 1966 so as to facilitate the implementation of his economic growth program. This step was followed by the 1967 passage of a controversial election law, which allowed PNC supporters resident overseas to vote. By 1975, it was widely accepted that the government was supervised by the party bureaucracy.[72] Although the 1984 passage of an industrial relations bill that amended the country's constitution

Table 5.1 Economic Growth Indicators, East Asian and Caricom States

Country	Population (millions, 1990 est.)	Area (thousands of square km.)	GNP per capita ($ U.S. 1988) [a]	GNP per capita Growth rate 1965–1988 (%)	Exports 1990 ($ U.S. million)	Imports 1990 ($ U.S. million)
Hong Kong	5.9	1	9,220	6.3	82,144	82,482
Korea	42.8	99	3,600	6.8	60,457	60,210
Singapore	2.7	1	9,070	7.2	52,753	60,984
Taiwan	20.4	36	6,280	8.9 [b]	66,426	55,438
Barbados	0.3	0.4	6,010	2.3	218	749
Guyana	0.8	215	420	−5.5 [c]	234	238
Jamaica	2.5	11	1,070	−1.5	1,218	1,848
Trinidad and Tobago	1.3	5	3,350	0.9	1,986	1,230

Sources: World Bank, *World Development Report 1990* (New York: Oxford University Press, 1990), pp. 178–179, 243; United Nations Development Program (UNDP), *Human Development Report 1991* (New York: Oxford University Press, 1991), pp. 160, 164; International Monetary Fund, *Direction of Trade Statistics Yearbook 1991* (Washington, D.C.: IMF, 1991); Keizai Koho Center, *Japan: An International Comparison 1990* (Tokyo: Japan Institute for Social and Economic Affairs, 1990), p. 12; "Taiwan," *Financial Times Survey*, October 10, 1989, p. 1.

[a] Gross domestic product.
[b] 1983–1987.
[c] 1980–1988.

to limit drastically the right to strike is reminiscent of Singapore's 1968 labor legislation, Guyana's subsequent pattern of economic growth and development was dramatically distinctive.

The country's GDP fell sharply (by 9.3 percent) in 1983; marginal recovery came between 1984 and 1987, although production declined by 30 percent in the sugar, rice, and bauxite sectors, which together represented about one-third of total output. When President Burnham died in 1985, Desmond Hoyte assumed leadership of the party and government and set about introducing several reforms, including an apparent rapprochement with the private sector. In 1987, the Guyanese dollar was devalued by 50 percent for official transactions, the maximum income tax rate was reduced from 70 percent to 33 percent, and improved public sector management allowed the nation's state enterprises for the first time to achieve an overall surplus.[73]

However, in 1988, sugar production fell by 24 percent, to its lowest level in forty years, as a result of frequent strikes, shortages of cane cutters, and unseasonable weather. In addition, bauxite production fell by 4 percent when flooded mines delayed ore extraction and foreign exchange shortages limited the remedial measures the Guyana Bauxite Corporation could take. As overall GDP fell by 3 percent, the PNC government negotiated an economic recovery program with the International Monetary Fund (IMF). This included a further 70 percent currency devaluation, tight monetary and credit policies, and increased public-sector investment.[74] However, Guyana's GDP fell further, (by 4 percent in 1989); the inflation level mounted to 85 percent per annum; and external debt rose to $1.75 billion one of the region's highest on a per capita basis. In January 1990, when a Commonwealth advisory group suggested a significant degree of deregulation and privatization, the annual emigration rate was 3 percent of the labor force, and fifty Guyana dollars were offered on the parallel market for one U.S. dollar (the official exchange rate was G$1.00 = U.S.$0.03).[75] By January 1992, the Guyana dollar had fallen to a rate of $135 to U.S.$1.00.

Barbados

Barbados's GDP grew by 3.5 percent in 1988 and 1989, mainly as a result of expansion in the tourism and manufacturing sectors, and the island's unemployment rate was 17.4 and 15.6 percent respectively in those years.[76] Although the 1988–1993 Barbados development plan projected GDP growth at an annual average rate of 2.5 percent, the economy declined in 1990 (by 3.5 percent) for the first time in seven years and again in 1991.[77] This performance resulted from reduced earnings from tourism and sugar. The agricultural sector's performance has been highly variable, as exemplified by sharp declines in production in the last few years (except 1990) and a decrease in the sector's contribution to GDP. (In 1991, sugar production reached a sixty-year low of 65,670 tons.)[78] Decreased production was largely a result of persistent difficulties in matching marginal costs in the sugar industry with domestic as well as export demand. Export performance has also been variable: During 1987, the value of total merchandise exports also fell by almost 50 percent as electronic components and clothing exports contracted,[79] but modest increases were registered through 1990. Barbados has a very small economy and scarce natural resources. The island's import dependence remains underlined by the consistent expansion of its merchandise trade deficit, which totaled $361 million in 1988 and $424 million in 1989. Foreign investment dependence was also demonstrated during winter 1989–1990 when several electronics components firms closed down in succession, and more than 200 workers were laid off, without immediate employment prospects. The debt burden has also increased—external debt incurred reached $552 million in 1990.[80] All these difficulties forced Barbados into a credit agreement with the IMF in 1991 based on an eighteen-month austerity package. Nevertheless, the convertible Barbadian dollar has been stabilized at an official rate of B$2.0113 = U.S.$1.00, and devaluation has been fended off. The nation's annual inflation rate was only 4.7 percent in 1988. It rose to 6 percent in 1989 but again declined to only 3.1 percent in 1990.[81]

Trinidad and Tobago

Between 1974 and 1980, Trinidad and Tobago experienced an "economic miracle": Annual real GDP growth averaged 7 percent, unemployment levels gradually decreased to 8.8 percent, and per capita GNP expanded from $1,231 to $4,370.[82] This growth was based upon a tremendous inflow of petrodollar earnings, which encouraged the People's National Movement (PNM) government to expand the size of the public sector significantly while engaging in a massive school-building program and increasing old-age pensions as well as food-stamp provision. By the beginning of the 1980s, however, when the public sector accounted for two-thirds of all employment in the economy, oil prices, production, and revenues were falling precipitously.[83] Nevertheless, the twin-island republic became ineligible for World Bank support in 1984 when its income per capita amounted to $6,450.

In December 1986, Prime Minister A.N.R. Robinson's National Alliance for Reconstruction (NAR) was elected to lead the government of Trinidad and Tobago. The NAR was faced with a catastrophic economic contraction that had continued since 1982, unemployment and inflation levels that exceeded 20 percent, and a sustained fall in investment. The new government attempted to combine export-led growth and selective import substitution while reducing the country's dependence on oil-sector revenues and public-sector spending. Nevertheless, foreign reserves, which had totaled $3.3 billion in 1981, declined to zero by 1988.

Meanwhile, the nation's GDP cumulatively diminished by 30 percent, and the contribution of the pivotal petroleum sector to current revenue fell sharply to less than a third. In response, the government devalued the Trinidad and Tobago dollar by 33 percent in 1986, and by an additional 18 percent in 1988. It also negotiated a structural adjustment program with the IMF, which included a controversial 10-percent wage cut for public-sector employees and import deregulation, despite the vocal opposition of the local manufacturers' association.[84] Although the country's disbursed external debt increased sharply, from U.S.$1.8 billion in 1987 to U.S.$2.06 billion in 1988, value of nonoil exports also exceeded TT$1.0 billion for the first time.[85] As the contraction of Trinidad and Tobago's GDP slowed from 4.3 percent in 1988 to 3.5 percent in 1989, and a positive trade balance of $80 million was recorded, the World Bank provided two structural adjustment loans totaling $44 million, funds intended primarily to increase public-sector efficiency and to alleviate the social costs of adjustment.[86] Economic performance continued to improve marginally in 1990, but the economic hardships that had been imposed by the NAR contributed to the return of the PNM to government in 1991.

Jamaica

Before 1972, Jamaica's economic growth was essentially driven by bauxite-alumina investment, tourism promotion, preferentially marketed primary product exports, and import substitution. Between 1972 and 1980, Prime Minister Michael Manley's People's National Party governed Jamaica on a democratic socialist platform, which emphasized both regulation and redistribution. After 1980, under the incoming conservative Jamaica Labour Party government led by Edward Seaga, taxes were increased and subsidies removed in order to balance the budget within the context of successive structural adjustment agreements with the IMF. Public corporations were privatized, interest rates increased, wages restricted, and imports rapidly liberalized—all with the intention of transferring resources from relatively inefficient to more competitive economic sectors.[87]

In any event, open unemployment averaged more than 26 percent of the labor force between 1980 and 1985.[88] After an extended decline, Jamaica's GDP grew by 1.9 percent in 1986, 5.2 percent in 1987, and between 1.6 and 2.5 percent through 1990.[89] In 1987, the island's merchandise exports rose by 31 percent to $529 million. At the same time, moderately higher petroleum prices and increased capital equipment purchases led to a 25 percent increase in merchandise imports, to $1.048 billion.[90] In addition, the pool of domestic savings available for investment remained minuscule. Between 1980 and 1988, the share of Jamaica's annual foreign exchange earnings that originated in the bauxite-alumina and tourism sectors declined from about 80 percent to 50 percent, or some $950 million. However, unemployment and inflation levels escalated. The island's consistently negative merchandise trade balance expanded (except for a surplus in 1988). Disbursed external debt increased from $3.4 billion in 1984 to $4.2 billion in 1988, when interest payments alone accounted for 20.3 percent of export proceeds.[91] The country's GDP grew by 4 percent in 1989, but the trade deficit also mounted to $444 million. By February 1990, the Jamaican dollar had been further devalued to a rate of J$7.00 = U.S.$1.00 in response to conditions the IMF attached to a new $108 million loan. Other related policy measures included hotel divestment and increases of 19.5 percent in food prices, 32 percent in electricity rates, and 34 percent in retail sales taxes on automobiles.[92] The Jamaican dollar depreciated further in 1991 to a rate of J$23 to U.S.$1.00 by January 1992.

Caribbean and Asian-Pacific Development Models: Economic Policy Recommendations

There is assuredly no shortage of economic policy recommendations for Caricom states. Winston Griffith argues that such countries cannot achieve the high growth rates observed in East Asia because of substantial sociopolitical differences, and distinctive industrial relations systems, quite apart from the fundamental changes that have taken place in the international business environment.[93] However, Clive Thomas proposes intensified regional integration, with an emphasis upon intraregional joint ventures, as well as greater political and legal cooperation within Caricom. This proposal is coupled with a call for expanded political participation, institutional reform, income redistribution, and tourism diversification and is intended in several senses.[94] Alluding to the example of Taiwan, Kempe Hope suggests vigorous land reform aimed at increasing the acreage available for agricultural production and expanding crop yields as well as rural incomes; the premise is to apply an integrated rural development strategy.[95] George Beckford and Michael Witter emphasize the importance of imaginative incentives for local production and export rather than reliance upon the process of "industrialization by invitation."[96]

In a similar spirit, David Bray envisages an emphasis upon labor-intensive import-substitution sectors, combined with the selective attraction of foreign investment within capital-intensive export sectors, mainly in order to access established international marketing networks.[97] Meanwhile, Compton Bourne contends that the Caricom countries must increase their international competitiveness by applying a series of measures, including product innovation, expanded investment, increased productivity, reduced import dependence, monetary policy restraint, and prudent public-sector management. Yet as Carl Stone comments, specific means of achieving such ends, which take account of the global economy's evolving structure, remain to be identified.[98] Many of these policy recommendations reflect the influence of the growth—if not necessarily development—models applied by the "four dragons" of Singapore, Hong Kong, South Korea, and Taiwan. International economic agencies, such as the International Monetary Fund and the World Bank, selectively emphasize elements of the East Asian experience in promoting domestic market liberalization and export-oriented growth across the Caribbean, but this approach produces false dichotomies.[99] Furthermore, in any relatively complex economy, the "butterfly effect" emerges: Economic policies that seem perfectly rational in the short-term produce perverse results and unintended consequences over time, as Peter Drucker argues.[100] The question remains of whether the East Asian model has substantial current applicability to Caricom states.

Since the 1960s, the East Asian model of economic growth has been based upon several interactive if differentially combined factors. These consist of high levels of domestic savings and investment, land reform, substantial market liberalization, export as well as foreign direct investment promotion, supportive cultural traditions, and strategic—if not always successful—policy direction by authoritarian governments. At least since 1987, the four NICs considered have also engaged in increasing external investment in an attempt to achieve several objectives: exorcise the specter of increasing protectionism within their major markets, control domestic inflation, and reduce labor costs.

Meanwhile, the Caricom model of economic growth has included import substitution, regional economic integration, public-sector expansion, limited market liberalization, export promotion, and the use of foreign investment incentives. Whereas the most successful NIC sectors involved consumer electronics, aerospace, steel, automobiles, petrochemicals, garments, and toys, the most dynamic Caricom sectors were tourism, clothing, and data processing. Economic policy emphases have shifted over time and from country to country; nevertheless, some generalizations remain practicable.

By NIC standards, the private sector has been subject to least regulation in Hong Kong. Within Caricom, the public sector has traditionally accounted for the least extensive proportion of GDP in Barbados. Each economy has achieved the greatest relative success in per capita income growth. Conversely, the most interventionist governments have been those of South Korea and Guyana: countries with the lowest per capita incomes within their group. Yet from a philosophy of science perspective, explanations and predictions cannot be equated. Each of the countries considered is unique, to some extent, in social, political, and economic structure—and it is simplistic, at best, to suggest that the "Taiwanization" of the Caribbean would generate a regional economic miracle. Equally important, it remains easiest, and least productive, to count the quantifiable, but the approach does not necessarily deal with the issues that matter most.

Economic growth and development are mutually reinforcing but not identical concepts. The antecedents, correlates, and consequences of the East Asian model include several significant negative sociopolitical and environmental factors. These development consequences are variably evidenced by what Albert Hirschman styled "voice" and "exit": popular demonstration and emigration.[101] Similarly, the various economic growth models employed by the Caricom countries have been implemented under the constraints of pluralistic democracy (aside from the anomaly of Guyana), dominant consumer interest groups, highly unequal domestic income-distribution patterns, and substantial primary product dependence. High import, consumption, and inflation levels continue to be accompanied by low savings, investment, and export ratios. Given that the prototypical pluralist political system is composed of constantly changing coalitions and cross-cutting interest groups, such a syndrome of policy failure might seem both readily summarized and intractable.

However, in considering the East Asian economic model, Caricom ministers might note the centrality of market incentives to work, save, and invest; largely unrestricted currency convertibility; agricultural reform; significant resource commitment to health and education; and policy continuity. Given such policy emphases, regional political leaders might more credibly promote among their electorates the need to transform domestic demand so as to balance net export earnings and consumption. Any successful policy equation must match competitiveness with consumer needs—getting both internal and external prices right while limiting the potential for corruption and elite rent-seeking. At the same time, an evaluation of Caricom's sociopolitical dynamics could well remind reflective East Asian leaders that if the linkage of market capitalism and political pluralism often produces unsatisfactory results, beyond the short term such a union might best guarantee that growth and development will ultimately underpin rather than undermine each other.

Notes

1. For example, see Laurence Whitehead, "Tigers in Latin America?" in *Annals of the American Academy of Political and Social Science,* special issue "The Pacific Region: Challenges to Policy and Theory," September 1989, p. 150. (This special issue is cited hereafter as *Annals.*)
2. See, for example, the discussion by Peter A. Gourevitch, "The Pacific Rim: Current Debates," in *Annals,* pp. 10–12.
3. Whitehead, "Tigers," p. 149.
4. For comparisons of East Asian and Latin American development strategies, see ibid., pp. 142–151, and Stephen Haggard, "The East Asian NICs in Comparative Perspective," in *Annals,* pp. 129–141.
5. "Hongkong: Weighing the Odds," *Economist,* June 3, 1989 (Special Survey of Hongkong), p. 5.

6. The U.S.-Canada trade relationship remains the most extensive in the world, generating exchanges of goods and services worth over $150 billion in 1988. During that year, the EC's external trade was twice as large as that of the United States and Japan combined.

7. General Agreement on Tariffs and Trade (GATT), *International Trade 1988-1989* (Geneva: GATT Secretariat, 1989), pp. 13-21.

8. For examples of these contrary approaches, see Kenneth Dam, "The Caribbean Basin Initiative and Central America," *Department of State Bulletin* 84, 2802 (1984): 80-83; and Paul Latortue, "The Taiwan Model and the Economic Development of Haiti," in Antonio Jorge et al., eds., *External Debt and Development Strategy in Latin America* (New York: Pergamon, 1985). Singapore has also been cited as a model for Latin America and the Caribbean, as exemplified by a letter to the editor of the *Wall Street Journal* on January 24, 1985, written by William Middendorf II, then U.S. ambassador to the Organization of American States.

9. For instance, in 1989, no less than five strongly contested elections were fought in Jamaica, Grenada, Antigua, St. Vincent, and Belize, as discussed by Don Bohning, "A Year of Elections," *Hemisphere*, 1, 2 (Winter 1989), 8-10.

10. W. Arthur Lewis, *The Theory of Economic Growth* (London: Allen and Unwin, 1955).

11. Norman Uphoff and Warren Ilchman, *The Political Economy of Development* (Princeton, N.J.: Princeton University Press, 1972).

12. "World Wire," *Wall Street Journal*, November 8, 1989, p. A15.

13. C. Hamilton, "Capitalist Industrialization in East Asia's Four Little Tigers," *Journal of Contemporary Asia* 13, (1983): 35-73; Bruce Cummings, "The Origins and Development of the Northeast Asian Political Economy: Industrial Sectors, Product Cycles, and Political Consequences," *International Organization* 38 (1984): 1-40; D. B. Bobrow and S. Chan, "Understanding Anomalous Successes: Japan, Taiwan, and South Korea," in Charles Hermann, Charles Kegley, and James Rosenau, eds., *New Directions in the Comparative Study of Foreign Policy* (Boston: Allen and Unwin, 1987), pp. 111-130; "Fruits of Gloom" (Third World Survey), *Economist*, September 23, 1989, p. 6.

14. "How to Leap a Frontier" (Third World Survey), *Economist*, September 23, 1989, p. 33.

15. Ching-yuan Lin, "East Asia and Latin America as Contrasting Models," *Economic Development and Cultural Change* 36 (April 1988): S157.

16. Bela Balassa, "The Lessons of East Asian Development: An Overview," *Economic Development and Cultural Change* 36 (April 1988): S280. See also S. B. Linder, *The Pacific Century: Economic and Political Consequences of Asian Pacific Dynamism* (Stanford, Calif.: Stanford University Press, 1986); K. T. Li, *The Evolution of Policy Behind Taiwan's Development Success* (New Haven, Conn.: Yale University Press, 1988).

17. A. H. Amsden, "The State and Taiwan's Economic Development," in Peter Evans, David Rueschemeyer, and Theda Skocpol, *Bringing the State Back In* (Cambridge: Cambridge University Press, 1985), pp. 78-104; Peter Evans, "Class, State, and Dependence in East Asia: Lessons for Latin Americanists," in Frederic C. Deyo, ed., *The Political Economy of the New Asian Industrialism* (Ithaca, N.Y., and London: Cornell University Press, 1987), pp. 203-226; T. J. Cheng and S. Haggard, *Newly Industrializing Asia in Transition: Policy Reform and American Response* (Berkeley: Institute of International Studies, University of California).

18. Roy Hofheinz, Jr., and Kent E. Calder, *The Eastasia Edge* (New York: Basic Books, 1982).

19. Steve Chan and Cal Clark, "Can Good Things Go Together? A Virtuous Cycle in East Asia," *International Studies Notes* 15, 1 (Winter 1990): 4–9.

20. L. W. Pye and M. W. Pye, *Asian Power and Politics: The Cultural Dimensions of Authority* (Cambridge, Mass.: Harvard University Press, 1985); J.C.H. Fei, "Economic Development and Traditional Chinese Cultural Values," *Journal of Chinese Studies* 3 (1986): 109–124; Dennis John Gayle, *The Small Developing State: Comparing Political Economies in Costa Rica, Singapore, and Jamaica* (Aldershot, England; Brookfield, Vt.: Gower, 1986), pp. 100–110; S. Greenhalgh, "Families and Networks in Taiwan's Economic Development," in E. A. Winkler and S. Greenhalgh, eds., *Contending Approaches to the Political Economy of Taiwan* (Armonk, N.Y.: M.E. Sharpe, 1988). Confucian traditions emphasize both deep respect for hierarchical authority and consistent equity for all citizens governed.

21. James Riedel, "Economic Development in East Asia: Doing What Comes Naturally?" in Helen Hughes et al., eds., *Explaining the Industrialization Success of East Asia* (Sydney, Australia: Cambridge University Press, 1987).

22. Balassa, "Lessons of East Asian Development," p. S280. The regression analysis included nonfuel exports and export market shares of Hong Kong, Korea, Singapore, Taiwan, Indonesia, Malaysia, Philippines, Thailand, Argentina, Brazil, Mexico, and India for the years 1963, 1973, 1980, and 1984.

23. Lin, "East Asia and Latin America," p. S157.

24. Cummings, "The Origins and Development of the Northeast Asian Political Economy," pp. 1–40. Some 98 percent of both Hong Kong's and Taiwan's population is Chinese. So is 75 percent of Singapore's population. The Confucian ethical system was officially adopted in Korea under the Yi dynasty, which ruled from 1392 until the Japanese annexation in 1910. During the fifteenth century, Korean scholars made several original contributions to the theoretical refinement of Confucianism.

25. Gary G. Hamilton and Nicole Woolsey Biggart, "Market, Culture, and Authority: A Comparative Analysis of Management and Organization in the Far East," *American Journal of Sociology* 94 (July 1988): S74.

26. A strong state can resist the pressure of private interest groups, persuade such groups to adopt and further its definition of the national interest, and even change domestic socioeconomic structure, over time. See Stephen D. Krasner, *Defending the National Interest: Raw Materials Investments and U.S. Foreign Policy* (Princeton, N.J.: Princeton University Press, 1978), pp. 56–57.

27. "A Survey of South Korea," *Economist*, May 21, 1988, p. 19.

28. As of January 1, 1990, South Korea has renounced its right under GATT to impose new import restrictions for balance-of-payments reasons and agreed to eliminate or bring all existing restrictions into conformity with GATT regulations by July 1, 1997.

29. "Survey: The Third World," *Economist*, September 23, 1989, p. 27.

30. "A Survey of South Korea," *Economist*, May 21, 1988, p. 20.

31. Chung-in Moon, "Beyond Statism: Rethinking the Political Economy of Growth in South Korea," *International Studies Notes* 15, 1 (Winter 1990): 24–27.

32. Opposition parties possess a majority in parliament, which cannot be dissolved by the president, although the ruling party has yet to be displaced in a free election. For further discussion, see G. Henderson, "Constitutional Changes from the First to the Sixth Republics: 1948–1987," in I. J. Kim and Y. W. Kihl, eds., *Political Change in South Korea* (New York: Korean PWPA, 1988), pp. 3–21.

33. Damon Darlin, "Korea's Goldstar Faces a Harsh New World Under

Democracy," *Wall Street Journal*, October 8, 1989, pp. A1, A14.

34. "South Korea: When Democracy Hits the Purse," *Economist*, March 10, 1990, p. 36.

35. *Wall Street Journal*, February 2, 1992, p. A10.

36. "The Other China Is Starting to Soar," *Business Week*, November 6, 1989, p. 61.

37. The "land-to-the-tiller" program was influenced by Sun Yat-sen's "Three Principles of the People": nationalism, democracy, and people's livelihood, which promoted the equalization of land rights.

38. "The Other China Is Starting to Soar," *Business Week*, November 6, 1989, pp. 60–61.

39. Lourdes Lee Valeriano, "Investment Spree by Taiwan Companies Is Expected with U.S. Firms as Target," *Wall Street Journal*, December 15, 1989, p. A11.

40. *Economist*, February 22, 1992, p. 28.

41. Until 1991, the KMT legislature was dominated by members who had been elected to represent mainland constituencies in 1947. In 1991, Taiwan began the process of democratization that included the first regular elections. See also "Taiwan Will Provide Forum for Defining Relationship with China," *Wall Street Journal*, December 1, 1989, p. A12.

42. See, for example, Morton L. Abramowitz, "One China, and the Moment of Truth," *New York Times*, January 18, 1992, p. 23.

43. "Taiwan's Transition: A Survey," *Economist*, March 5, 1988, p. 10.

44. W. Arnold, "Bureaucratic Politics, State Capacity and Taiwan's Automobile Industrial Policy," *Modern China* 15 (1989): 178–214.

45. Alison Maitland, "Anger Grows over Taiwan's Polluted Success Story," *Financial Times*, October 13, 1989, p. 4.

46. Alison Maitland, "Unpalatable Price of Success," *Financial Times Survey: Taiwan*, October 10, 1989, p. III.

47. Dennis J. Gayle, "Singaporean Market Socialism: Some Implications for Development Theory," *International Journal of Social Economics* 15, 7 (1988): 53.

48. Andrew Baxter, "Maintaining the Balance," *Financial Times*, November 13, 1989, Special Survey: Singapore, p. II.

49. P. S. Chen, *Singapore Development Policies and Trends* (Singapore: Oxford University Press, 1983); T. J. Cheng, "The Developmental State in Singapore: A Plato's Republic?" *IRPS Case Studies in Comparative Policy Environments* (Graduate School of International Relations and Pacific Studies, University of California, San Diego, 1987).

50. The technocratic development model is characterized by low levels of political participation, high foreign investment inputs, increasing income inequalities, and rapid economic growth. See Samuel P. Huntington and Joan M. Nelson, *No Easy Choice: Political Participation in Developing Countries* (Cambridge, Mass.: Harvard University Press, 1982), pp. 23–24.

51. "Birth of Another Nation," *Economist*, March 10, 1990, p. 37.

52. "Survey: Hongkong as a Business and Trading Centre," *Financial Times*, November 8, 1989, p. III.

53. "Weighing the Odds: A Survey of Hongkong," *Economist*, June 3, 1989, p. 12.

54. Some 70 percent of China's direct foreign investment, which totaled $12.0 billion in 1988, was routed through Hong Kong, with two-thirds originating within the British colony itself.

55. See Kenneth I. Boodhoo, "The Economic Dimension of U.S. Caribbean

Policy," in H. Michael Erisman, ed., *The Caribbean Challenge: U.S. Policy in a Volatile Region* (Boulder, Colo.: Westview, 1984), pp. 78–83.

56. See Juan A. Castaner and Angel L. Ruiz, "Puerto Rico's Trade Linkages with the Rest of the Caribbean," *Caribbean Affairs* 2, 4 (October–December 1989): 122–140.

57. Clive Thomas provides a summary discussion of these preferences in "Economic Crisis and the Commonwealth Caribbean: Impact and Response," *Caribbean Affairs* 2, 4 (October–December 1989): 27–29.

58. U.S. Department of Commerce statistics, cited by Kal Wagenheim, *Caribbean Update* (December 1989): 21.

59. Dennis J. Gayle, "Trade Issues in the Anglophone Caribbean," *Occasional Papers Series Dialogue*, no. 129, Latin American and Caribbean Center, Florida International University, August 1989, pp. 9–10. Under the "Super 807" program, U.S. imports of clothing assembled from fabrics formed and cut within the United States by the U.S. importing company were excluded from established country quotas and made subject only to bilaterally agreed limits.

60. See Caribbean Development Bank (CDB), *Annual Report 1989* (Bridgetown, Barbados, 1990), p. 21. (The annual CDB reports are cited hereafter as CDB, 19xx.) See also CDB, *1990*, p. 21.

61. Ibid. See also Caribbean Tourism Research and Development Center, (CTRDC), *Caribbean Tourism Statistical Report 1987* (Marine Gardens, Christ Church, Barbados: CTRDC, 1987), p. 5.

62. Canute James, "Revitalising Caribbean Farming," *Financial Times*, September 27, 1989, p. 36.

63. Rafael A. Trejos and Manuel Gollas, eds., *Industrialization and Trade in the Caribbean Basin* (San José, Costa Rica: Institute for Economic and Social Research, 1987), p. 74.

64. *Keesings Contemporary Archives*, September 1985, p. 33,849.

65. See Roderick G. Rainford (Caricom Secretary-General), "Reflections on the Lessons to Be Learnt from the Caribbean Community," *Caribbean Affairs* 2, 4 (October–December 1989): 10–11; CDB, *1990*, p. 39. The debt climbed to $9.5 billion in 1990.

66. Thomas, "Economic Crisis and the Commonwealth Caribbean," p. 22. By 1986, when the subregion was importing $1.3 billion in food, Caricom's net capital outflows had risen to $97 million, a sum that includes official aid, foreign investment, and debt-servicing costs. See also CDB, *1990*, p. 17.

67. In 1987 and 1988, aggregate GDP in the OECS states expanded by 5.5 percent as a consequence of continued growth in the agricultural, tourism, manufacturing, and construction sectors. Tourism earnings increased by 6 percent, to $365 million, helping to offset a $524 million merchandise trade deficit.

68. United Nations Development Program (UNDP), *Human Development Report 1991* (New York: Oxford University Press, 1991), pp. 164–165.

69. World Bank, *The Caribbean: Export Preferences and Performance* (Washington D.C: IBRD, 1988), p. 35.

70. Dominica's 1987 external trade surplus totaled $6.9 million.

71. Some 80 percent of the formal economy was included in the public sector by 1986 despite a succession of substantial public-sector deficits, which mounted to 52 percent of GDP in 1984 and were 39.6 percent of GDP in 1985. See Dennis J. Gayle, "Privatization and Deregulation in Global Perspective: The Caribbean Experience," *Gestion 2000* 3, 2 (1987): 50, 55.

72. Festus Brotherson, "The Politics of Permanent Fear: Guyana's

Authoritarianism in the Anglophone Caribbean," *Caribbean Affairs* 1, 3 (July–September 1988): 64–65.

73. Inter-American Development Bank (IDB), *Economic and Social Progress in Latin America: 1988 Report* (Washington, D.C.: IDB, 1988), pp. 425–427. (These IDB annual reports on Latin America are cited hereafter as IDB, 19xx.)

74. IDB, *1989*, pp. 349–352.

75. Kal Wagenheim, "Guyana," *Caribbean Update*, January 1990, pp. 10–11.

76. CDB, *1989*, pp. 15, 25; CDB, *1990*, p. 15.

77. CDB, *1990*, p. 24.

78. *Trinidad Guardian*, January 2, 1992, p. 7.

79. IDB, *1988*, pp. 345–346. The late 1986 closure of a single large electronic components firm, Intel, depressed manufacturing value–added by almost 7 percent in 1987, when real output in this sector plummeted by approximately 67 percent.

80. CDB, *1990*, p. 17.

81. CDB, *1989*, p. 26; CDB, *1990*, p. 25.

82. Central Bank of Trinidad and Tobago, *Annual Report for Year Ended 31st December 1976* (Port of Spain: College Press, 1977), p. 11; World Bank, *World Development Report 1982* (New York: Oxford University Press, 1982), p. 111.

83. Scott B. MacDonald, *Trinidad and Tobago: Democracy and Development in the Caribbean* (Westport, Conn.: Praeger, 1986), pp. 191–193, 206–207. The first clear indication of trouble occurred when oil output fell by 11 percent, from 212,066 barrels/day in 1980 to 189,487 barrels/day in 1981.

84. Canute James, "Trinidad and Tobago Seeks to Counter Treachery of Oil Plunge," *Financial Times*, November 9, 1989, p. 8.

85. Kal Wagenheim, "Trinidad and Tobago," *Caribbean Update* (December 1989): 17.

86. Kal Wagenheim, "Trinidad and Tobago," *Caribbean Update* (February 1990): 18–19.

87. Robert E. Loomey, *The Jamaican Economy in the 1980s: Economic Decline and Structural Adjustment* (Boulder, Colo.: Westview, 1987), pp. 200–202.

88. As living standards deteriorated, compounded by the persistence of high unemployment and successive currency devaluations in the period 1983–1985, Jamaica's electorate increasingly supported the opposition People's National Party. For a detailed discussion, see Evelyne Huber Stephens and John D. Stephens, "Manley Prepares to Return: PNP Options in Today's Jamaica," *Caribbean Review* 16, 2 (Winter 1988): 16–19, 39–44.

89. IDB, *1988*, pp. 449–450; CDB, *1989*, p. 32; CDB, *1990*, p. 32.

90. IDB, *1988*, pp. 449–450.

91. IDB, *1989*, p. 372. By 1985, external debt amounted to over 180 percent of the island's GDP, and Jamaica's 49 percent debt service export earnings ratio, including short-term obligations, was one of the world's highest. Also, Jamaica has not undertaken the import compression characteristic of most other indebted countries of the hemisphere: Since 1975, import values per capita have remained relatively stable, at just over $500.

92. Kal Wagenheim, "Jamaica," *Caribbean Update* (March 1990): 12–13.

93. Winston H. Griffith, "The Applicability of the East Asian Experience to Caribbean Countries," in Yin-Kann Wen and Jayshree Sengupta, eds., *Increasing the International Competitiveness of Exports from Caribbean Countries* (Washington, D.C.: World Bank, 1991), pp. 91–100.

94 Thomas, "Economic Crisis and the Commonwealth Caribbean," pp. 45–

48; Clive Thomas, *The Poor and the Powerless* (Washington, D.C.: Monthly Review, 1987), pp. 162–167.

95. Kempe Ronald Hope, *Economic Development in the Caribbean* (New York: Praeger, 1986), pp. 52–65.

96. George Beckford and Michael Witter, *Small Garden, Bitter Weed: Struggle and Change in Jamaica* (London: Zed, 1980).

97. David Bray, "Industrialization, Labor Migration, and Employment Crises: A Comparison of Jamaica and the Dominican Republic," in Richard Tardanico, ed., *Crises in the Caribbean Basin* (Newbury Park, Calif.: Sage, 1987), pp. 79–93.

98. Carl Stone, "Caribbean Development in the Year 2000: A Review of the Bourne Report," *Caribbean Affairs* 2, 4 (October–December 1989): 71–79.

99. Kari Levitt, "Stabilisation and Structural Adjustment: Rhetoric and Reality," *Caribbean Affairs* 3, 1 (January–March 1990): 11–25.

100. Peter F. Drucker, *The New Realities in Government and Politics/Economics and Business/Society and World View* (New York: Harper & Row, 1989), pp. 165–170.

101. Albert Hirschman, *Exit, Voice and Loyalty* (Princeton, N.J.: Princeton University, 1965).

6

Security for Development: Caribbean–Asia Pacific Regional Mechanisms

Ivelaw L. Griffith

The preceding chapter compared the economic development strategies adopted by the English-speaking Caribbean and the Asian-Pacific NICs and suggested some aspects of the East Asian model that might be usefully considered by Caribbean policymakers. There is, however, an aspect of Asian development that must also be addressed: the relationship between military-political security and economic security and development.

It was noted in Chapter 5 that national security, as much as economics, played a role in determining the outward-oriented development path of the Asian NICs. For example, South Korea was forced to look away both from its traditional partner China and from North Korea. Because it did not wish to enter into a semicolonial relationship with Japan, the former colonizing power, Korea had to look to other horizons.[1] Similarly, Taiwan was cut off from China; Singapore was expelled from Malaysia and forced to find markets further afield; and Hong Kong was compelled to expand outward after the communist takeover of China and the trade embargo imposed on Beijing during the Korean War. Interestingly, these countries have achieved economic growth despite the high military budgets they have been forced to maintain.

As for the Association of Southeast Asian Nations (ASEAN), security concerns—about China, about the war in Vietnam and, later, the fall of Vietnam, and about the withdrawal of the British from the region—played a large role in bringing the countries together and in intensifying the relationship in the 1970s. The situation in Kampuchea (Cambodia) and the continuing influx of Vietnamese refugees required major ASEAN coordination in the 1980s that has continued into the 1990s. ASEAN success in the security field has provided a climate of stability needed for economic growth.

In East Asia as a whole, the security interests of the United States have also facilitated economic development. The United States played an important role in redirecting Japan's postwar energies into economic growth, and Japan's development has been facilitated by the postwar U.S. security umbrella. South Korea also developed a close relationship with a United States interested in keeping the communist North at bay. For similar reasons, Taiwan has been protected and aided economically by the United States. ASEAN countries were given a sense of security (and room to develop) by U.S. involvement in Vietnam at a time when they were facing communist insurgencies and regional insecurity vis-à-vis China. Thailand hosted U.S. troops until 1975; the Philippines did the same until 1992. In addition, U.S. open markets and financial assistance were important to the success of the East Asian model of development. (The British presence should also be mentioned. Although Britain reduced its involvement after the independence of Malaysia, Britain assisted Singapore financially and remained in control of Hong Kong.)

These close ties between Asian states and the United States have diminished over the years. Japan has been replacing the United States as the major economic presence in Asia; Southeast Asian states have been normalizing their relations with China; and the United States, having pulled out of Indochina in the 1970s, is reducing its remaining military presence in the post–Cold War climate of the 1990s. In 1991, the Philippines Senate rejected a new accord on military bases, thus forcing the United States out of its bases in that country. (One base, Clark Air Base, had already been abandoned, mainly because of damage from a volcanic eruption; one small naval operation was to be transferred to Singapore.) Moreover, negotiations were begun that could lead to reduced troop deployments in South Korea if North Korea agrees to abandon its nuclear program.

The reduction in the U.S. presence raises new security concerns on the part of the East Asians, despite various bilateral security accords that exist between the United States and Asian states. They are also, based on historical experience, so wary of Japanese dominance, whether economic or military, that a Japanese plan (tabled in 1991) for formal regional meetings on defense issues has not been adopted as of mid-1992.[2] Newly industrializing Hong Kong had its own specific security and economic concerns raised by the return of the territory to China, scheduled for 1997. Asian-Pacific states are well aware of the need for external and internal stability in the interest of continuing their "economic miracle." Although Taiwan and Korea will continue to rely on U.S. guarantees, and Hong Kong will fall under China's military jurisdiction, ASEAN states have developed their own regional procedures for ensuring some environmental predictability. In addition, they are seeking in the early 1990s to strengthen regional cooperation, as discussed in this chapter.

As a prelude to the search for suitable security recommendations, it is useful to consider Asian-Caribbean similarities. The English-speaking Caribbean countries resemble the East Asian ones in their historically outward economic orientation: These are states that have been integrated into the global economy through colonialism and, given their small size and vulnerabilities, have been forced to maintain links with larger powers for both military and economic survival. But small size also has protected them from major military involvements, and until the 1970s, there were no overriding military-security concerns that could impel these nations toward ASEAN-type regional security collaboration. Nevertheless, economic self-interest did lead them to create an economic integration movement. Threats to internal stability and the perception of an ideological security threat from Grenada after 1979 (and until 1983) finally provided the catalyst not only for security cooperation but also the revival of regional economic integration, and the deepening of the more successful subregional integration movement. Like the Asian-Pacific states, the Caribbean has relied heavily on the United States for its economic and military survival. Nevertheless, in this era of post–Cold War reductions in U.S. attention, the Caribbean is seeking to strengthen regional capabilities as a coping mechanism.

Regional arrangements, then, seem to be gaining new visibility in the 1990s, both in the economic and military security arenas. As noted in one of the few major studies on the security of small states to date:

> Regional cooperation provides a framework within which, especially in the absence of deep ideological division, member states can feel far less need for military protection from major powers. . . . In security terms, a closely integrated region is less likely to be vulnerable to divisive fears, or to experience intervention, than one which is fragmented. . . . We feel strongly that a cooperative regional environment provides one of the major contributions to enhancing security.[3]

With this recommendation in mind, I concentrate in this chapter on a comparison between ASEAN and Caribbean security mechanisms to address the focal question: Can the Caribbean learn from the ASEAN security model?

Problems of Third World Security

Although states in Asia and the Caribbean have institutional and resource differences, they share some common problems—geopolitical vulnerability and actual and potential instability resulting from ethnic and political discontent as well as economic deprivation. States in both areas have been sensitized to the futility of individualistic action and have resorted to subregional and regional initiatives. A discussion of the core problems facing Third World nations enables us to appreciate some of the challenges facing the states that are the subject of this book. We can then look specifically at the security mechanisms within ASEAN and various Caribbean security organizations in the context of a broader discussion on regionalism and security.

Third World states are confronted with four main security dilemmas:

vulnerability, internal instability, intervention, and militarization. Vulnerability arises when geographic, political, economic, or other factors cause a nation's security to be compromised; it is not usually a function of any single factor. The factors that combine to create vulnerability (geography, perception, poor economy, weak military, and so on) result in the removal or reduction of the influence or power of the state in question, thereby opening it up to internal subversion or external incursion.

Among Third World states, small states are particularly vulnerable; in fact, some writers feel they are "inherently vulnerable" because they may be perceived as potentially easy victims for external aggression in all its guises.[4] This, however, is only part of the problem. What other states perceive is certainly important. But vulnerability relates as well to objective geographical, economic, and political factors and to organizational deficiencies, including populations too small to meet security needs, limited ability to acquire defense-related material, and fragile economic infrastructure.

A report by Sheila Harden points to a half dozen factors of vulnerability: great-power rivalries, territorial claims, possession of rich resources, provision of refuge to refugees or freedom fighters, corruption, and suppression of democracy.[5] Military and political vulnerability often dominates the analysis of this dilemma. However, it is increasingly recognized that questions of economic vulnerability are significant in their own right, and they affect military and political vulnerability.[6] Edward Azar and Chung-in Moon, for example, identify three kinds of threats related to economic vulnerability: systemic vulnerability threats, sensitivity dependence threats, and structural dependence threats. In the first, states are exposed to the transmission of external economic disturbances originating in the international system. The second type stems from transactions among states based on asymmetric relationships. The third compromises economic sovereignty by the existence of distorted economic structures and production relationships.

The second dilemma is internal instability. Protracted in some places, recurring in others, it is for many Third World states (and particularly for small states), the most dangerous security threat. Instability can result from political factionalism, economic deprivation, military coups, ethnic or racial conflict, civil war, or insurgency. Sri Lanka, Haiti, the Sudan, Liberia, Guyana, Lebanon, and Suriname are but a few examples of Third World states with differing kinds of political instability during the late 1980s and early 1990s. Whatever its source or explanation, political instability undermines domestic order and sometimes external security.[7]

Political stability requires attention to at least four matters: political authority, political equality, political participation, and political legitimacy. The first relates to a reciprocal relationship between government and people—the government manages the society and the people accept and consent to that rule. The second issue implies the possession of rights by citizens to participate actively in the political process. The third involves the ability of citizens to influence the nature and operation of the political system through institutions such as political parties, unions, and free media. Political legitimacy, the fourth, requires that the governing body be appropriate and widely representative and have the capability to govern. It is the absence of all or some of these factors in small states that creates problems of internal instability.[8]

Intervention, the third problem area, is the intrusion by a state or entities from it, such as mercenary or terrorist groups, into the territorial and political jurisdiction of another state, often with the use of force. Societies that are victims of military intervention are generally politically unstable and in dispute over a central political authority. Panama in 1989, Grenada in 1983, Seychelles in 1981, Uganda in 1979, and Lebanon since 1975 are examples of this. States intervene in the affairs of others for a variety of reasons: to fulfill ideological commitments, to secure influence, and to achieve strategic considerations.[9]

Potential interveners must consider the degree of cohesion in the target society. They could be constrained by adversaries, their own military limitations, economic costs, and the state of international relations at the time. Changes in international politics since World War II have led to a climate in which the international community frowns on unilateral intervention by big powers. But intervention by Third World states in the affairs of others has been a matter of increasing concern.[10] Among some of the more notable cases are Vietnam in Laos and Cambodia; Indonesia in Malaysia and in West Irian and East Timor; Jamaica, Barbados, Dominica, and others (alongside the United States) in Grenada; Tanzania in Uganda; and Libya in Chad. The latest case of significance was in the Middle East. Iraqi troops stormed into Kuwait on August 2, 1990, plunging the area into a new crisis involving confrontation with the international community, especially the United States and Egypt, when Iraq seemed poised to invade Saudi Arabia.[11] The result was a forty-two-day war that ended February 27, 1991, although the permanent cease-fire was not settled until April 11 with Iraqi acceptance of U.N. Security Council Resolution 687, adopted April 3, 1991. Iraq was expelled from Kuwait and made to comply with all the Security Council resolutions dealing with compensation, recognition of Kuwaiti's sovereignty, restitution of its government, and other issues.[12]

Finally, there is the problem of militarization. It involves increasing the allocation of resources to the development, purchase, and deployment of military equipment and forces. Betty Sedoc-Dahlberg identifies several indexes of this phenomenon: percentage of budget allocated for military purposes; total size of armed forces; level, number, and kind of political positions held by military officials; and the status of the military in the decisionmaking process.[13] Some writers argue that militarization was an option chosen by some states because of a fear of neocolonialism. Others contend that in many cases it was inevitable because the military was the institution to which ex-colonial powers transferred authority. But one critic presents this argument:

> In most Third World states, however, the quest for arms is often unrelated to security needs; hypothetical external threats and the responsibility to preserve law and order are only convenient arguments for extravagant militarization. The desire for prestige and the determination to stay in power have been, more often than not, the true incentives of many governments to build up armed forces and acquire unnecessary sophisticated and expensive military hardware.[14]

The militarization phenomenon has led to a debate about the relationship between militarization and modernization and about the nexus between militarization and economic growth.[15] The growth of military budgets and forces is said to present significant opportunity costs in diverting resources away from other sectors of society. It also creates psychological tensions and facilitates the violation of civil rights, among other effects. The counterargument is that with militarization comes the prospect for expanded employment, education, and health care and a general spillover from the military to the civilian sectors, to the benefit of the entire society. Argentina, Pakistan, Brazil, South Korea, and other countries have used the military as engines of growth. Nevertheless, as those same countries attest, the problem with militarization is that it breeds a climate of power politics in which the military leaders tend to become arbiters of state politics, coups and countercoups become normal political behavior, and the civil and political rights of citizens are trampled on—all of this leading to very tenuous internal security circumstances.

I am not suggesting here that vulnerability, internal instability, intervention, and militarization are security concerns exclusive to Third World states. Some of these are faced by the more developed countries as well. Vulnerability has been a problem for France, Poland, and others. Romania, Yugoslavia, and the now-defunct USSR are among the many states that experienced instability in recent times; intervention has been a concern for many East European states; and militarization has been an issue for all great powers, especially the former USSR. But developmental weaknesses make these concerns especially problematic for developing states such as India and Vietnam (which have dealt with the "militarization" issue) or the Southeast Asian states (which have had particular concerns about intervention). Moreover, in small developing states, the "soft" nature of the state, the capability limitations from which small states suffer, and the extent to which they could be subordinated to others in the international community make these problems all the more acute. A word of caution is, therefore, in order. Despite the common security concerns of Southeast Asian and Caribbean states, the small nations of the English-speaking Caribbean have security needs that differ in intensity, if not in content, from those of their larger ASEAN colleagues.

The scholarship on Third World security has undergone some change of emphasis over recent years. First, the preoccupation with external security has given way to recognition that internal security questions not only are important in their own right, but also they complicate (and sometimes aggravate) external problems. Second, the tendency to cast security analysis in military-political terms has been replaced by acceptance that security concerns go beyond these to the economic arena. Some scholars address ecological and environmental issues as well, arguing that these also qualify for substantive security treatment because of their impact on the survival of states.[16] The third change lies in the recognition of and emphasis on the link between security and development.[17] One scholar whose work now reflects a departure from the conventional approach to which he once subscribed describes part of the change this way: "The traditional concern with territorial integrity and political independence has had to be broadened to include a concern with domestic stability—and thus also a concern with prospects for, and means of, domestic development."[18]

Third World Responses: Regionalism and Security

Recommendations on how Third World states should deal with their problems have been as wide-ranging and sensitive as the debate on the nature of the problems. Suggestions and policy options abound: nonalignment, alternative economic strategies, alliances with middle powers and with more powerful states, greater functional cooperation, domestic legitimation, and regional cooperation.

The last is particularly relevant to this study. Shown in Table 6.1 are some regional security endeavors undertaken by Third World states. Such initiatives vary in their nature and scope—some deal with several pursuits, others concentrate on one—and membership varies. The record of performance by regional organizations over the years is mixed. For example, in the Asian-Pacific area, the expansion of economic links among market economy states has brought growing interdependence yet has not dealt adequately with the vulnerability problem. But in Southeast Asia ASEAN has been successful in enhancing economic viability and internal political stability despite the difficulties encountered by the Philippines and other countries in the 1980s.

In contrast, one examination of Latin America found that although the elites there have greater understanding of the potential benefits of regional trade liberalization and industrial cooperation than do most Third World regions, there has not been commensurate success in collaborative endeavors.

Table 6.1 Regional Initiatives Involving Third World Nations

Region	Organization	Year Formed	Membership	Major Concerns
Africa	Economic Community of West African States (ECOWAS)	1976	16	ES, PS
	Organization of African Unity (OAU)	1963	51	PS, ES
	Organization of Front Line States (OFLS)	1976	6	PS
	Southern Africa Development Coordination Conference (SADCC)	1979	9	ES, PS
Asia	League of Arab Nations (Arab League)	1945	22	PS, MS, ES
	Gulf Cooperation Council (GCC)	1981	6	MS, PS
	Association of Southeast Asian Nations (ASEAN)	1967	6	ES, PS
	South Pacific Forum (SPF)	1971	10	ES
Latin America/The Caribbean	Organization of American States (OAS)	1948	34	PS, MS, ES
	Latin American Economic System (SELA)	1975	27	ES
	Caribbean Community and Common Market (CARICOM)	1973	13	ES, PS
	Organization of Eastern Caribbean States (OECS)	1981	7	ES, PS
	Regional Security System (RSS)	1982	7	MS, PS

Sources: Gavin Boyd, ed., *Regionalism and Global Security* (Lexington: Lexington Books, 1984); Henry Dagenhardt, compiler, *Treaties and Alliances of the World* (Detroit: Gale Research, 1986); *New York Times* (1991).

Notes: MS – Military Security; PS – Political Security; ES – Economic Security

Also, cooperation for military security has not fared well in Latin America's regional community-building.[19] And the following observation about Africa is true about other areas:

> The primary concern is the development of their own states while at the same time maintaining maximum freedom to maneuver. . . . Continental and regional associations may limit the effectiveness of efforts at the state level. Regional associations may provide greater political and economic leverage to deal with problems within the continent and with external powers, but they do tend to become entangled in a variety of political issues.[20]

In the Caribbean, the formation of the Organization of Eastern Caribbean States (OECS) in 1981 and the Regional Security System (RSS) in 1982 reflects an awareness that a two-track approach—military and economic—is often advisable if not necessary. This approach is also reflected in the Gulf Cooperation Council (GCC), though this group does not fall within the area under consideration.[21] Both the RSS and the GCC are composed of very small states, except for Saudi Arabia in the latter case. Because of the capability limitations of the states in these groups, there is skepticism about their military value. In the case of the GCC, this attitude was confirmed in 1990 when the group was paralyzed by the Iraqi intervention in Kuwait, a GCC member. Such regional mechanisms are nevertheless useful: They can facilitate contacts with other regional and international groups and serve as moral deterrents to potential extraregional aggressors, and they have the potential to handle some cases of intraregional political instability.

ASEAN and Other Regional Arrangements

The regional option has been exercised by states in both Southeast Asia and the Caribbean. The former established ASEAN, and the latter created the Caribbean Community and Common Market (Caricom), the OECS, and the RSS.

ASEAN was formed in August 1967 by Thailand, Malaysia, Indonesia, Singapore, and the Philippines. Brunei joined in 1984. Papua New Guinea is an observer. The formation of this organization was a collective response to problems of security that involved elements of the four problems previously mentioned. ASEAN members felt militarily and politically vulnerable vis-à-vis the People's Republic of China. There were problems of internal instability based on ethnic as well as political disputes in the Philippines, Singapore, Malaysia, and elsewhere. The intervention dilemma was manifested in disputes involving Malaysia and the Philippines, and Singapore and Malaysia. At the time, there was no imminent threat from outside the region, but a significant threat developed later from within Southeast Asia itself. In December 1978, a unified communist Vietnam, with the largest and most battle-tested military force in the area, invaded Kampuchea, turning the area into a conflict zone for more than a decade. This gave rise to new geopolitical and international problems.[22]

In structural and operational terms, the highest authority of ASEAN derives from the meeting of the heads of government, but the annual ministerial meeting, composed mostly of foreign ministers, generally sets policy. Continuing supervision of ASEAN activities is the responsibility of the standing committee which includes the foreign minister of the host country as chair, the ASEAN directors-general, and the ASEAN secretary-general. Of importance are the following eight technical committees, the titles of which reflect ASEAN's broad view of security issues: Finance and Banking; Food, Agriculture, and Forestry; Minerals and Energy; Trade and Tourism; Transport and Communications; Culture and Information; Science and Technology; and Social Development.

The record of ASEAN summits is a poor one. The heads of government have met on only four occasions: February 1976 in Bali, Indonesia; February 1977 in Kuala Lumpur, Malaysia; December 1987 in Manila, the Philippines; and in January 1992 in Singapore. At the end of the 1987 meeting, ASEAN leaders affirmed the belief that future meetings should be held about every three to five years—hence the 1992 Singapore meeting.

This failure to hold summits more frequently was the result of several factors. One cause was the preoccupation of some leaders with their own domestic political battles, as in the Philippines, Malaysia, and, to a lesser extent, Singapore. There was also difficulty in getting consensus on summit agendas. Perhaps most crucial, though, was that the business of the group and the interests of its members were settled by the other ASEAN institutional mechanisms as well as outside the ASEAN framework. William Tow is therefore correct in describing ASEAN summits as "largely cosmetic" and "merely the product of compromise" already reached at lower levels.[23]

ASEAN is headquartered in Indonesia. It has been described as a security organization without the structure of an alliance.[24] One Malaysian defense minister underscored the fact that although ASEAN is not a military pact and each member state is responsible for its own defense, cooperation in defense matters is crucial to an effective defense against any potential threat. This sentiment is shared by all member states. The Thais have characterized the organization as a mechanism for "collective political defense" to indicate their reluctance to having a military security community. ASEAN is concerned with security in military, political, and economic terms, but it places a premium on economic and political security. The concentration on economic security is predicated on the belief that comprehensive security will evolve from successful national and regional economic development. In January 1992, ASEAN further advanced this notion with the creation of a free-trade area, to become operational January 1, 1993. This is intended as a precursor to a common market.[25]

This economic emphasis and some practical problems have made ASEAN decline to pursue a regional military establishment. Among the problems have been a diversity among member countries of weapons systems, military doctrine, training, logistics, and languages. All this has made it difficult to coordinate joint deployment of forces from the six states. Member states are also conscious of the political hazards of stationing mixed contingents in any member country to deal with internal instability, especially insurgency, a concern of many ASEAN members. The obstacles to close multilateral military cooperation have occasioned the development of ad hoc structured mechanisms for intelligence exchanges, occasional joint military exercises, and common-border operations.

Defense officials at different levels of the military hierarchies exchange visits, and officers from one member state train in the military schools of another. Resource sharing is also a feature of ASEAN security cooperation. For example, Singapore soldiers do jungle training in Brunei, Brunei's navy uses Malaysia's Lumut Naval Base, and Malaysia's air force holds stagings through Indonesian air bases. Joint bilateral military exercises, especially naval and air exercises, have been held. Singapore and Indonesia, as well as Thailand and Malaysia, now have annual air exercises aimed at familiarizing air force personnel with procedures of joint air force operations and joint air strike strategy planning. Indonesia holds annual exercises with Malaysia, Thailand, and Singapore. A series of other bilateral exercises have also been held between Singapore and Thailand (naval), Thailand and Malaysia (air), Malaysia and Singapore (naval), and Singapore and Brunei (naval). Only Malaysia and Indonesia have regular bilateral army exercises.[26]

States in ASEAN subscribe to the concept of "national resilience." This concept advocates complete mobilization and utilization of a nation's total tangible and intangible resources in defense of its interests. National resilience is complemented by the notion of "regional resilience," which posits that as each member increases its capabilities to defend itself, the region as a whole becomes more capable of withstanding external aggression. Indonesia's President Suharto is the original proponent of these concepts.

Vietnam remained a key potential military threat until reforms there in the late 1980s resulted in a scaling back of the military and troop withdrawals from Kampuchea. The military weakness vis-à-vis Vietnam, societal fissures, and the geopolitical realities of the area gave rise to increasing reliance on nonregional forces in security planning. Although states such as Brunei, Indonesia, and Singapore adhere strongly to the concept of nonalignment, ASEAN as a whole has been reluctant to have a diminution of U.S. and British presence in the area. Two ASEAN members, Thailand and the Philippines, maintain alliances with the United States, and all member states benefit from U.S. security assistance, training, and weapons sales.

ASEAN welcomes the five-powers defense arrangement (FPDA), which involves Britain, New Zealand, Australia, and two ASEAN members, Malaysia and Singapore. FPDA was dormant for much of the 1980s and was weakened by New Zealand's withdrawal of its 740-member military detachment from Singapore and by Australia's rotation of its fighters (the initial plan was for them to maintain permanent deployment). Earlier, in 1976, Britain had removed its troops from Malaysia and Singapore. Yet states within FPDA saw its deterrence value and were confident of the ability of some members, especially Britain and Australia, to transform it quickly into a credible security mechanism. In September of that year, FPDA members undertook their first major maritime defense exercise. As part of the four-day event, code-named Lima Bersatu, Britain provided four Tornado jets directly from England, a naval task force headed by the aircraft carrier HMS *Royal*, and 1,500 British commandos.[27] That exercise significantly enhanced the military preparedness and credibility of FPDA members.

Although states within ASEAN welcomed the outside role to meet their vulnerability to Vietnamese, Soviet, and other potential designs, they desired to end the competition between the United States and the now-defunct USSR involving the region. Fifteen years after the Kuala Lumpur declaration calling for a zone of peace, freedom, and neutrality (ZOPFRAN), the proposal was adopted in 1986. It called for an end to hegemonic competition in the area by the big powers and for the settlement of the Kampuchean problem. The Soviets endorsed ZOPFRAN in 1987, stressing its importance in pursuit of an East Asian nuclear-free zone, and in 1988 proposed the mutual elimination of Soviet and U.S. bases in Southeast Asia. The United States rejected the trade as one of "unequal value." The demise of the USSR and the end of the Cold War, however, have changed the geopolitics of the region dramatically, effectively removing the concerns about superpower rivalry.

Caribbean Security Arrangements

Like Southeast Asia, the English-speaking Caribbean has faced the four security dilemmas discussed earlier. As small states, the countries of the region have been especially vulnerable to military, political, and economic measures taken by larger neighbors, such as the United States, Cuba, and Venezuela. Guyana and Trinidad and Tobago are susceptible to racially based internal instability, and there has been political instability in Jamaica, Grenada, Dominica, and Trinidad and Tobago, and other states. The United States has a long record of direct and indirect intervention in the Caribbean area as a whole; the 1983 intervention in Grenada and the 1989 intervention in Panama are the most recent instances. Militarization, the fourth security problem previously discussed, was a concern during the 1970s and the 1980s, particularly in Guyana and Grenada.

Caribbean states, including the English-speaking ones, have depended on several sources for their security: bilateral arrangements with the United States and Britain; the hemispheric umbrella organization, the Organization of American States (OAS); the Rio Treaty, formally known as the Inter-American Treaty of Reciprocal Assistance; membership in multilateral groups such as the nonaligned movement (NAM) and the British Commonwealth; and regional mechanisms such as those described in this section.

Like parts of the Asian-Pacific area, the Caribbean demonstrates the multidimensional and overlapping nature of Third World security concerns, characteristics that necessitate complementary and concentric initiatives. In the larger English-speaking Caribbean region, the major organizational initiative has been Caricom. Created by the Treaty of Chaguaramas in July 1973, its members are Antigua and Barbuda, the Bahamas, Barbados, Belize, Dominica, Grenada, Guyana, Jamaica, Montserrat (still a British colony), St. Kitts/Nevis, St. Lucia, St. Vincent and the Grenadines, and Trinidad and Tobago. Colombia, the Dominican Republic, Haiti, Puerto Rico, Suriname, Aruba, and Venezuela are observers. Cuba's bid for similar status was denied in 1992 but Caricom heads of state agreed to establish a Cuba-Caricom commission to establish cooperative links in a number of sectors. Caricom is concerned with deepening political and functional cooperation as well as reducing intraregional trade barriers, creating a common external tariff, and coordinating policies on joint ventures and foreign trade.

Institutionally, as in ASEAN, the heads of government conference act as the final authority on policy and on relations and treaties with other groups or with states. Because this is a full-fledged common market (unlike ASEAN), there is a Common Market Council responsible for its development and smooth running. There are also functional committees. These include the Conference of Ministers Responsible for Health and several ministerial standing Committees: Education; Labor; Foreign Affairs; Finance; Agriculture; Industry; Transport; Energy; Mines and Natural Resources; and Science and Technology. The Secretariat is in Guyana's capital, Georgetown.

Caricom is not backed by any military mechanism, a fact that has hampered its ability to solve regional conflicts. In fact, political and ideological disagreements among states prevented leaders from holding any summit between 1975 and 1982. Disparate national-interest pursuits among member states also so undermined foreign policy coordination that for a long time strong collective positions could not be articulated in such crucial regional conflicts as Haiti and Suriname. The 1983 crisis in Grenada was a dramatic instance of policy incapacity: Caricom states were divided over the best course of action to take, and the Community was almost destroyed by the subsequent bickering among members.[28] However, in the early 1990s,

Caricom states have displayed a measure of cohesiveness, especially with regard to the adoption of an active stance on the resolution of Haiti's political problems.

Caricom's primary security concern remains economic. In that area, although there have been some notable achievements, the institution has been unable to cushion appreciably the impact of the region's economic vulnerability. This vulnerability is not merely operational but also structural: It involves heavy reliance on foreign trade, limited production and export diversification, low savings, and heavy reliance on foreign capital. Moreover, the expansion of Caribbean trade has been frustrated by import restrictions, especially by the larger states, a situation occasioned by their adverse balance-of-payments position. In addition, industrial policies and regional labor mobility are still areas of disagreement.

The situation regarding imports should be improved with the implementation of a common external tariff (CET) by all member states. Originally scheduled for 1992, implementation was postponed until January 1, 1993 because of disagreements over the most appropriate CET rate. At their 1992 summit meeting, heads of government agreed to lower the tariff rate from the original 45 percent to a level that would be more attractive to dissenting member states. As for labor mobility, the Grand Anse Declaration adopted at the 1989 Caricom summit called for free intraregional movement of skilled and professional personnel and contract workers "on a season and project basis." Although such freedom of movement had not been implemented by mid-1992, most countries had by then introduced measures to facilitate travel by Caricom nationals within the region, and those that had not were committed to doing so as soon as possible. Like ASEAN leaders, Caricom leaders are aware that unless action is taken to strengthen their economic viability, Third World countries are in danger of marginalization, in an era of large economic blocs in Europe and North America. The problem is more acute for Caricom than for ASEAN, given the marginality already inherent in small size and limited resources. Awareness of this problem has led Caricom to renew action on the common external tariff and a regional stock exchange and to strengthen other economic linkages within Caricom.[29]

The smaller eastern Caribbean countries within Caricom are more closely interlinked politically and economically. In June 1981, Antigua and Barbuda, Dominica, Grenada, Montserrat, St. Kitts/Nevis, St. Lucia, and St. Vincent and the Grenadines formed the OECS.[30] The work of the organization is conducted through five "institutions": the Authority of Heads of Government; the Foreign Affairs Committee; the Defense and Security Committee; the Economic Affairs Committee; and the Central Secretariat, based in Castries, the capital of St. Lucia. The treaty provides for OECS members to "coordinate, harmonize, and pursue joint policies" in several areas, among them foreign policy, international trade, currency and central banking, the judiciary, and (unlike in Caricom) mutual defense and security.

The OECS treaty outlines defense and security matters under Article 8. The fourth section of that provision is a key one and worthy of full reproduction here:

> The Defense and Security Committee shall have responsibility for coordinating the efforts of Member States for collective defense and the preservation of peace and security against external aggression and for the development of close ties among Member States of the Organization in matters of external defense and security, including measures to combat the activities of mercenaries operating with or without the support of internal or national elements, in the exercise of the inherent right of individual or collective self-defense recognized by Article 51 of the Charter of the United Nations.

This provision—the subject of much controversy involving OECS participation in the Grenada intervention—is the legal and political framework for the creation of the RSS.[31]

The RSS was created on October 29, 1982, by Antigua and Barbuda, Barbados, Dominica, St. Lucia, and St. Vincent and the Grenadines through a memorandum of understanding signed originally in Roseau, Dominica. The document was signed by St. Lucia later (November 4, 1982), and the RSS became operational between January and April 1983, with heads of RSS member states formalizing arrangements at a February 1983 meeting in St. Lucia. St. Kitts/Nevis joined officially in February 1984, but had begun participating in the organization since the previous September. Grenada joined in January 1985. Establishment of the RSS came in the wake of security problems in the eastern Caribbean. The Tom Adams government in Barbados was the alleged intended victim of a planned mercenary expedition in 1978. There was an insurrection on Union Island, in St. Vincent and the Grenadines, which the Barbados Defense Force helped to quell. In March 1979, the government in Grenada was removed by a coup, and later, in 1981, the government in Dominica was the target of mercenary and coup attempts. These events and experiences naturally worried eastern Caribbean leaders. They were fully aware of their individual limitations and were amenable to adopting a collective scheme to secure themselves.

As shown in Figure 6.1, the RSS is headed by a Council of Ministers (composed of defense ministers) as the central policymaking body. Operational command falls under a Central Liaison Office headed by a Regional Security Coordinator. A linkage exists between the Regional Security Coordinator and the U.S. Military Liaison Office in the Eastern Caribbean (USMLOEC) and the British High Commission in the area (UKHCEC) because these are the principal foreign agencies to which the coordinator relates on behalf of the RSS. The RSS headquarters is in Barbados which also provides the Regional Security Coordinator.

Technically, the overall force level of the RSS is the sum of the security establishments of all participating states. But most states are reluctant to

116　　　　　　　　　　　　　　　　Development

Figure 6.1 Structure of the Regional Security System

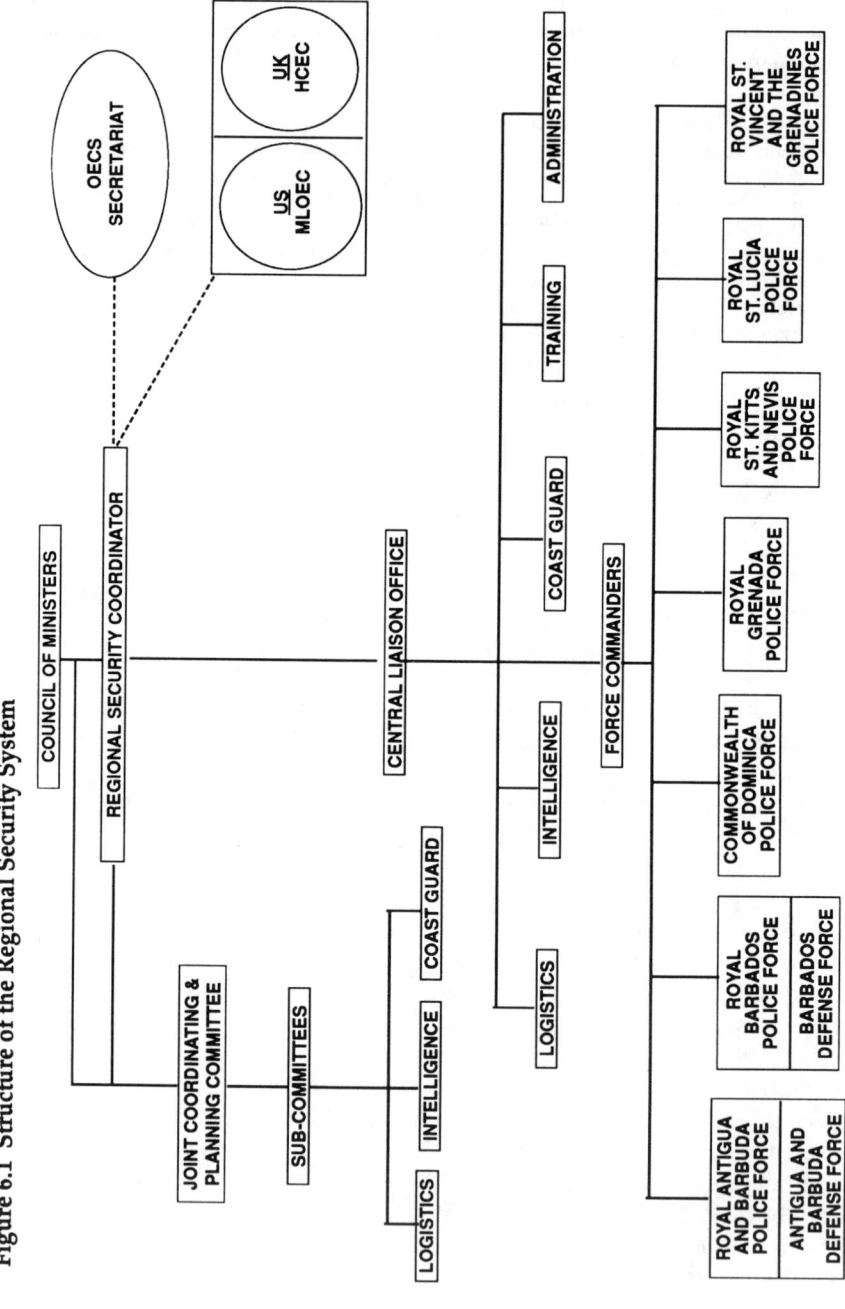

Notes: OECS - Organization of Eastern Caribbean States; MLOEC - Military Liaison Office, Eastern Caribbean; HCEC - High Commission, Eastern Caribbean; - - - - indirect relations have their entire security establishment identified for RSS purposes and, therefore, designate a complement of forces for potential RSS activity. The security establishments appear in the bottom row of Figure 6.1.

RSS officials are conscious of the system's limitations. They consider its greatest value to be the potential for deterrence, acknowledging that "The RSS does not pretend to have the capacity to deter or defeat any large-scale foreign aggression against any of its members. Should such an attack take place, a substantial outside support would be essential."[32] They also regard the mechanism as a form of security insurance: "The RSS can be likened to an insurance policy designed to meet the more likely threat to the peace and security of the area. Without peace and security, no development can take place at all, and a suitable balance must be struck between [having] nothing and having a large standing army."[33]

The weapons and equipment at the disposal of the RSS are essentially light armor, basic communications equipment, and patrol vessels. Much of the arms arsenal is old, some of World War II vintage. However, since 1984, the United States and Britain have been providing more up-to-date equipment; still, none of it is very sophisticated. Although initially financed on the basis of 49 percent contribution by Barbados and 51 percent contribution by the other states, the RSS is now financed on the basis of 40 percent by Barbados and 10 percent each by the other six states. RSS funds may not be used for normal operational purposes within participating states, but RSS supplies may be loaned to those states. Financial contributions go to a central fund; according to RSS sources, several states have been delinquent in contributing to the fund.

The capability limitations of RSS member states make foreign support necessary. Foreign assistance comes mainly from the United States but also from Britain and Canada. The United States is prohibited legally from financing the RSS as an institution, but it provides training and equipment of considerable value to RSS member states. U.S. commitment to assisting the RSS was reaffirmed in February 1991 by Admiral Leon Edney, Commander in Chief of the United States Atlantic Command. Admiral Edney visited the eastern Caribbean, meeting in Barbados with political and military officials from the area to discuss Caribbean-U.S. cooperation.[34]

There have been several attempts to expand the RSS, all futile so far. The first was a 1985 proposal by St. Lucia's prime minister, John Compton. The second initiative came the following year with a proposal to upgrade the RSS agreement to a full security treaty. A draft treaty was circulated to heads of RSS member governments and received the endorsement of most of them. The treaty was seen by RSS officials as part of the institution's evolution. It would also have given the RSS an international personality, simultaneously permitting direct security cooperation with the United States, France, Britain, Venezuela, and other states. The treaty proposal encountered strong resistance from two prime ministers, James Mitchell of St. Vincent and the Grenadines and the late Errol Barrow of Barbados, both of whom were wary of militarization.[35]

The most recent attempt at RSS expansion derived from a heightened security consciousness in the region following the 1990 coup attempt in Trinidad and Tobago. Prime Minister Erskine Sandiford of Barbados has been a strong advocate of expansion, arguing as follows at the 1990 Caricom summit in Jamaica:

> I think the time is now for us to look at the creation of a broader regional system of security. I should like to propose for the consideration of my fellow Heads of Government, the expansion and consolidation of the existing Regional Security System in the Eastern Caribbean to include as many Caricom states as possible. I would urge that the RSS be invested with the authority and resources to deal with all aspects of regional security including the interdiction of drug trafficking, surveillance of our coastal zones, mutual assistance in the event of natural disasters, as well as threats to constitutional democracy from criminals, terrorists, mercenaries, and other enemies of democracy.[36]

As a result of Sandiford's lobbying, Caricom leaders "agreed on the need to review existing arrangements in support of regional security and decided to establish a Committee of Member States to look into the matter and report before the Twelfth Meeting of Conference."[37] The matter was still pending in mid-1992.

RSS units participated in the Caribbean peacekeeping force that kept internal security in Grenada after the 1983 intervention by the United States. RSS officials also coordinated the deployment of army and police contingents from several Caricom countries in Trinidad and Tobago after the aborted coup there in 1990. RSS forces have also been deployed annually since 1985 in military exercises. These are designed to train and professionalize RSS personnel and to reinforce the idea of defending democracy in the region. The first exercise, Operation Exotic Palm, was held in St. Lucia September 11–15, 1985. It involved units from all RSS members except St. Vincent and the Grenadines, along with forces from Britain and the United States, for a total of 600 troops. The 1991 maneuvers, Tradewinds 91, involved military and police units from thirteen Caricom nations and units from the United States and Britain.[38]

What one analyst said about collective security efforts of small states in Africa and in the Persian Gulf has direct relevance to collective efforts in the Caribbean:

> Their strength lies in their ability to diffuse local conflagrations and thus to avoid superpower interference, in their ability to project a strong, collective voice, and in their talent for gaining support of major powers with compatible interests in the region. But the major threats to their areas—local powers or outside actors—will probably best such

arrangements. They have not been able and will not be able to cope alone. In the near term, they will remain halfway houses on the road to security cooperation, dependent on the interest and support of outside powers, and absorbed, first and foremost, by their own political and economic instabilities.[39]

The RSS fits much of this characterization. However, the events of October 1983 in Grenada and the geopolitical realities of the area cast doubt on its ability to diffuse military tensions of any significance without the involvement of the proximate superpower or a middle power such as Venezuela. There is no guarantee that the RSS states' "strong, collective voice" and "talent for gaining the support of major powers with compatible interests" would attract the United States or other military powers to help with conflict resolution in the region. Countries such as the United States, Britain, or Venezuela will be inclined to act because of their geopolitical interests—and because they can subordinate the Caribbean to those interests. Nevertheless, there is little doubt that the RSS is a security halfway house, dependent on the interests and support of outside powers, and preoccupied with the political and other challenges facing its members.[40]

One other security response of Caribbean states can be mentioned: the proposal for a zone of peace. At the 1979 OAS General Assembly in Bolivia, a resolution was adopted calling for the Caribbean to be declared a zone of peace. In the resolution, sponsored by Grenada, the OAS General Assembly expressed "deep concern over the heightening of tensions in the subregion resulting from recent increases in military activity in the Caribbean area." It repudiated the concept of the region as a sphere of influence and voiced support for the principles of ideological pluralism and peaceful coexistence. The resolution also called urged states to devote efforts "in regional and international forums to the advancement of this concept."[41]

Advancement of the proposal to designate the Caribbean a zone of peace has been stymied by various problems. The resolution could only be meaningful if the military powers of the hemisphere consent to respect its terms and requirements. It would require the elimination of foreign military bases, the end of foreign military maneuvers, adoption of a policy of nonintervention, and adherence to the Treaty of Tlatelolco that proscribes nuclear weapons from the region. To date, the United States and other military powers in the area have been unwilling to make these concessions.

Comparisons and Recommendations for the English-speaking Caribbean

ASEAN states have long accepted the thesis that military stability is a prerequisite for development. Despite the changes in the post–Cold War world, threats to the peace are still present in Asia, and the reduction of the U.S. military presence has necessitated reliance on national and regional security approaches initiated in the 1960s. The noncommunist nations of Southeast Asia are intent on integrating their security and economic planning, even if that means asserting more independence from Washington.[42] In the Caribbean, there is a historically strong orientation toward the United States, both in terms of economic and military security needs. Nevertheless, regional efforts have been perceived as necessary for survival and are likely to play a more crucial role in the 1990s. Economic integration is considered necessary to prevent marginalization in a global economy characterized by large trading blocs, and regional security is needed increasingly to confront challenges that are domestic as well as regional—challenges such as drugs, the environment, and illegal immigration.

Although states in Southeast Asia and the Caribbean share some common security problems and responses, the circumstances of the two regions differ in several ways. There are small weak states in each group, but the profiles of the two groups reflect greater size and resource limitations in the Caribbean—in population, productive capacity, and military strength (see Table 6.2). The security problems as defined by the leaders of the states in the two groups share some commonality in that vulnerability, internal instability, intervention, and militarization have been dilemmas for both regions. But the sources and intensities of threats have varied. Both regions are geopolitically important, and in the recent age of superpower rivalry, both have experienced superpower activity. However, the difference in the geography-security nexus in the two cases relates essentially to the proximity of the United States to the Caribbean and to the limitations placed on the Caribbean by its subordinate status.

The United States is obviously the dominant state in the Western Hemisphere. Dominant-subordinate relations involving the United States and Caribbean (and other) countries are primarily the result of disproportions in the economic and military capabilities of the states involved, with the balance tipped strongly in favor of the United States. However, the United States has much more than greater military capability, a capacity to destabilize, and mechanisms for economic control. It also has what Paul Johnson calls "ideological, cultural and other normative mechanisms of manipulation." Johnson explains:

> Essentially, I am referring to those recurrent social processes whereby decision-making elites in subordinate states come to share the values, beliefs, and attitudes of the elites of the hegemonic power and hence are spontaneously predisposed to identify their own and their country's interests with those of the hegemon, and to devise their policies accordingly. These elites of subordinate states may be educated abroad, rely on foreign technical experts, read mass media dominated by

imported wire service reports, attend movies imported from the hegemonic country, travel extensively there, associate with the foreign diplomatic community, adopt a foreign life-style, and so on.[43]

Table 6.2 Profile of ASEAN and Caricom

Country	Population (1989, thousands)	GDP Per Capita[a] ($ U.S. 1989)	Armed Forces[b] (1991)
ASEAN			
Brunei	398	9,600	6,900
Indonesia	170,179	430	458,000 [c]
Malaysia	16,942	2,130	330,600
The Philippines	60,685 [d]	700	196,500
Singapore	2,685	10,450	67,100 [e]
Thailand	56,340 [d]	1,170	424,700
CARICOM			
Antigua and Barbuda [f]	78	4,595	470
Bahamas	249	10,088	2,868
Barbados [f]	256	6,673	2,300
Belize	183	1,665	1,400
Dominica [f]	82	1,842	370
Grenada [f]	100	1,820	655
Guyana	755	337	9,800
Jamaica	2,375	1,636	9,297
Montserrat	12	6,133	106
St. Kitts/Nevis [f]	43	2,477	415
St. Lucia [f]	148	1,510	590
St. Vincent and Grenadines [f]	115	1,463	570
Trinidad and Tobago	1,213	3,576	6,600

Sources: Caribbean Development Bank, *Annual Report 1990* (Bridgetown, Barbados, 1991); *Europa World Yearbook 1991* (London: Europa, 1991); *Military Balance 1991–1992* (London: International Institute for Strategic Studies, 1991); Ivelaw L. Griffith, *The Quest for Security in the Caribbean* (New York: M. E. Sharpe, 1993).
[a] ASEAN figures are for GNP.
[b] Armed forces figures include active military, paramilitary, and police forces.
[c] This figure does not include WANRA (Civil Guard), a part-time local military auxiliary, or KAMRA (People's Security), a part-time police auxiliary with about 1.5 million members.
[d] Figure for 1990.
[e] This figure does not include the Civil Defense Force of about 100,000.
[f] Member of the Regional Security System (RSS).

The U.S. subordination of the Caribbean affects the area's regional initiatives generally and its security initiatives in particular. Diplomatic hostility, economic ostracism, and military intervention have been the fate of Caribbean states that have pursued political and economic security measures considered by the United States to be inimical to its interests. For example, between 1979 and 1983, Grenada's efforts to secure financing from the

International Monetary Fund (IMF), the European Community (EC), and the Caribbean Development Bank (CDB) for a variety of projects were either blocked or otherwise frustrated by the United States. Jamaica, during Michael Manley's first two terms as prime minister (1972–1980), faced considerable political and economic hostility. The Caribbean Basin Initiative launched by the United States in 1982 initially excluded Grenada, Guyana, and Nicaragua as a punitive measure. And, of course, there was the October 1983 intervention in Grenada.

Caribbean leaders were conscious of the effects of these measures. They were often unable to mitigate the impact of the measures, but they acted when they could to salvage regional initiatives and preserve some of their integrity. One such case occurred in June 1981 when the United States attempted to exclude Grenada from a CDB loan to the eastern Caribbean. The political pressures the United States put simultaneously on some states—Jamaica, Dominica, and Antigua and Barbuda in particular—caused a strain in the regional integration movement. But Caribbean leaders decided to forgo the loan rather than have a blatant dictation that would further subvert their efforts at political and economic security.

Despite differences in geopolitics, capabilities, and other circumstances of Asia Pacific and the Caribbean, the Caribbean may be able to profit from adoption of the twin concepts of national and regional resilience practiced in Southeast Asia. A novel way of increasing capabilities in the economic and political arena is to redefine the region's economic and political space to take advantage of the potential economic and political support of Caribbean citizens in places such as the United States, Britain, and Canada. The tendency of some Caribbean political elites to adopt a hostile attitude to citizens who emigrate and establish themselves in Europe and North America (for whatever reason) should be changed to one of encouraging a partnership. This partnership could serve Caribbean states by having citizens abroad help lobby foreign governments and businesses in pursuit of specific political and economic goals. Foreign nationals could also be encouraged to invest in the region and to promote foreign investment there.

The economic problems of the Caribbean now present states there with some of the greatest security threats, and these have political as well as military implications. James Mitchell, prime minister of St. Vincent and the Grenadines, outlined some of the implications:

> Fundamentally, in my view, the sores of poverty in our region cannot be cured by military therapy. I lead a popular government and I need to deliver the goods. Opportunities for subversion will soon emerge when the people are frustrated again. It is the collapse of social institutions that creates avenues for international intrigues. If the people's expectations are not fulfilled through channels that people like me create, we will, in due course, be inviting the colonels and the

commissars. And the more arms we have available in the country, the greater will be the temptation to solve our problems with a coup.[44]

In summary, states in Asia Pacific and the Caribbean have had problems that are common to Third World nations generally: problems of military, political, and economic vulnerability; internal instability; intervention; and militarization. The extent of these problems varies by region as well as in the institutional and resource capacities of states to deal with them. For the regions under consideration, both sets of states are conscious of the limitations of individual action, and both have devised ways to structure collective action. Southeast Asian states have a track record of a quarter century in ASEAN, and Caribbean states can learn from this experience. The ASEAN states have adhered to the notions of national and regional resilience: Without creating a formal military mechanism, they have sought to increase national and regional military and political capabilities, and in doing so, have engendered the necessary climate for economic growth. The smallest Caribbean states, by virtue of resource limitations not experienced by ASEAN, have been forced to pool their efforts in military as well as economic arenas, but for the larger Caribbean Community, priority has always been given to economic security. To further their economic goals, however, Caricom states may find that the ASEAN notion of "resilience" offers possibilities for political coordination that will complement and further the prime goal of strengthening regional economic integration.

Notes

1. Laurence Whitehead, "Tigers in Latin America?" *Annals of the American Academy of Political and Social Science*, special issue "The Pacific Region: Challenges to Policy and Theory," September 1989, p. 150.
2. *New York Times*, July 25, 1991, p. A14.
3. Commonwealth Study Group, *Vulnerability: Small States in the Global Society* (London: Commonwealth Secretariat, 1985), p. 65 (hereafter cited as *Vulnerability*).
4. *Vulnerability*, p. 15.
5. Sheila Harden, ed., *Small Is Dangerous: Micro-States in a Macro-World* (New York: St. Martin's, 1985), p. 13. Also see William T. Tow, *Subregional Security Cooperation in the Third World* (Boulder, Colo.: Lynne Rienner, 1990), ch. 1, esp. pp. 18–19.
6. *Vulnerability;* Edward Azar and Chung-in Moon, "Third World National Security: Toward a New Conceptual Framework," *International Interactions* 11, 2 (1984): 103–135; Stephen Krasner, "Third World Vulnerability and Global Negotiations," in Robert Art and Robert Jervis, eds., *International Politics: Anarchy, Force, Political Economy, and Decision-Making* (Boston: Little, Brown, 1985): and York Bradshaw and Zwelakhe Tsandu, "Foreign Capital Penetration, State Intervention, and Development in Sub-Saharan Africa," *International Studies Quarterly* 34, (June 1990): 229–251.

7. Zalmay Khalilzad, "The Politics of Ethnicity in Southwest Asia: Political Development or Political Decay?" *Political Science Quarterly* 99 (Winter 1984–1985): 657–679; Edward Azar and Chung-in Moon, "Managing Protracted Social Conflict in the Third World: Facilitation and Development Diplomacy," *Millennium: Journal of International Studies* 15, 3 (1986): 393–406; Anthony Maingot, "Haiti: Problems of a Transition to Democracy in an Authoritarian Soft State," *Journal of Interamerican Studies and World Affairs* 28, 4 (1987–1988): 75–102; and Ivelaw L. Griffith, "The Military and the Politics of Change in Guyana," *Journal of Interamerican Studies and World Affairs* 33 (Summer 1991): 141–173.

8. Perry Mars, "The Conditions of Political Stability," (Journal of the Guyana Institute for Social Research and Action) *GISRA* 6, 1 (1975): 1–6; Samuel Huntington, *Political Order in Changing Societies* (New Haven: Yale University Press, 1968); and Charles Andrain, *Political Change in the Third World* (Boston: Unwin Hyman, 1988).

9. See Neil MacFarlene, *Intervention and Regional Security*, Adelphi Papers no. 196 (London: International Institute for Strategic Studies, 1985); Zalmay Khalilzad, "Intervention in Afghanistan: Implications for the Security of Southwest Asia," in William Dowdy and Russel Trood, eds., *The Indian Ocean: Perspectives on a Strategic Arena* (Durham, N.C.: Duke University Press, 1985); and Peter Schraeder, ed., *Intervention in the 1980s: U.S. Foreign Policy in the Third World* (Boulder, Colo.: Lynne Rienner, 1989).

10. See Talukder Maniruzzaman, *The Security of Small States in the Third World*, Canberra Papers on Strategy and Defense no. 25 (Canberra, Australia: Strategic and Defense Studies Center, 1982); and Jagat Mehta, ed., *Third World Militarization* (Austin, Tex.: LBJ School of Public Affairs, 1985).

11. See R. W. Apple, Jr., "Invading Iraqis Seize Kuwait and Its Oil; U.S. Condemns Attack, Urges United Action," *New York Times*, August 3, 1990, pp. A1, A8; Youssef Ibrahim, "A New Gulf Alignment," *New York Times*, August 3, 1990, pp. A1, A10; and William Quandt, "The Middle East in 1990," *Foreign Affairs* 70 (America and the World 1990/1991): 49–69.

12. See R. W. Apple, Jr., "Allies Destroy Iraqis' Main Force; Kuwait Is Retaken After Seven Months," *New York Times*, February 28, 1991, pp. A1, A9; Andrew Rosenthal, "Military Aims Met; Firing Ending After 100 Hours of Ground War, President Declares," *New York Times*, February 28, 1991, pp. A1, A12; and Allan Crowell, "Truce Now Official," *New York Times*, April 7, 1991, pp. L1, L14. For a comprehensive analysis of the crisis, the war, and the subsequent settlement, see Micah L. Sifry and Christopher Cerf, eds., *The Gulf War Reader: History, Documents, Opinions* (New York: Times Books, 1991).

13. See Betty Sedoc-Dahlberg, "Interest Groups and the Military in Suriname," in Alma H. Young and Dion E. Phillips, eds., *Militarization in the Non-Hispanic Caribbean* (Boulder, Colo.: Lynne Rienner, 1986).

14. Mehta, *Third World Militarization*, p. 17.

15. See, for example, Emile Benoit, *Defense and Economic Growth in Developing Countries* (Lexington, Mass.: Lexington Books, 1973); Alfred Maizels and Machiko Nissanke, "The Determinants of Military Expenditure in Developing Countries," *World Development* 14, 9 (1986): 1125–1140; and Nicole Ball, *Security and Economy in the Third World* (Princeton: Princeton University Press, 1988).

16. See Azar and Moon, "Third World National Security"; Jessica Tuchman Mathews, "Redefining Security," *Foreign Affairs* 68 (Spring 1989): 162–177; and Peter Gleick, "The Growing Links Among Environment, Resources, and Security," paper delivered at 1991 topical symposium, National Defense

University, Washington, D.C., November 14–15, 1991.

17. See *Vulnerability;* Colin Clarke and Tony Payne, eds., *Politics, Security, and Development in Small States* (London: Allen and Unwin, 1987); Robert Rothstein, "The Security Dilemma and the 'Poverty Trap' in the Third World," *Jerusalem Journal of International Relations* 38 (Summer 1986): 1–38; and Anthony T. Bryan, J. E. Greene, and Timothy M. Shaw, eds., *Peace, Development, and Security in the Caribbean* (New York: St. Martin's, 1990).

18. Rothstein, "The Security Dilemma," pp. 8–9.

19. Gavin Boyd, ed., *Regionalism and Global Society* (Lexington, Mass.: Lexington Books, 1984), pp. 118–121.

20. Ibid., p. 63.

21. For assessment of the GCC, see Mahnaz Zehra Ispahani, "Alone Together: Regional Security Arrangements in Southern Africa and the Persian Gulf," *International Security* 8 (Spring 1984): 152–175; Erik Peterson, *The Gulf Cooperation Council: Search for Unity in a Dynamic Region* (Boulder, Colo.: Westview, 1988); and Tow, *Subregional Security Cooperation,* pp. 26–28, 46–56, 92–94.

22. For a discussion of the genesis and development of ASEAN, see Sheldon Simon, *The ASEAN States and Regional Security* (Stanford, Calif.: Hoover Institution, 1982); Michael Leifer, *ASEAN and the Security of South-East Asia* (London: Routledge, 1989); and Tow, *Subregional Security Cooperation,* pp. 23–25, 37–45. For an examination of the role of elite perceptions in the shaping of ASEAN and its security activities over the years, see Robert Tillman, *Southeast Asia and the Enemy Beyond* (Boulder, Colo.: Westview, 1987).

23. Tow, *Subregional Security Cooperation,* p. 23.

24. See Michael Leifer, "The Paradox of ASEAN: A Security Organization Without the Structure of an Alliance," *Round Table,* July 1978, pp. 361–368.

25. Philip Shenon, "Southeast Asia Nations Sign Free-Trade Accord," *New York Times,* January 29, 1992, p. D1.

26. For more on recent military and political cooperation within ASEAN, see Donald Weatherbee, "ASEAN: Patterns of National and Regional Resilience," in Young Whan Kihl and Lawrence Grinter, eds., *Asian-Pacific Security: Emerging Challenges and Responses* (Boulder, Colo.: Lynne Rienner, 1986); Sheldon Simon, "ASEAN Security in the 1990s," *Asian Survey* 29, 6 (1989): 580–600; Donald Weatherbee, "ASEAN Defense Programs: Military Patterns of National and Regional Resilience," in Young Whan Kihl and Lawrence Grinter, eds., *Security, Strategy, and Policy Responses in the Pacific Rim* (Boulder, Colo.: Lynne Rienner, 1989); and T. M. Cheung, "Shoulder to Shoulder: ASEAN Members Strengthen Defense Ties," *Far Eastern Economic Review* 147 (March 22, 1990): 25–26.

27. Tow, *Subregional Security Cooperation,* p. 101.

28. For more on this, see Jacqueline Braveboy-Wagner, *The Caribbean in World Affairs* (Boulder, Colo.: Westview, 1989), pp. 179–194; and Vaughan Lewis, "Small States, Eastern Caribbean Security, and the Grenada Intervention," in Jorge Heine, ed., *A Revolution Aborted: The Lessons of Grenada* (Pittsburgh: University of Pittsburgh Press, 1991).

29. For more on Caricom, see *Ten Years of CARICOM* (Washington, D.C.: Inter-American Development Bank, 1984); Mirlande Manigat, "CARICOM at Ten," in Jorge Heine and Leslie Manigat, eds., *The Caribbean and World Politics* (New York: Holmes and Meier, 1988); Vaughan Lewis, "Some Perspectives on Caribbean Community Integration," *Caribbean Affairs* 1, 1 (1988): 85–100; and West Indian Commission (WIC), *Reaching for the Future: Statements by the Prime Ministers of Barbados, Jamaica, and St. Vincent and the Grenadines.*

Occasional Paper no. 2 (St. James, Barbados: WIC, 1991).

30. See "Treaty Establishing the Organization of Eastern Caribbean States," 20 *International Legal Materials* 1166 (September 1981). The treaty is also reproduced in Jack Hopkins, ed., *Latin American and Caribbean Contemporary Records 1981–1982* (New York: Holmes and Meier, 1983).

31. For assessment of the OECS, see William Gilmore, "Legal and Institutional Aspects of the Organization of Eastern Caribbean States," *Review of International Studies* 11 (October 1985): 311–328; Patrick Emmanuel, "Community Within a Community: The OECS Countries," in *Ten Years of CARICOM*; and Tow, *Subregional Security Cooperation*, pp. 15–16, 28–30, 57–63.

32. RSS Staff, "The Roles of the Regional Security System in the East Caribbean," *Bulletin of Eastern Caribbean Affairs* 11 (January–February 1986): 6.

33. Ibid., p. 7.

34. See "Expansion of Security System Being Considered," *Sunday Advocate* (Barbados), February 24, 1991, p. 5.

35. "Barrow and Mitchell Put the Brakes on a Security Treaty," *Caribbean Insight* 9 (October 1986): 1–2; and Rex A. Hudson, "Strategic and Regional Security Perspectives," in Sandra W. Meditz and Dennis M. Hanratty, eds., *Islands of the Commonwealth Caribbean* (Washington, D.C.: Library of Congress, 1989), p. 628.

36. "Communique and Addresses: Eleventh Meeting of the Heads of Government of the Caribbean Community," *CARICOM Perspective* (special supplement) 49 (July–December 1990): 6.

37. "Communique and Addresses," p. 16.

38. "Caribbean, U.S. Set Joint Military Exercise," *San Juan Star*, May 19, 1991, p. 11; "UK Will Also Participate in Caribbean Military Exercise," *Guyana Chronicle*, May 21, 1991, pp. 2, 7; and "War Games," *Sunday Advocate* (Barbados), June 23, 1991, p. 3.

39. Ispahani, "Alone Together," p. 175.

40. For more on the RSS, see Gary Lewis, "Prospects for a Regional Security System in the Eastern Caribbean," *Millennium: Journal of International Studies* 15, (1986): 73–90; RSS Staff, "Roles of the Regional Security System"; and Ivelaw L. Griffith, *The Quest for Security in the Caribbean: Problems and Promises of Subordinate States* (Armonk, N.Y.: M. E. Sharpe, 1993).

41. See "The Caribbean as a Zone of Peace," in *OAS Documents— AG/RES.456(IX–0/79)*.

42. See *New York Times*, July 25, 1991, p. A14.

43. Paul Johnson, "The Subordinate States and Their Strategies," in Jan Triska, ed., *Dominant Powers and Subordinate States: The U.S. in Latin America and the Soviet Union in Eastern Europe* (Durham, N.C.: Duke University Press, 1986), p. 297.

44. Gary Brana-Shute, "An Eastern Caribbean Centrist: Interviewing Prime Minister James F. 'Son' Mitchell," *Caribbean Review* 14, 4 (1985): 28.

PART 3

THE SMALL STATES OF THE PACIFIC AND THE CARIBBEAN: COMMON PROBLEMS AND POTENTIAL LINKS

7

No Easy Choices: Comparing the Political Economies of the Newer Caribbean and Pacific States

W. Marvin Will

Although the Pacific islands are not part of the dynamic core of Asian-Pacific countries, they are beginning to diversify their relations, moving away from their traditional European linkages fostered by colonialism and looking more in the direction of East and Southeast Asia. Japan, for example, has become the major export partner for many of the Pacific countries and compares only with Australia as an import partner. (In fact, Australia and New Zealand, which have developed strong security and trading links with the islands, are themselves looking toward Asia.)[1] Moreover, ASEAN nations, led by Indonesia, have for some time been forging closer ties with the Pacific countries, especially the larger nations like Papua New Guinea (PNG), which has participated in ASEAN activities, and Fiji.[2]

The argument presented in Parts 1 and 2 has been that Caribbean countries could gain from having stronger links with the Asian-Pacific region and drawing on the Asian-Pacific economic and security experience. The fact is, however, that the Asian-Pacific economic experience is more relevant to the larger countries of the Caribbean and the circum-Caribbean, whereas Belize and the smaller islands of the eastern Caribbean share far more with the insular Pacific than with East and Southeast Asia: a limited economic base; dependence on agriculture and tourism; financial, trade, and security dependence on former colonial powers (including, in the case of the Pacific, the intermediate powers Australia and New Zealand); and vulnerability to political interventions from larger nations. Although distance has kept the Pacific and Caribbean nation-states rather isolated from each other, they (and this includes the larger nations of both regions) share adequate commonalities to make their closer cooperation a useful strategy for improving their economic and political position in the global environment. Such cooperation is, and will continue to be for the foreseeable future, primarily of a strategic nature (bargaining strength) rather than real economic interchange because of the competitiveness of Pacific and Caribbean economies.[3] But deeper cross-Basin cooperation is likely to occur as the Caribbean nations develop a greater cognizance of the benefits accruing from the economic strategies and growth of some of their Asian and Pacific neighbors. Likewise, Pacific states may find that there are lessons to be gleaned from the greater national and regional institutionalization of the Caribbean. If this projection is to be realized, however, each area must expand its knowledge of the other—especially how the newer states in each basin differ, where there is similarity, and, of greatest importance, what are the appropriate lessons each can learn from the other. A primary goal of Part 3 is to contribute to this multifaceted goal.

A major argument in this chapter is that policymakers in small weak states have very little margin for error in policy maneuvers, especially when their region is situated in the shadow of ambitious metropolitan actors. Even when blessed with substantial potential for economic development—certainly not the case in most of the recently decolonized states of the Caribbean and Pacific basins—options appear to be severely limited. And yet under-development may have its virtues. A further hypothesis of this chapter is that downturns in the largely subsistence economies of the new states in the Pacific appear to impact political systems less harshly than do economic reversals among the more developed countries (MDCs) within the Caribbean. Finally, contemporary politicians must be acutely cognizant of the inextricably intertwined nature of small-state domestic and external policies and the resultant pressures on leaders to expand employment; to start and restart the engines of prosperity; or, that failing, to extinguish or at least retard the flames of unrest that can result. The historical legacy of the nations of the Caribbean and Pacific has had an impact on the problems and policy alternatives presented to the political leaders of these two Third World blocs; therefore, we must first direct a brief comparative glance at the colonial history of the Caribbean and Oceania.

The Newer American States

The most recently independent American states are spread throughout the insular and littoral Caribbean Basin: from the Bahamas—(which extend within fifty miles of Florida)—and Jamaica (just ninety miles south of Cuba) to Belize, sandwiched between Mexico and a still-disputed border with Guatemala; and from insular Barbados, on the Atlantic rim of the Basin approximately 1,700 miles southeast of Belize, to the South American states of Guyana and Suriname, which share a common border with Brazil. The total population of this group of states is approximately 6 million, remarkably similar to the population in the newly independent Pacific states. All but Suriname are English-speaking. These Caribbean territories were among the first to experience European colonization, serving as seventeenth- and eighteenth-century pawns in power struggles among a severely weakening Spain and the emerging empires of Britain, France, and the Netherlands. (See Chapter 3 for map of Caribbean region.)

Power-balancing and Colonial Neglect

When British Foreign Secretary George Canning bragged "I called the New World into existence to redress the balance of the Old!"[4] he no doubt exaggerated, but this assertion pinpoints the almost constant exposure to the metropolitan power game the small territories of this region have experienced. St. Lucia, it is said, changed hands some fourteen times—most frequently between France and Britain. Almost all of the Caribbean territories and many Pacific states experienced rotation between two or three colonial masters, often but not entirely as an outgrowth of the many European wars. As "pieces in Elizabethan schemes of empire, objects of Caroline and Cromwellian enterprise, loot of eighteenth-century wars," an island governor observed, "the West Indies have been prized with an excessive enthusiasm in one century and left to decay . . . in the next."[5] And these alternating patterns of power/dependency and metropolitan attention/neglect have not been limited to past centuries. Although the initial metropolitan actors were Spain and Portugal, followed by Britain, France, the Netherlands, the United States, and even Scandinavian, the latest entrants into the power game are the regional intermediate powers, Mexico, Canada, and Venezuela—and many analysts also include Brazil, Colombia, and even Cuba.

A special period of neglect by the metropolitan colonial powers occurred in the years preceding World War II. By the 1930s, the island systems, which had developed as slave-powered plantation-organized appendages of European mercantilism, had not yet engendered strong support among the primarily black masses either for the political or economic structures or for the need for active participation by the masses. With the severe commodity price downturns related to the Great Depression and continued restrictions on suffrage, however, came a period of worker insurrection and violence in six West Indian territories that led to substantial political-economic mobilization and a stress-adaptation reaction by the British, a response highlighted by a belated official investigation of the region's massive socioeconomic problems by a commission headed by Walter Moyne. The resultant Moyne report was so critical of British neglect that public release of it was delayed until after World War II, at which time meaningful responses finally were initiated in selected territories.

These responses came both in the form of economic assistance and in support for labor and political party institution building. British-sanctioned experimentation with self-governance occurred—initially in Jamaica, then in Barbados, and eventually in other territories—albeit usually tinged with race- and class-based tensions.[6] The independence movement in the West Indies in the post–World War II era would ultimately receive support from Whitehall, first via federation, then in terms of singular units. This decolonization process is still evolving.

Decolonization in the Caribbean

Jamaica, with a population then of 1.6 million (now 2.45 million), was the initial member of the English-speaking Caribbean to achieve political independence, the first new state to emerge in the Americas in the twentieth century. This occurred in 1962 following a 1961 national plebiscite in which Jamaicans voted to withdraw from the faltering 1958–1962 ten-territory West Indies Federation (WIF). The federation, established with a meager infrastructural and sociopolitical-economic base, had been promoted as a means for collective West Indies independence in this initial period of decolonization following World War II. [7]

Jamaica was followed quickly into independence by Trinidad and Tobago (1962), an action emulated by other English-speaking territories: Guyana and Barbados in 1966; the Bahamas in 1973; and Belize, on the Central American littoral, in 1981. After the failure in 1967 of an attempted federation with Barbados and a subsequent period of semiautonomous, self-governing status, six of the "little seven" insular states of the eastern Caribbean were granted statehood: Grenada (1974), Dominica (1978), St. Vincent and the Grenadines (1979), St. Lucia (1979), Antigua and Barbuda (1981), and St. Kitts/Nevis (1983).[8] Tiny Montserrat (population 12,000), which saw its quest for independence delayed by the ravages of hurricane Hugo in 1989, remains a dependency. Although the English-speaking states have been unsuccessful in their attempts to unite politically, they early saw the need to unite economically to enlarge their limited markets. This issue has already been discussed and will be touched on later in the chapter in the context of a comparison of Caribbean and Pacific integration movements. At this point, however, the data presented in Table 7.1 give an economic picture of these small states.

Although the Anglophone group is the focus of this chapter, the newer Caribbean nations also include Suriname, which was granted independence from the Netherlands in 1975. Slated for independence by 1996 as one or more states are the Dutch colonies of Aruba, Curaçao, and Bonaire, plus the smaller possessions of Saba, St. Eustatius, and St. Martin, the latter an island the Netherlands divides with France. There is a possibility the three smaller possessions may elect to become the thirteenth province of the Netherlands. The French territories in the Caribbean include three of the four official Overseas Departments of France: Martinique, Guadeloupe, and French Guiana, plus a number of islands governed by Guadeloupe (Marie Galante, Les Saintes, Saint Barthélemy, and the French portion of St. Martin). As in the Pacific, the French cling tenaciously to their overseas territories.

The status of the Commonwealth of Puerto Rico remains uncertain. First claimed by Columbus in 1493 and settled by Ponce de León in 1508, this third largest Caribbean island passed to U.S. control in 1898 and gained commonwealth status in 1952. A plebiscite on three options—commonwealth status, U.S. statehood, and independence—originally scheduled for June 1991 was deferred. Before the deferral, it was anticipated that Puerto

Table 7.1 Economic Indicators for the Caribbean Community and Suriname

Country	Area (sq. km.)	Population 1989 (thousands)	GDP per Capita ($ U.S. 1988)	GDP Average Annual Increase % (1984–1988)	Annual Rate of Inflation (%) (1980–1988)	Life Expectancy 1988
Antigua and Barbuda	440	82.9	4,123	9.6	6.0	73
Bahamas	13,942	249.0	8,802	3.9 [a]	6.2	68
Barbados	431	255.8	5,740	3.2	5.2	75
Belize	22,960	183.2	1,587	7.7	4.0	68
Dominica	750	82.4	1,692	5.5	6.0	74
Grenada	345	100.0	1,675	5.5	5.0	69
Guyana	244,970	754.8	547	1.0 [a]	19.8	64
Jamaica	11,424	2,374.9	1,351	1.6	18.7	73
Montserrat	10.2	12.0	4,516	6.9	3.6 [c]	—
St. Kitts/Nevis	469	43.0	2,521	6.0	5.0	69
St. Lucia	616	148.2	1,454	4.8 [a]	4.0	71
St. Vincent	388	115.0	1,365	6.5	5.0	70
Trinidad and Tobago	5,128	1,213.3	3,699	-4.6	5.3	71
Suriname [b]	163,265	437.0	3,010 [c]	1.2 [d]	4.0	67

Sources: World Bank, *World Development Report 1990* (New York: Oxford University Press, 1990); United Nations Development Program (UNDP), *Human Development Report 1991* (New York: Oxford University Press, 1991); Caribbean Development Bank (CDB), *Annual Report 1989, 1990* (St. Michael, Barbados: CDB, 1990, 1991); *The Universal Almanac 1990* (Kansas City: Andrews and McMeel, 1989).

[a] 1984–1987.
[b] Suriname holds observer status in the Caribbean Community.
[c] 1989.
[d] 1965–1989.

Rican voters would vote to retain commonwealth status, perceiving that as the least risky short-term choice.[9]

The extremely small British Virgin Islands, Cayman Islands, and Turk and Caicos Islands have atypically high per capita incomes and, as a partial result, apparently perceive it to be in their interest to remain British dependencies for the foreseeable future.[10] Much the same—relatively high income and reluctance to change political status—is applicable to the unincorporated U.S. Virgin Islands.

The Pacific: An Emerging Community?

As emphasized in this book, the economic dynamism of many Pacific countries during the 1970s and into the 1990s, especially those along the western littoral or rimland, has generated euphoria on both sides of the Pacific. This has contributed significantly to the emergence among metropolitan interests of concepts of a Pacific Community, of the twenty-first century as the Pacific Century.[11] Nonetheless, the idea of a Pacific Basin that links blocs of developmentally disparate states (for example, the NICs with the smallest Pacific nations) in any real sense of community has, at least in the past, been more of a geopolitical conception generated by the metropole than an empirically based reality. This idea reflects a close similarity to the socalled Caribbean Basin concept, although the Basin concept in the Caribbean was largely inspired by geopolitical military considerations, whereas in the Pacific, as discussed in Chapter 1, evidence suggests the first usage of the basin/community concept originated with Japan, primarily to enhance the acceptability of its exports and investments and to fend off threatened protectionist practices by the United States. Australia, Japan's principal supplier of raw materials, followed suit as did the United States, with its strong security interest in the region, and South Korea, the second most industrial economy in the western Pacific.[12]

As an outgrowth of colonization, institutional arrangements and concepts in both the Caribbean and Pacific regions have often been induced by the metropole. Yet there does appear to be a growing sense of indigenous community and regional institution-building among the newly independent states of the Pacific.

One Ocean: Three Cultures

The Pacific insular region is customarily divided into three predominant cultural groups of peoples who inhabit these areas: (1) the Polynesian triangle that extends from New Zealand to Easter Island to Hawaii, encompassing the world's largest ocean expanse, and includes tiny Niue (population under 3,000), Tahiti, Tonga, Samoa, and the Easter Islands (a dependency of Chile

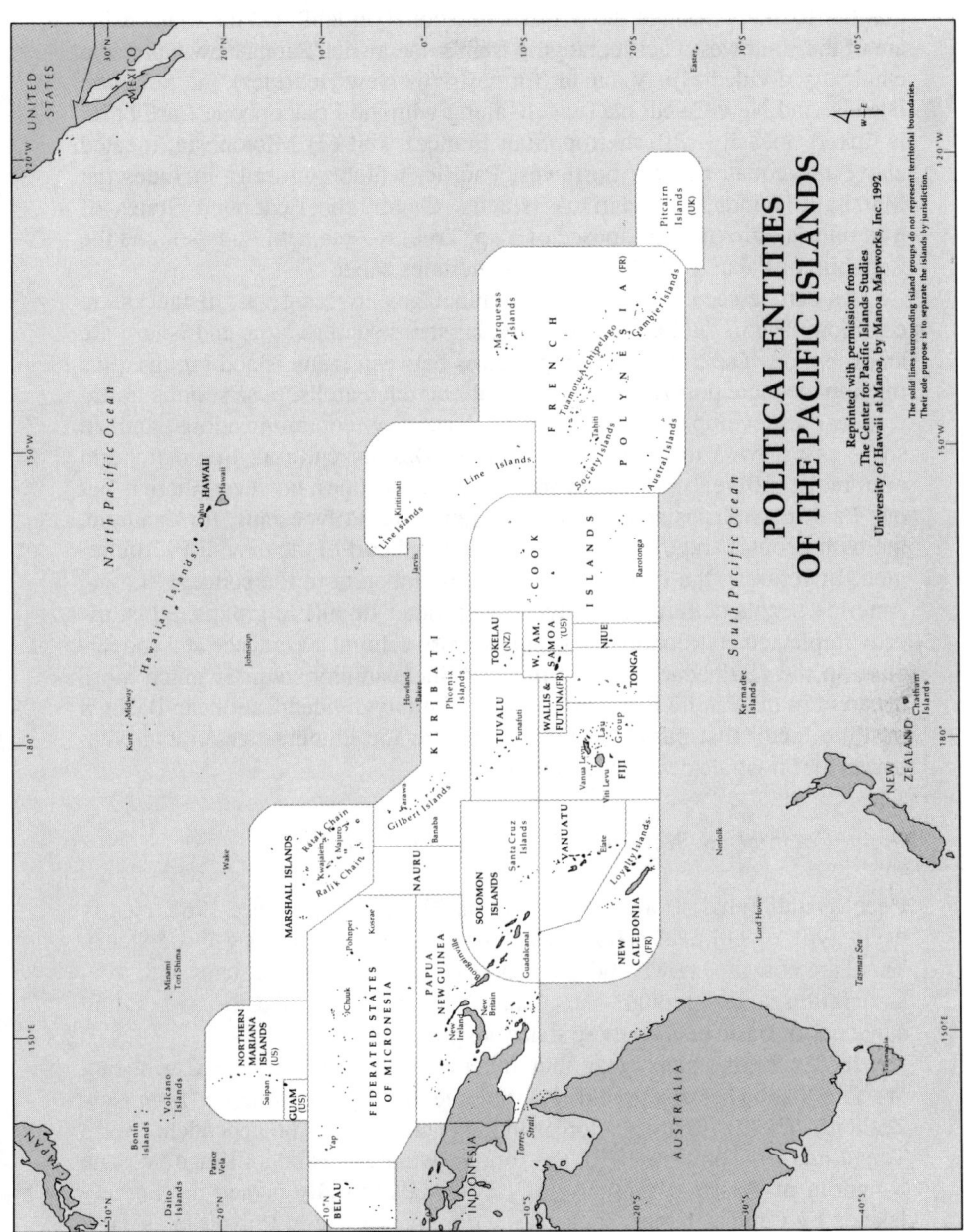

familiar to many through the writings of Thor Hyerdahl); (2) the Melanesian arc of the southwest Pacific, ranging from mineral-rich Papua New Guinea to ethnically divided Fiji, Vanuatu (formerly the New Hebrides), the Solomon Islands, and New Caledonia (which, along with the Francophone Caribbean, is linked uneasily with metropolitan France); and (3) Micronesia, located above the equator in the northwest Pacific, which culturally includes the Marshall Islands, the Mariana Islands, Guam, the Federated States of Micronesia (currently composed of Yap, Truk, Kosrae, and Ponape), and the Republic of Palau (or Belau, as it is sometimes called).[13]

As can be seen in Figure 7.1, archipelagos covering vast distances are commonplace in the Pacific, and singular states such as Niue and Nauru are an exception. The truly massive distances between many island groups, plus often inadequate port facilities and coral-encircled atolls, pose serious obstacles to the development of commercial activity, communications, and, in some cases, even to national integration. Despite cultural, linguistic, and even racial differences and metropolitan security zones, however, there is but one Pacific. Melanesians may be different from Polynesians, for example, but both peoples and their states are considered part of the overall Pacific region. In contrast, the cultural exclusiveness inherent in the concept "Latin" America begets cultural exclusiveness by other linguistic groups, a historically implanted conception that hampers cross-cultural acceptance and cooperation in the Caribbean Basin.[14] In short, inclusionary status is much more apparent in the Pacific Basin than in the culturally divided Caribbean Basin, a positive factor that partially compensates for the immense geographic distances that frustrate development in the Pacific.

From Colonial to Statehood Status in the Pacific

Decolonization has strongly impacted the Pacific islands since 1962. Nearly every type of political status may currently be found among these states. There are now nine newly independent Pacific states and five states with free-association status (though one, Pelau, has not yet ratified the association agreement). Basic data on these states are presented in Table 7.2.

In 1962, the same year that independence came to the Caribbean, Western Samoa became the first Pacific state to gain independence (from New Zealand). The first British colonies in the Pacific to attain independence were Tonga and Fiji, both in 1970, the former as an independent kingdom. The Kingdom of Tonga, a grouping of 172 islands initially named the Society Islands by Captain James Cook, was a dominant force in Polynesia as early as the thirteenth century and became a British protectorate in 1900. Fiji, composed of more than 300 islands, was annexed as a British Crown Colony in 1874 and, as many other Pacific islands were, was formally ceded to the colonizer.[15]

Papua New Guinea (PNG), the largest of the new Pacific states in area and population, achieved full independence from Australia, its trustee, in

Table 7.2 Economic Indicators for Independent and Freely Associated Pacific States

Country	Area (sq. km.)	Population 1989 (thousands)	GDP per capita ($ U.S.1988)	GDP Average Annual Increase % (1965–1988)	Annual Rate of Inflation (%) (1980–1988)	Life Expectancy 1988
Cook Islands *	237	17,600 [a]	698 [b]	n.a.	n.a.	69
Micronesia (FSM) *	702	99,000	1,249 [c]	n.a.	n.a.	n.a.
Fiji	18,376	740,000	1,520 [d]	1.9	5.7	71
Kiribati	861	89,000	650 [d]	3.7	5.7	55
Marshall Islands *	180	41,000	1,121 [e]	n.a.	n.a.	n.a.
Papua New Guinea	462,840	3,800,000	810 [d]	0.5	4.7	54
Solomon Islands	27,556	313,000	630 [d]	3.5 [f]	13.1	64
Tonga	748	98,000	830 [d]	n.a.	n.a.	67
Tuvalu	26	8,458 [a]	326 [c]	n.a.	n.a.	64
Vanuatu	12,190	152,000	840 [d]	n.a.	4.3	64
Western Samoa	2,831	163,000	640 [d]	n.a.	10.5	66
Nauru	21	8,400 [a]	20,000	n.a.	n.a.	n.a.
Niue *	259	2,900 [a]	1,069 [c]	n.a.	n.a.	n.a.
Palau *	458	14,106 [a]	2,257 [g]	n.a.	n.a.	n.a.

Sources: World Bank, *World Development Report*, for years 1987–1990 (New York: Oxford University Press, 1987–1990); *The Universal Almanac 1990* (Kansas City: Andrews and McMeel, 1989); Michael P. Hamnett and Robert C. Kiste, eds., *Issues and Interest Groups in the Pacific Islands* (Washington, D.C.: U.S. Information Service, Office of Research, 1988); *Oceanic Economic Handbook* (London: Euromonitor, 1990).

* Freely Associated States. Palau, however, has not yet accepted U.S. conditions for genuine free association.
[a] 1987.
[b] 1980.
[c] 1985.
[d] Data are GNP not GDP.
[e] 1983.
[f] 1965–1985.
[g] 1986.

Table 7.3 Economic Change in the Caribbean per Capita GDP at Current Market Prices ($ U.S.)

	1981	1982	1983	1984	1985	1986	1987	1988
Bahamas	5,920	6,497	7,447	7,061	7,822	9,462	11,447	11,316 [a]
Barbados	3,701	3,982	4,200	4,570	4,894	5,288	5,747	5,740
Guyana	777	696	596	565	584	654	455	547
Jamaica	1,353	1,425	1,524	1,034	858	1,042	1,219	1,351
Trinidad and Tobago	6,668	6,609	7,558	6,962	6,538	3,959	3,782	3,699
Belize	1,055	1,024	1,131	970	1,110	1,226	—	1,587
Antigua and Barbuda	1,649	1,776	1,493	2,037	2,244	2,935	3,399	4,123
Dominica	798	898	966	1,105	1,132	1,423	1,550	1,692
Grenada	883	1,002	1,065	938	961	1,013	1,346	1,675
Montserrat	1,736	2,479	2,513	2,952	3,118	3,555	3,997	4,516
St. Kitts/Nevis	1,062	951	980	1,358	1,469	1,670	2,119	2,521
St. Lucia	1,071	1,081	1,096	1,127	1,245	1,388	1,400	1,454
St. Vincent and Grenadines	657	611	794	860	933	883	1,210	1,365
Suriname[a]	3,722 [b]	—	2,792	2,642	2,836	2,767	3,366	3,420

Sources: Caribbean Development Bank (CDB), *Annual Report(s)*, (St. Michael, Barbados: CDB, 1983–1990); Inter-American Development Bank (IDB), *Annual Report 1989*, (Washington, D.C.: IDB, 1990).
[a] Data from Inter-American Development Bank.
[b] 1980.

Note: CDB and IDB data do not always agree. For example, per capita GDP figures for the Bahamas in 1988 are $8,802 according to the CDB, a seemingly inordinate decline from 1987—hence the use of IDB data.

1975, after it had passed from the late-blooming German empire to a Class C mandate under the League of Nations.[16] Minuscule Nauru (21 square kilometers) received independence from Australia in 1968; Tuvalu (formerly the Ellice Islands) and the Solomon Islands cast off British colonial status in 1978; and Kiribati (formerly the Gilbert Islands) left the British fold in 1979. Both Nauru and Tuvalu currently have populations of less than 9,000. In 1980, Vanuatu received independence from France and the United Kingdom, under whose joint governance it had been the awkwardly administered international condominium of New Hebrides.

In 1965, the fifteen small Cook Islands became the first freely associated Pacific nation (in association with New Zealand)—a status just short of defacto independence. This status, or linkage, is now shared by Niue (1974), while the Marshall Islands (1986), the Federated States of Micronesia (1986), and Palau/Belau (pending ratification of the agreement) are also freely associated states in conjunction with the United States, although Palan has yet to ratify the agreement, laced as it is with military conditionalities attached by the United States. Continuing as dependencies are French Polynesia, Wallace and Futura, American Samoa, Guam, and the Commonwealth of the Northern Marianas.

New Caledonia and all France's Pacific holdings remain Overseas Territories rather than Overseas Departments; Tokelau remains a territory of New Zealand. At least one Pacific state is actively seeking independence; others are "holding" in self-governing free-association status; and still others— typically the smallest and least viable—remain dependencies. Although Britain once possessed the largest number of insular colonies in the region, the only remaining British colony in the Pacific, with the apparent legal resolution of the Hong Kong dilemma by 1997, will be the tiny Pitcairn Islands with a mere population of 50.[17] In the Pacific, as in the Caribbean, the United States and France have proved to be the most stubborn decolonizers.

Caribbean and Pacific Political Economies: Limitations and Vulnerabilities

Despite their developmental pluses, the small, highly dependent states of the Caribbean and Pacific basins find their economic development options severely restricted and their socioeconomic-political vulnerability exacerbated by their limited natural resource base and an often frustrating international economic climate. In addition, systemic vulnerability is fostered by the relatively high degree of political openness these states enjoy, an openness that at the same time contributes positively to both the democratic process and political legitimacy of governance.

Most Caricom states, for example, have faced a rising tide of debt and International Monetary Fund (IMF) conditionalities, particularly since the late 1970s, a second wave of which struck in the early 1990s. In addition, many regional commodities suffered sharp international pricing declines during the 1980s—whether the resource product was petroleum, which only Trinidad and Tobago produces in sufficient quantity for export; bauxite/alumina, plentiful in both Guyana and Jamaica; sugar, still a multiterritorial mainstay although especially important to Barbados where it fails to command a world price commensurate with its unsubsidized cost of production; or coffee, which is produced in Jamaica and several smaller countries. Fluctuations in commodity prices produce major stress on regional political systems. In the small-state Pacific, only Papua New Guinea has both a variety and a substantial quantity of mineral resources. Nauru has a diminishing supply of phosphate, Fiji some gold, and others astride the Pacific "rim of fire" have some miscellaneous mineral deposits. The economy of most insular Pacific states is based on the production of tropical oils, timber, and—as in the Caribbean—coffee, sugar, and tourism (the latter a very mixed blessing worldwide but especially so in the smallest and weakest of these developing nations). Unlike the Caribbean, the Pacific states are relatively free of standby or extended IMF arrangements and accompanying conditionalities, although Tuvalu is nearly totally aid-dependent and several other states receive 20–30 percent of their GNP from external assistance, primarily from Australia (see Figure 7.2). The economies of the Pacific states, although fragile, grew by more than 3 percent in the late 1980s. As a result, most of these states are more stable economically than developing states in general, and because of the continued, though faltering, importance of peasant agriculture, they face fewer boom-bust cycles than the Caribbean. Relatively little land has been alienated, and most islands still have viable subsistence sectors, although some are slipping into the ranks of the very poor and the very vulnerable. The smallest Pacific islands, as Michael Ogden notes, may be unable ever to achieve sustainable growth and probably will require permanent assistance from metropolitan countries or migration and remittances for mere survival.[18] Although present and deepening, class differences are less marked than in most Caribbean states. Nonetheless, spiraling drug use and suicides in some of the present and former U.S. trust territories are extremely worrisome.[19]

When political participation outraces a political system's ability to respond satisfactorily, and especially when crisis situations develop, the vulnerability level of the regime escalates dramatically, as Samuel Huntington and others have generalized. Open political systems in general and small democracies in particular appear extremely vulnerable to such stress, especially when sustained economic growth periods have been incorporated as part of the national memory. Somewhat ironically, this problem appears to be particularly prevalent among the "Big Four" states of the Caribbean Community (Caricom) and thus impacts severely on regional trade and overall cooperation. The discussion that follows is an examination of specifics, and pertinent economic data are presented in Tables 7.1, 7.2, and 7.3.

Figure 7.2 Estimated Economic Dependence and External Assistance in Selected Pacific States and Territories

Country	
Papua New Guinea	~5
French Polynesia	~18
Tonga	~22
Vanuatu	~30
Kiribati	~33
New Caledonia [a]	~35
Western Somoa	~37
Solomon Islands	~42
Cook Islands	~70
Tuvalu [b]	~100

Sources: Organization for Economic Cooperation and Development, International Bank for Reconstruction and Development, and *The Economist*, October 13, 1990, p. 36.

Note: Figures represent aid as a percentage of GNP in 1988 except [a] = 1987 and [b] = 1983

The Caribbean States

The "Big Four." Discussion of the political economies of Guyana, Barbados, Trinidad and Tobago, and Jamaica—the "Big Four" economies in the English-speaking Caribbean—is limited in this chapter because these countries were treated extensively in Chapter 5. What follows is a brief review: The four larger English-speaking territories all suffered severe economic downturns in the 1980s and early 1990s. Guyana's per capita GDP declined from $800 in 1975 to $547 in 1988, and $337 in 1989. During the 1970s and 1980s, political corruption and economic mismanagement led to an almost perennial shortage of capital and entrepreneurship that, in turn, led to major problems in the country's rice, fish, forestry, mining, and manufacturing industries. After achieving a 1.4 percent economic growth rate in 1986, the economy has suffered consistent declines, although modest growth was finally achieved in 1991 and 1992 after some years of efforts to liberalize the economy.[20] Hand in hand with economic liberalization came efforts at political liberalization: No general elections were held in Guyana between 1973 and 1980 and the general elections of 1980 and 1985 were marred by irregularities and fraud. In October 1992, after a much-needed revision of the voter lists, Guyana finally held an election that was free and fair (according to foreign observers). A disaffected electorate voted out the incumbent People's National Congress (PNC) regime in favor of the perennial opposition party, the People's Progressive Party (PPP). However, social divisions continue, and communal and personal violence persist as polarizing and debilitating forces in Guyana.

In Barbados, two decades of steady growth have been followed by an economic downturn characterized by much lower growth rates, contraction of exports and foreign investment, and resort to IMF credits. Most of Barbados' troubles can be traced to the recession in the industrial world (particularly the United States), which has led to decreased earnings from tourism, sugar, and manufacturing. By 1992, GDP reversals, budgetary contractions, and mounting debt had induced Barbadian workers—from police, nurses, and educators to unemployed youth—to march against the Democratic Labour Party (DLP) government of Erskine Sandiford. There have been opposition calls for an early general election. (The DLP had been returned to power, with a reduced parliamentary majority, in early elections called in 1991 just before the imposition of IMF conditionalities.) [21]

Trinidad and Tobago's oil boom ended in the early 1980s, to be followed by a period of austerity and political and social instability. GDP declines of 5–6 percent in the mid-1980s and of 3–4 percent in the late 1980s were arrested by a series of measures that included two devaluations of the dollar and access to IMF structural adjustment lending. However, increased borrowing also increased the debt burden, and social disaffection manifested itself in unrest and an aborted coup in July 1990. Whereas in 1986, the ruling People's National Movement (PNM) had suffered its first parliamentary defeat partly as a result of the economic downturn, the party that replaced them in government, the National Alliance for Reconstruction (NAR), was itself defeated in 1991 in popular reaction against the harsh austerity measures and internal personality-based divisions within the NAR.[22]

Finally, Jamaica's economy has foundered amid declining bauxite and tourism earnings, resultant negative trade balances, and high external debt. GDP declines were arrested in 1986, but growth has been modest. Unemployment hovers near 19 percent, and the weakness of the Jamaican dollar continued into 1992 despite devaluations undertaken as a response to IMF conditionalities. (The currency stabilized somewhat in 1992.) Poor economic performance in Jamaica is all the more problematic because this state is beset by the sharpest class cleavages in the English-speaking Caribbean and also strongly embraces the politics of economic-political patronage or clientelism. The depressed and flat economy triggered electoral reversals for both the People's National Party (PNP) and the Jamaica Labour Party (JLP) during the 1980s and seems likely to do the same in the mid-1990s. Opinion polls in the early 1990s suggest that an electoral reversal could be pending should currency stabilization fail and the economy continue to contract.[23] (In 1992, partly because of Jamaica's continuing economic difficulties, Prime Minister Michael Manley resigned in favor of his long-time deputy party leader, P. J. Patterson.)

The Commonwealth of the Bahamas. The Bahamas proved to be an exception among the Caricom MDCs by registering a 5 percent GDP growth rate during the period 1982–1984 (the largest increase of any Caricom state) and 3.5 percent in 1985 and 1986 despite sharp trade reversals with the United States, a major variable in the GDP reversals of other Caricom MDCs. In 1988–1992 the economy experienced lackluster performance and a sluggish GDP. Economic uncertainty contributed directly to the defeat of the Progressive Liberal Party (PLP), led by Prime Minister Lynden O. Pindling, in general elections held in October 1992. The defeat at the hands of the Free National Movement (FNM), led by Herbert Ingraham, was the first defeat for the PLP, which had held power since independence.

Still, by regional standards, the Bahamian economy has remained relatively buoyant, especially in populous Nassau, as a result of the ability of these islands to attract U.S. tourists, plus its income bonanza from restrictive offshore banking. Because oil refining is a major Bahamian industry, the resurgence of oil prices in 1990 has also been of some benefit.

Many informed Bahamian and U.S. sources acknowledge that drug money is also a major revenue source for the Bahamas. A major Nassau shopping center is alleged to be a recent drug payoff. The hundreds of islands, many uninhabited, and their proximity to the U.S. mainland make drug smuggling a popular activity for a range of participants, from the "whiskey class" booze runners of the 1920s to the cocaine runners of the present. Despite major drug/corruption allegations levied against both the government and the party during the 1987 electoral campaign, Prime Minister Lynden O. Pindling and his Progressive Liberal Party (PLP) survived a major electoral threat from the Free National Movement (FNM). The economy once again proved to be a key factor in electoral politics; in this instance, however, it protected the PLP incumbency.[24] However, in 1992, both the economy and the drug issue contributed to the defeat of the PLP.

The Caricom LDCs. Ironically, the lack of industrial development that has hampered progress within the Caricom LDCs has also insulated them somewhat from the repercussions of the economic downturns and the sharp drop in trade with the United States that have beset the four largest Caricom states. GDP gains realized by some of the LDCs have also related positively to a redirection in tourism and to a nominal resurgence in the export price of coffee and other locally produced commodities. Interestingly, the group of small eastern Caribbean islands, now organized into the Organization of Eastern Caribbean States (OECS), also experienced increases in exports to the United States during much of the 1980s.

This combination of factors induced modest to high economic growth in Antigua, Dominica, St. Lucia, and St. Vincent during the 1980s, although a downturn in St. Vincent in the early 1980s was partially instrumental for bringing James F. "Son" Mitchell and his New Democratic Party to power in 1984. By 1988, the economy of St. Vincent registered growth of 8.4 percent, and the 1989 balloting saw the Mitchell team sweep all parliamentary seats, a remarkable electoral feat in the Caribbean. St. Kitts/Nevis also began the decade with economic reversals, but rebounded with modest steady growth beginning in 1984. In Dominica, the GDP declined in 1989 because of hurricane damage to the key banana industry, although there were some slight gains in 1990. Still, Eugenia Charles and her Freedom Party tumbled to a one-seat margin in the May 1990 election.[25] Other Caricom LDCs that experienced GDP fluctuations in the 1980s and early 1990s included Belize and Grenada.

Belize, the newest Central American littoral state, experienced constant flux in its economy following independence in 1981, despite achieving a positive trade balance with the United States between 1983 and 1985. Per capita income between 1982 and 1984 fell below the preindependence level. The economic declines substantially contributed to the electoral defeat of George Price and his People's United Party (PUP) in the nation's first postindependence election in 1984, which brought to power the United Democratic Party (UDP) led by Manuel Esquivel. "Baby Belize," to paraphrase a campaign ditty, had become so seriously deprived of revenue-producing commodities—from citrus to sugar—that not even the palliative of North American television (with which the country is inundated) beaming from Chicago could revive the patient; only new leaders could resuscitate the country, was the decree of an aroused electorate. The economy grew toward the end of the Esquivel regime, but not enough to save the UDP government in the 1989 election, which restored Price and the PUP to parliamentary leadership by a two-vote margin.[26] Belize has continued to enjoy economic expansion into the 1990s.[27]

Grenada's economic performance deserves special mention given the political problems experienced in the early 1980s. After recording modest but steady gains through 1983, the economy fell in 1984 and did not again reach the 1983 per capita GDP level until 1987.[28] During this period, Grenada's trade volume with the United States, although increasing modestly, was the smallest of any Caricom country. These factors, combined with controversial governmental measures perceived to be antilabor, produced defections and fragmentation in the postintervention coalition government headed by Herbert Blaize; the result was political stagnation and a crisis of leadership.

Relatively strong GDP growth (more than 4 percent) has been reported in Grenada since 1986; however, it did not necessarily produce economic development because the expansion was unevenly distributed among Grenada's people and also among its agricultural, tourist, and manufacturing sectors. This lack of development, together with soaring unemployment, contributed to extensive party fragmentation in the 1989–1990 election period and threatened Grenada's "return to democracy and development," which the Reagan-Bush (U.S.) administration pledged following the 1983 intervention. In 1990, the ruling party retained but two seats when a pragmatic and modernizing coalition, the National Democratic Congress (NDC), headed by reformist Nicholas Brathwaite, won the day. Shortly after the elections, however, the NDC government began losing support primarily as the result of a weakening economy.[29] Grenada was forced to turn to the IMF in late 1991.

Despite leading the Caricom LDCs with a GDP growth of nearly 5 percent from its independence year (1981) to 1985, and 7.5 percent from 1986 to 1989, the political economy of Antigua and Barbuda has experienced a slowdown in economic activity, and private investment has reduced growth in the early 1990s. Moreover, this two-island state accumulated the largest external debt among the LDCs—$239 million at its height in 1988—and an economic policy that might be termed "government by overdraft." In 1983, when this nation's debt figure was one-third lower, it already totaled nearly two-thirds of the country's GNP, and repayment obligations, according to World Bank estimates, were consuming one-third of the government's total revenue. The debt still stood at an estimated $110 million in early 1992.

Antigua's main problems, however, have been political in nature: The government of the aged Vere Bird has been beset by allegations of corruption and mismanagement, including a recent arms scandal involving the illegal purchase of arms and ammunition from Israel for export to Colombian drug dealers.[30] By mid-1992, Prime Minister Bird was considering retirement.

St. Lucia, a Caricom LDC with positive GDP growth between 1982 and 1991 (6.8 percent in 1988 but dropping to about 4 percent since), faced near paralysis of government in the late 1980s as a result of attempted electoral manipulation by the government of Prime Minister John Compton and the United Workers' Party (UWP). Two elections were called in 1987 in a vain attempt to increase the UWP's one-seat margin. This case demonstrates that economic performance is not always the major determinant of electoral outcome. Indeed, during the 1992 general election campaign, the opposition was primarily preoccupied with forestalling further attempts at political manipulation, such as the gerrymandering of existing constituency boundaries. It was, however, on platform and performance issues that the electorate rejected the opposition in the April elections and returned the UWP to power with a decisive parliamentary majority (11 of 17 seats).

The Republic of Suriname. Settled by the Dutch in 1667, this littoral South American state was the first non-British colony in the Caribbean to receive independence in the last three decades (1975). Its population, just under one-half million, is highly fragmented culturally—East Indians (37 percent), Creole blacks (31 percent), Javanese (15 percent), and Bush blacks or Maroons (10 percent). Its economy, based on bauxite mining, fish, timber, rice, and palm oil, faltered during the 1980s because of frequent spates of governmental instability and violence. After posting a 6.5 percent GDP growth in 1981, the economy turned sour until the period 1987–1989, when positive gains were again realized, albeit with 53 percent inflation in 1987 (which declined to pre-1980 levels of 7–10 percent after 1987). Per capita income increased to $3,524 by 1989, but 25–30 percent unemployment continues to haunt Suriname.

Economic development in Suriname has been hampered by political instability. As rising expectations outdistanced both resources and political legitimacy, a bloodless military coup led by Desi Bouterse overturned the civilian government in 1980. An internal war followed, precipitated by the torture and execution of prominent Surinamese citizens in 1982, and not until 1988 was there a return to elected governance. In 1991, however, elements linked to the Bouterse military regime again placed Suriname under military rule, with ensuing violence and restrictions of civil liberties. Suriname returned to civilian rule following elections in mid-1991. Although not currently a member of Caricom, Suriname has observer status and anticipates eventual membership.[31]

The Pacific Basin States

Papua New Guinea (PNG). The largest newly independent country in the Pacific island region (with half the total population of the new Pacific states), and frequently the only state with a positive trade balance, Papua New Guinea has significant economic potential because of its mineral wealth. Although PNG's per capita GDP growth-rate was negative in the early l980s, it has experienced a recent pattern of annual growth (approximately 3.4 percent); however, World Bank data indicate but marginal per capita income growth per annum since the colonial period. Still, only a few other small Pacific states have positive growth rates.[32]

Papua New Guinea has three large copper and gold mines in production, with at least three additional gold mines in the final planning stages. A major gold field that came into production in 1989 stimulated an almost Klondike mentality. PNG is now the world's seventh largest gold producer; not surprisingly, one-third of governmental revenues are derived from this industry. In addition to proven ore deposits, PNG has substantial coffee plantations, timber for export, and potential oil reserves. As a result, there are active investment efforts by Asian interests, especially Japanese transnational corporations (TNCs). There is danger of timber depletion, however, on this large island that Papua New Guinea divides with Indonesia. With 85 percent of PNG's citizens engaged in subsistence farming, agricultural development is also important, as it is in the smaller states of the south Pacific. To promote this industry, PNG is cross-breeding black-bellied sheep from Barbados with Australian breeds—an excellent example of Caribbean-to-Pacific technology transfer.

Political instability results from ethnic pluralism, and in late 1989, a strong and potentially separatist resistance from insular Bougainville began that led to closure of the large Panguna copper mine and prompted a blockade by the national government and some bloody skirmishes in the early 1990s.[33] Uneven development, fragmented parties and factions, and labor friction also counteract much of the economic health of this geographically and culturally diverse island state. These factors make it difficult to command a majority, and as a result, most PNG governments are short-lived. There have been five governments and six administrations since independence in 1975, including 1992 when more than half of the 100-seat legislature was defeated. Pais Wingti was returned to the office of prime minister by a single tie-breaking vote cast by the Speaker of the House. Like some previous parliaments, the present government may not survive beyond the one-year minimum for a constitutionally permitted "no confidence" vote. Such political uncertainty can be very destructive to a national economy, and one can only imagine the ensuing problems were the economy of PNG to weaken significantly. In addition to grappling with the economy in the 1990s, and attempting to legitimize its fledging political institutions—including the expanding military—the new government must respond to insular secessionist sentiment that will likely result in a weakened federation.[34]

The Republic of Fiji. This former British colony has enjoyed the Pacific region's most developed economy; however, much of this advantage was relinquished when the economy declined 11 percent in 1987 following political turmoil associated with two coups and the imposition of a military government. Led by Col. (now Major General) Sitiveni Rabuka, the irregular change in government was intended to prevent the Indian plurality in Fiji from assuming power. Partly as a result, inflation jumped from 1.6 percent in 1986 to 14.5 percent in 1987 before declining to 8.7 percent in 1988. An INF report for May 1989 listed Fiji (as well as the Cook Islands) as unlikely "to make economic recovery." However, the Fijian economy rebounded in 1989 with a growth rate of about 12 percent, and lower but steady growth in the early 1990s.

But with the promulgation in mid-1990 by President Ratu Sir Penaia Ganilau of a new Fijian constitution (the self-proclaimed high note of the interim government led by Prime Minister Ratu Sir Kamisese Mara), some improvement of regional political and economic relations followed. Both Australia and New Zealand, for example, accepted the new constitution, and this induced New Zealand to resume air force surveillance cooperation and regular ministerial contact.[35]

Modernization of Fiji has been accelerated by the fact that it is the only new country in the Pacific to have major manufacturing capacity. It was the political turmoil in Fiji in the late 1980s that triggered the sharp economic downturn, as contrasted with the more developed countries in the Caribbean where economic downturns tend to induce political change.

Agriculture, forestry, and fisheries make up 22 percent of Fiji's economy, but sugar continues to be dominant. Fiji, along with the Solomon Islands, has the only operating fish canneries in the region as well as the region's largest manufacturing sector, including sugar refining. Tourism, although initially adversely affected by the political turmoil of the late 1980s, contributes approximately 12 percent of the national GDP.

Although Fiji returned to constitutional governance and the trappings of democracy in the early 1990s, its new rules continue to ensure permanent secondary or underclass status for nonnatives. This disparity obviously casts a cloud over Fiji's political and economic future.[36]

Solomon Islands. The per capita income of the former British Solomons was only $380 in 1986, a sum reflecting a decline of 54 percent in economic growth since 1982, partially the result of cyclone-inflicted damage. By 1988, however, per capita income in the Solomons had nearly doubled, reaching $630. Subsistence agriculture and fishing are economic mainstays. Principal exports of the Solomons are fish (46 percent), forestry products (31 percent), and agricultural products (16 percent); specific export products are copra, cocoa, and palm oil. Pressure to stop large-scale logging operations by TNCs was mounted in the early 1990s by the lone female member of the island's parliament. The Solomons have some mineral potential, and the World War II battlegrounds on Guadalcanal are attracting an increasing number of tourists.

Even though the economy has not been as robust as that of Papua New Guinea or precoup Fiji, the political scene for the 312,000 Solomon Islanders is more highly legitimated despite the proliferation of more than 100 indigenous dialects and languages. Governmental change in the Solomons occurs in a more orderly manner, with considerable rotation of the office of prime minister. In the April 1989 general election, Solomon Mamaloni became prime minister when his People's Alliance Party (PAP) secured 22 of 38 seats. Governments routinely remain in office the full term, and relative social stability is the norm in the Solomon Islands even in the face of severe economic downturns. This pattern is at variance with much of the Caribbean.

In the early 1990s, Prime Minister Mamaloni survived a no-confidence vote in parliament as well as a plot to oust him from the leadership of PAP. Like Herbert Blaize, the late prime minister of Grenada in the Caribbean, Mamaloni survived by leaving the party, keeping some loyal members, and attracting opposition members to cross the floor—including former Prime Minister Sir Peter Kenilorea.[37]

The Republic of Vanuatu. Based on its major exports of copra, beef, and fish, on its forestry products industry, and on tourism, the per capita income of Vanuatu in 1985 was $863, in 1988 down slightly to $840. This partly aid-dependent nation of twelve principal and some sixty smaller islands also received extensive cyclone damage in 1987 that crippled its economy, which had been expanding by 3–5 percent since independence in 1980. The economy continued to decline in 1988 and 1989, prompted by the fallout from an attempted coup in 1988. The IMF now discounts an early economic recovery for this proud new nation. Inflation also has become a major problem in Vanuatu, increasing dramatically from a relatively low percentage in the period 1983–1985 to 16 percent in 1988.[38] Australia has made charges that

Vanuatu serves as a heroin route from Southeast Asia. In early 1992, Vanuatu expelled the acting Australian ambassador, who had been accused of meddling in Venuatu's internal politics—although the reasons included a revenge factor by the Francophone faction in this multicultural island.

Vanuatu maintains political ties with both Britain (as a member of the Commonwealth) and France, its former dual colonial masters, and both English and French are official languages in this island group. Vanuatu has also in the past cultivated relations with the former Soviet Union, Vietnam, Cuba, and even Libya. In fact, the fishing treaties Vanuatu negotiated with the Soviets (together with a Kiribati/Soviet fishing treaty) were sparks that redirected U.S. attention toward the region—just as the spate of revolutionary activity in the Caribbean and the real and potential Eastern European bloc linkages during the late 1970s attracted Washington's attention to those areas. Vanuatu is also the only member of the nonaligned movement from the Pacific as compared with eight members from the newly independent Caribbean.[39]

The 1990s brought political change, however, change that was probably linked more to personality politics than to divine will—as speculated by some Vanuatu religious leaders. Father Walter Lini, an independence leader who had also led the Vanua'aku Party (VP) and the government since 1980, was removed by a no-confidence vote from both the VP leadership and the prime ministership in late 1990. In the ensuing election (1991), the post-Lini VP retained a plurality but was replaced in government by a weak coalition of the Francophone Union of Moderate Parties (UMP) and Lini's new National Union Party (NUP) plus some church-linked factions. The UMP's Maxime Carlot became prime minister. The change suggests greater efforts to improve relations and attract loans and investments from the United States and Europe. With the vacating of Clark Air Force Base and Subic Bay in the Philippines and no solid support for base relocation in Palau, there is even a possibility of cooperation between Vanuatu and the United States on a military base. Indeed, income from such a base may be required to pay for the expanded education and health services promised by the government.[40]

Federated States of Micronesia (FSM). The Federated States of Micronesia had a per capita GDP of $1,249 in 1985, and the World Bank estimates that their income will continue to be in the high-income range. However, as in the Marshall Islands (and Puerto Rico in the Caribbean), a significant percentage of this income has emanated from U.S budgetary assistance, including the food-stamp program, under the FSM compact of free association. The bulk of the relatively low U.S. economic assistance to the region flows to former U.S. trust territories, including the FSM, which receives nearly three-fourths of its GDP (72 percent) from this source. Another aspect of remaining under the dependent umbrella of the giant metropole is that FSM commodity demands and imports are sixteen times greater than island exports, a less than enviable position for this emerging state.

Copra is virtually the only export of the Federated States of Micronesia. Licensing of foreign fishing fleets garners some governmental revenue. Economic development has been so minimal under the U.S. tutelage, in fact, that many older Micronesians recall Japanese rule with some nostalgia.

Principal unrest in the FSM states has resulted from and resistance to U.S. military demands for an increased presence. Alcoholism and a near-epidemic increase in suicides are negative phenomena now impacting the FSM under the leadership of President John Haglegam.[41] Still, in late 1990, the United Nations terminated its trusteeship relationship with the FSM and in 1991 admitted the former trust territory to membership in the organization. There was a doubling of U.N. development funds to Micronesia as well as to the neighboring Marshall Islands, which also moved from U.N. trustee to U.N. member.

The smaller Pacific states. The remaining smaller island countries (SICs) of the region had annual GDPs of less than $100 million in the 1980s: the Cook Islands, $21 million; Kiribati, $27.7 million; the Marshall Islands, $37.9 million; Niue, $3.1 million; Tonga, $68 million; Tuvalu, $2.8 million; and Western Samoa, $81.4 million. The Republic of Nauru has an unusually high per capita income, higher than the top-ranking Bahamas in the Caribbean, which has led to a lifestyle emphasizing "instant gratification and consumerism."[42] Its economy, historically based on phosphate mining and, later, revenue from hotels and a government-owned shopping center in Australia, is now declining primarily because of mine exhaustion and also partially as a result of costly overruns on its national airline, the aging of its real estate holdings, and its costly import policies. These factors present a concern for the government of President Bernard Dowiyogo.

Peaceful electoral change has occurred in most of the SICs, including Kiribati, French Polynesia, Western Samoa, and Micronesia. Elections in the Kingdom of Tonga in 1990 were won by the Reformists, a victory that, according to Rodney Hills, puts the region's most traditional governments on notice.[43] However, Taufa'ahau Tupou IV still dominates the Tongan government.

The smallest Pacific countries share many of the problems of the larger economies but to an accentuated degree: flat and declining economic growth; increasing inflation and unemployment; negative trade balances; declines in primary commodity prices; limited economic resources; expanding national debts, although these are still relatively small (except in the Republic of Palau, which by 1985 had moved into the ranks of seriously indebted nations with a $35 million debt owed by its 15,000 citizens as the result of a bankrupt electric power project); and continuing dependence on and vulnerability to overseas aid (again the Palau bankruptcy makes it vulnerable to U.S. demands that it discard its antinuclear constitution in return for aid).

One regional scholar feels Kiribati, Niue, Tuvalu, and the Cook Islands are SICs that have reached such a grave crisis level of requiring permanent assistance that the "business of government has become the aid business."[44] Global warming poses a massive potential disaster to this region because several of these island states just break the ocean surface. There is also the ever-present vulnerability to cyclones, volcanic eruptions, and other recurrent natural disasters that, though faced by all, are felt most harshly by the poorest, the SICs. They are particularly vulnerable because even the rare advancing economy is extremely fragile in an extremely weak state, and they are subject to immediate dislocation whenever political or economic ripples occur.

Kiribati is such an example. With only copra and fish as export products, it has one of the lowest incomes in the Pacific and is now considered, as are Haiti and Guyana in the Caribbean, a "least developed country" by the United Nations. Still, it is not a country that has given up. In the words of its president, Ieremia Tabai: "There is no alternative to developing our country so we can stand on our God-given feet." Kiribati managed to become self-sufficient from British aid seven years after independence, although it took a fishing pact with the former Soviet Union to enable the island to turn this corner—an act that provoked great suspicion in Washington and Whitehall. Now, because of reduced export earnings, conditions have returned to a crisis level. Hope remains, however, that four garment factories and a palm syrup industry will again fire the engines of development. Life in small, poor countries is constantly on the margin. Larger countries can suffer reverses and survive, but there are few easy choices for these small states.[45]

Despite the special problems inherent among the smallest and weakest states, there also is surprising cooperation, such as that between Kiribati and Tuvalu. In this case, the cooperation results largely from the fact that these two states were once one British colony, the Gilbert and Ellice Islands. Such cooperative patterns are also found in the eastern Caribbean because there too the territories once were linked in common colonial groupings. Perhaps this activity, together with overall regional integration movements, bodes well for the future in both the Pacific and the Caribbean.

Strategies for Economic Survival

Integration Movements in Two Regions

Caribbean regionalism: From Carifta to Caricom and the OECS. The ten-nation West Indies Federation (1958–1962) and subsequent abortive "little eight" federation effort, which marked the initial path from colonial status for the British Caribbean, may have been short-lived; nonetheless, these federation schemes provided the basic integration structures for the widely scattered West Indies. These moves, together with the earlier metropolitan-imposed, now defunct Caribbean Commission,[46] proved to be harbingers of later regionalism, including the integrative attempts of the late 1980s and the early 1990s.

Upon achieving singular independence, the Caribbean states, almost as a second rite of passage following membership in the United Nations, routinely participated in the (British) Commonwealth, the loosely linked association of ex-British colonies, and joined the Organization of American States (OAS), the predominant regional intergovernmental organization. The Commonwealth Caribbean states have experienced frustration with these organizations—the focus, pace, and accessibility to primary leadership roles within the Hispanic-dominated OAS have been especially vexatious. To better address cooperative goals and especially to stimulate local trade, indigenous IGOs were formed, including the Caribbean Free Trade Association (Carifta) in 1968, from which Caricom evolved in 1973. Subsequently, the small eastern Caribbean states, which had experienced considerable collective governance under British colonialization as the Windward and Leeward island groupings, coalesced into the OECS, a sub-Caricom grouping. (Chapter 6 contained details on these organizations; this chapter briefly reviews that discussion.) The Caricom-affiliated Caribbean Development Bank (CDB), of great importance to economic development and planning by both Caricom and the OECS, was formed in 1969.

Some early achievements of Caricom included substantial expansion of regional trade, considerable cross-national institutional integration, and foreign policy coordination/consultation, including a strong leadership role in negotiations with the European Community in formation of the multiregional African-Caribbean-Pacific (ACP) group. Caricom's pace in these cooperative endeavors slowed dramatically by the late 1970s, however, as a result of (1) the drastic economic downturns that buffeted the region and (2) the 1979–1983 ideological rift resulting from the Marxist revolution in Grenada, together with the attendant ideological policies of Washington throughout the 1980s.

Somewhat ironically, the OECS has taken the lead in promoting such supranational concerns as the sharing of selected diplomatic posts and economic policies among member nations. Important recent developments promoted by the OECS include the emergence of a general secretariat and the development of overarching economic and political sectors. Other entities created include a common central bank and a subregional court. OECS member states also share a common eastern Caribbean currency (EC$). As discussed earlier, the OECS, in conjunction with Barbados, in 1982 formed a defense mechanism, the Regional Security System (RSS), which Barbados hosts. This mechanism, established with the assistance of a major funding grant from the United States, competes for scarce tax revenues and may be perceived as presenting a viable but illegal alternative to electoral governance. Somewhat similar to U.S. military expansion in the Pacific, U.S. support for the RSS paralleled its concern about percieved Marxist penetration of the region.

By 1986, Caricom trade had plummeted to less than half its 1981 level. In addition to damage inflicted on the institution by ideology related to the intervention in Grenada, the severe declines of the three largest Caricom economies in the region—Guyana, Trinidad and Tobago, and Jamaica—produced havoc in its overall trade patterns.

A significant beginning to the resurgence of the fourteen-year-old Caricom structure was made in July 1987 at the eighth heads-of-government summit in Castries, St. Lucia, when an agreement was reached calling for the early removal of "all measures restricting intra-regional trade." The summit participants also formulated a plan for development of a Caribbean Export Bank (CEB), operated as a separate facility of the Caribbean Development Bank, to replace the now-defunct Caribbean Multilateral Clearing Facility.

In the human resource area, plans were initiated for a limited "Caribbean citizenship" status for Caricom notables. At subsequent summit meetings, Caricom heads of government agreed, among other things, to implement a common external tariff, create a regional stock exchange, and to ease restrictions on regional labor mobility. In 1990, plans for a CEB were shelved because of a lack of funding. But by 1992, although none of the other measures had been fully implemented, some progress in all could be discerned. The 13th Caricom summit, held in June–July 1992, marked another juncture in the resurgence of the organization: Leaders agreed to implement the CET fully by January 1, 1993 and to move toward a common currency by the end of the century. They also agreed to continue to facilitate easier travel for Caricom nationals. Moreover, a West Indian Commission of regional experts, established in 1989 to review the progress toward integration in all sectoral and policy, delivered to summit leaders a substantial report containing suggestions for improved Caricom decisionmaking and implementation and more effective economic and functional cooperation. Included in the latter is a call for implementation of a long discussed Caribbean Court of Appeals.[47] It should be noted that the current impetus for stronger integration owes much to the recognition that small states need to cooperate to survive in a world of three large blocs: an increasingly united Europe, the North American Free Trade Area, and a strong Pacific trading bloc.

An intra-OECS political union of up to seven states was first promoted by prime ministers James Mitchell of St. Vincent and James Compton of St. Lucia at a May 1987 regional conference in Tortola, British Virgin Islands. Noting a "strong sense of worry about the twentieth century closing and leaving us all stranded," and feeling that such integration would probably facilitate increased U.S. assistance (a point by no means assured), Mitchell made the case for a unitary nation-state to the assembled delegates.

At one point, six of the seven OECS leaders were endorsing union by the year 1989, but momentum cooled as opposition surfaced from Vere Bird, the prime minister of Antigua; from a bevy of OECS opposition party leaders; and from the always vocal local press—and as perceptions rose that this latest integration idea was inspired by Washington.[48]

Unity discussions have continued, but it has sometimes appeared that rhetoric may be dominating reality: Only a planned referendum in the Windwards, scheduled for early 1993, and growing favor for a Caribbean appellate court are approaching reality.[49]

The Pacific: Slower-paced movements. Despite enduring diverse colonial masters, the continued presence of metropolitan-spawned regional structures, and a vast expanse of ocean—all of which are obstacles to true regional integration—the Pacific has realized significant movement in regional cooperation in the brief period since formal decolonization. Of the approximately 200 regional intergovernmental organizations operating in the Pacific today, the South Pacific Commission (SPC) and the South Pacific Forum (SPF) rank as the most important for promoting regional integration and cooperation on trade and development issues; both organizations meet annually. As yet, there is no regional bank in the Pacific, although many states belong to the Asian Development Bank. A development of major importance is the expanding judicial cooperation under which the supreme courts of several islands presently are made up of the chief justices from neighboring states.

Six colonial or metropolitan powers administered the Pacific at the end of World War II: the United Kingdom, the United States, France, the Netherlands, Australia, and New Zealand, with the last two countries being regional intermediate powers as well as U.N. trust holders. The South Pacific Commission (SPC), similar in scope and metropolitan paternalism to the U.S.-U.K.-France-Netherlands Caribbean Commission (1946–1961), was established in 1947 under the Canberra Agreement by these same six metropolitan countries. It was designed to function as a mutually reinforcing consulting, advising, and technical assistance agency. The SPC Secretariat, located in Noumea, New Caledonia, provides additional services such as technical training and dissemination of socio-cultural and socio-economic information and assistance. In 1950, the SPC began to sponsor regional conferences that are credited with "playing a crucial [role] in the development of islander awareness of the region and other islanders within it. . . . For the first time [there was] a regional outlook."[50]

To provide needed institutional flexibility, the SPC expanded the traditional number of commissioners (twelve) after 1970 to accommodate representation from the emerging small island states. After 1975, the SPC constitution was altered to permit commissioners from each new state. The change brought the number of commissioners to the current twenty-seven: a commissioner from each of the five remaining metropolitan countries (the Dutch having departed with the loss of the Dutch East Indies, now Indonesia), plus a commissioner from each of the twenty-two Pacific member states and territories. Metropolitan powers contribute a massive 92 percent of the SPC budget; Australia provides the lion's share—more than twice the amount of any other actor in the region—in keeping with its post–World War II role as a rising intermediate power.[51]

Despite these adaptations by the SPC, dissatisfaction surfaced about the "colonial mentality" of the commission and also the organization's nonpolitical stance. Decolonization issues and mounting reservations among the small states regarding metropolitan nuclear policies were kept off the SPC agenda, and vitally important topics relating to the expansion of interisland trade also failed to be given sufficiently high priority. In response, the new Pacific states developed their own subregional grouping, the South Pacific Forum (SPF), to provide a greater sociopolitical and socio-economic focus (much as the small non-Hispanic states in the Caribbean felt a need to develop Caricom and the OECS, to focus on their indigenous political-economic problems after the demise of the metropolitan-sponsored Caribbean Commission in 1961). Principal SPF goals are to encourage economic and political cooperation among the membership and between the less developed and more developed members.

The organizational impetus for the SPF, which includes its Secretariat in Suva, Fiji, came from within the new states of the region. Formative dialogue was initiated after the independence movements of the 1960s, and the SPF came to fruition in discussions at Fiji's independence celebrations in 1970. The first SPF conference was held the following year in Wellington, New Zealand, the second in 1972 in Australia. Membership includes the independent Pacific states, plus Australia and New Zealand.

Into the early 1990s, Australia was still carrying primary financial responsibility in the SPF (as in the SPC)—yet another indication of the importance of Pacific regionalism and insular stability to this South Pacific intermediate power. The SPF, lacking a formal constitution, relies on self-regulating rules supplied by the regional heads of government. The organization has significant accomplishments to its credit, including establishment of the Pacific Forum Line based in Western Samoa, a shipping service initiated in 1978, and a Forum Fisheries Agency (FFA) created in 1979 and based in the Solomon Islands that recently negotiated a fishing agreement with the United States. As early as 1980, the SPF negotiated the South Pacific Regional Trade and Economic Agreement, which permits nonreciprocal access to the markets of Australia and New Zealand. Pacific states also have access to each other's markets, but tend to trade with outside partners because of transportation and marketing obstacles. Probably the major accomplishment in economic diplomacy of both the SPF and Caricom has been their successful negotiations with the European Community under the Lomé conventions to create the African-Caribbean-Pacific (ACP) marketing organization.

The SPF meets annually, and its agenda includes discussion of common concerns and the issuance of joint policy proclamations. One such agreement that has been strongly countered by the United States—but not by Australia and New Zealand—is a declaration of the South Pacific as a nuclear-free zone. This action was formalized by treaty (Raratonga) in 1985. The Pacific states also issued a statement opposing French nuclear testing in its Pacific colonies, initiated a plan for cultural linkage that has some similarities to the Caribbean Festival (CARIFESTA), and in 1986 drafted a noteworthy environmental treaty.[52] At the Forum's 1992 meeting, economic development and pollution control shared the agenda.

Although most Pacific states consider the SPF to be the natural successor of the unforgivably procolonial SPC, most states continue to accept both organizations. As much of the real action has shifted from the SPC, however, metropolitan representatives to the organization seem less and less empowered to negotiate seriously for their governments, one of many examples of the tendency of metropolitan actors to downplay multilateral politics.[53]

Bilateral Initiatives for Development

The pursuit of improvements in the domestic economy explains why diplomats and leaders from the small states of both the Caribbean and the Pacific have given almost undivided effort in the 1980s and early 1990s to a search for external markets, capital for investments and loans, and financial aid and, for many states, to the not-always-fruitful quest of the fickle tourist—the hope being that anticipated income from the tourism sector will continue to cover much of the perennial visible trade imbalances in both regions. Put more crassly, for too many new states, the business of governments becomes the aid business at both the multilateral and bilateral levels. In view of the severe economic downturns of the 1980s and early 1990s, this contributes to embarrassingly dependent relations on the bilateral level.[54]

The Caribbean Basin Initiative. Bilateral diplomacy took on added prominence in the English-speaking Caribbean during the administration of U.S. President Reagan, which, in sharp contrast with the earlier Carter administration, deemphasized multilateral relations. In addition to the United States, important non-Caricom state-to-state contacts during this period were pursued with traditional friends Canada and Britain; with selected "new" friends in the EC, important for both trade and aid programs; with Japan, prompted by its growing economic importance; with intermediate Hispanic powers in the Caribbean Basin, especially Venezuela and Mexico as a result of their significant multilateral assistance in providing low-cost petroleum to most Caricom and Central American states under the San José accords during the early to mid 1980s;[55] and with selected African and Asian states, especially if linked to national population groups.

Since World War II, Britain has been replaced by the United States as the most important actor among the small Caricom states. Thus, when the United States announced a proposed "Marshall Plan" for the region—the Caribbean Basin Initiative (CBI)—in the early days of the Reagan administration, strong interest was expressed both by the Caribbean Community and by individual states (especially Jamaica, whose leader was the first foreign head of government hosted by the Reagan White House). Much of this subregion perceives a need for outside economic assistance in the form of trade, loans, and investment, and the CBI seemed to promise all three, with the opportunities for trade especially attractive. Officially titled the Caribbean Basin Economic Recovery Act (Public Law 98-67, Title II), the plan was announced in a speech to the Organization of American States on February 24, 1982, in which President Reagan promoted CBI as "a program that integrates trade, aid and investment . . . to the countries of the Caribbean and Central America to make use of the magic of the marketplace . . . to earn their own way towards self-sustaining growth."[56]

This CBI, now in its third round, remains the centerpiece of U.S.-Caribbean relations today. Although initially promoted as a multilateral endeavor to be cosponsored by Canada, Venezuela, and Mexico, the CBI was developed without the support of these intermediate powers largely because of Washington's insistence on specifically eliminating Cuba from participation and effectively excluding the then-revolutionary regimes of Nicaragua and Grenada, an exclusion that also was strongly opposed in specific requests from Caricom foreign ministers.[57] Key provisions of CBI I were for (1) one-way, duty-free access to U.S. markets for selected Basin exports for a period of twelve years; (2) allocation of $350 million for emergency assistance, in addition to $474.6 million already committed as aid for fiscal year 1982; and (3) U.S. tax incentives for U.S. investments in the region. These provisions were incorporated into several U.S. House and Senate bills passed between September 1982 and August 1983 with modifications that, unfortunately for Caricom, included elimination of the tax incentive and related credits.[58]

U.S. bilateral aid to the region doubled between 1981 and 1984, but the emphasis placed on military aid and other forms of security assistance led many Caribbean leaders to believe the Reagan-Bush administration was more interested in promoting militarism than economic development. As noted by Earl Bousquet, Washington was "more interested in doling out military aid and assistance than ensuring that the . . . CBI operates."[59] And only a tiny fraction of the development funds reached the eastern Caribbean. Of the $350 million in supplemental CBI emergency funds requested by the Reagan administration to assist with trade and IMF imbalances in fiscal year 1982, for example, $128 million was slated for then-insurrectionist El Salvador alone; $105 million for Costa Rica and Honduras, the two Central American states bordering Nicaragua; and only $10 million for ten English-speaking Caribbean states. The fact that Belize (bordering Guatemala) and Jamaica, then led by the strongly pro-U.S. Edward Seaga, were slated to receive $10 million and $50 million, respectively, did not detract from this obvious slighting of the eastern Caribbean democracies for which Caricom had identified $580 million in emergency needs. This pattern continued through the decade.

Other problems that have seriously hampered success of the CBI include price declines (and product substitutions) for bauxite and sugar; the collapse of the computer chip market; and, for Trinidad, the sluggish world price for oil during most of the 1980s. As if the low world price for these commodities and goods did not present sufficiently formidable roadblocks, the faltering program was still further undercut by restrictive quotas imposed by the United States against Caribbean sugar in 1985 in response to pressures from its domestic sugar producers, an action that cost the Caribbean region up to $300 million and 130,000 badly needed jobs. Such policies especially impacted Jamaica and Barbados. At least partly because of these policies, Barbadian exports to the United States have dropped from more than 50 percent of total exports (up to 1985) to less than 20 percent in 1990, the largest percentage drop between this Caribbean country and any of its major trading partners. The United States, one conservative journal concluded in the mid-1980s, "should pursue trade policies that, at a minimum, do not sabotage the goals of foreign aid programs, and that, ideally, serve these goals. The need to support foreign friends would not be so pressing . . . if this country practiced the free market principles we so often preach."[60] Thus, the export of free-market principles has been an enduring although controversial aspect of the CBI.

Although less restrictive versions of the CBI were passed in the late 1980s and early 1990s, the most basic problem with the CBI has remained its integral tie to the export of U.S. economic models. Despite the general adherence to such models in the early 1990s, these development programs are not necessarily compatible with the long-term needs of the Anglophone states. Some comments made in the 1980s are still relevant to the 1990s: For example, a test of appropriateness and "of U.S. sincerity," stated Atherton Martin, a former minister of agriculture from Dominica, "would be to let us sit down as partners and say this will work, this will not work, this is what is . . . possible in our countries."[61] Joan French, a Jamaican analyst, presented a similar point: The United States should "ask us what we produce and help us make it more efficiently, rather than turning our whole economy around to suit what [the United States] wants."[62]

In the early 1990s, the trade relationship with the United States took a new turn with the offer by President Bush, in what he termed the Enterprise for the Americas Initiative (EAI), to negotiate free-trade agreements with interested countries of the hemisphere.[63] The EAI is underwritten by the same principles of economic development as the CBI, but goes beyond its one-way free-trade rules and projects free-trade linkages into South America. Whether the Caribbean can preserve CBI preferences while negotiating under the EAI remains to be seen.

Dependence on the United States has limited the Caribbean's ability to develop indigenous models of development. In the Cold War era, experimentation brought hostility and economic sanction from the United States. Michael Manley, for example, claims he attempted to extricate Jamaica from imposed Western models by "construct[ing] economic alliances that give us the greatest chance to underwrite our economic independence."[64] In the process, he lost support among his own middle- and upper-class constituencies and, most significantly, from Washington as well. Likewise, the late Maurice Bishop of Grenada asserted that extricating his small island from Western models and dependency was the raison d'être for the Grenadian revolution. With the replacement of Eric Gairy by the People's Revolutionary Government (PRG) in Grenada, the chill from Washington became overpowering, well before a Leninist direction became an established reality for the PRG[65]—just as had occurred nearly two decades earlier when Cheddi Jagan, the U.S.-educated constitutional Marxist from Guyana, attempted a partially non–Western-oriented approach to development in his country on the eve of its independence. Jagan's government was summarily "destabilized" by a combination of U.S. and British intelligence activities. His successor, the corrupt and largely authoritarian Forbes Burnham, could later flirt with non-Western models only because Jagan was perceived to be to his left. A newer version of the search for independence, characterized by efforts to escape the "debt trap" and the "jaws of the IMF" has proved to be as unsuccessful as the earlier stance toward ideological independence.[66]

In short, care and finesse are the operative words if so-called indigenous economic models are ever to be introduced successfully in the Caribbean Basin. For the would-be indigenous developer, tactics may have to be drawn from, among others, the late Omar Torrijos of Panama, who is credited with balancing Washington (as well as his own elites) by "signaling one way and going another."[67] And it is almost self-evident that the ability to balance, is infinitely more difficult in periods of economic austerity such as the Caribbean small states are experiencing today.

Pacific bilateralism. The bilateral relations of the Pacific states reflect former colonial ties and postcolonial realities. One of these realities has been a desire by the United States and other major and intermediate powers to maintain the Pacific as a security zone, or at least as a tranquillity zone, in an attempt to frustrate regional adventurers—defined in the 1970s and 1980s as the Soviet Union, China, Vietnam, and Libya. This pursuit accounted for much of the increased U.S. attention to the region in that period. U.S. aid to the south Pacific increased from $6 million in 1978 to $29 million in 1988; however, this still constituted only 4 percent of the total economic assistance to this subregion, well behind the contributions of Australia, Japan, New Zealand, France, Britain, and the European Community. Such a low level of assistance by the resident superpower "generated islander perceptions of American insensitivity to regional needs, and a belief that Washington has not adequately reciprocated island state support for U.S. interests and policies."[68]

In contrast, approximately half the total asssistance to the subregion comes from Australia, including funding of the military in the four newest Pacific states that maintain forces. New Zealand is also a major donor. Most significant, both Australia and New Zealand open their markets to goods produced in the Pacific, and both fund programs that service selected health and educational needs of the new insular states. France has substantially increased its assistance to the Pacific through its South Pacific Cooperation Fund, which has funded projects in Tonga and the Cook Islands as well as in its own remaining Pacific colonies. In 1989, France paid out $753 million just to cover French Polynesia's trade deficit. "You cannot put a price on a myth," according to one commentator, "or on la gloire of keeping the Tricolour flying among the Palms!"[69]

Despite efforts to diversify aid sources, most Pacific states remain firmly tied to the West. China, Libya, Vietnam, and the former USSR have, however, offered programs and minor assistance to Pacific states, since realizing that a very few dollars go a long way when dealing with very small states—a lesson previously learned by Venezuela, Mexico, and Canada in their dealings with the small states of the Caribbean. Foreign aid is criticized, especially at the region's two universities (Fiji and PNG), but the criticism is more muted than in the Caribbean. Such differences between the two regions result from differing levels of socioeconomic development, the Pacific being the less developed. At the same time, however, the Pacific states are more cushioned from consumer demands, unemployment, and perceived inequality. Moreover, the Pacific actors are not located a mere fifty or even ninety miles from the United States. The much greater distance permits greater maneuverability for the Pacific states than is enjoyed by its eastern counterparts. Finally, the Pacific has enjoyed greater insulation from great-power rivalry than has the Caribbean as a result of the strongly protective and cooperative roles played by the intermediate powers of New Zealand and Australia. These middle powers have been more effective in this capacity than have Canada, Mexico, Venezuela, and, at times, Colombia and Brazil, their counterparts in the Caribbean.[70]

Multilateral Diplomacy for Development

The quest for development assistance and the need for cooperative efforts traditionally place membership in intergovernmental organizations high on the policy agenda of the newer states in both the Caribbean and Pacific. Membership in these organizations has enormous value, according to George Reid, a West Indian foreign policy official, by providing valuable technological and data services. They also offer the most cost- and personnel-effective form of diplomacy. Further, these states "in their search for economic assistance . . . tend to look to the multilateral agencies and the United Nations as a counterweight to dependency on unilateral arrangements."[71]

For the small and weak, the rites of passage to independent nationhood almost by definition include joining the United Nations and the appropriate regional organizations. In addition to significant economic and technological assistance from U.N. development agencies and U.N.-associated agencies such as the Food and Agriculture Organization (FAO), there is the direct political function of low-cost diplomatic representation. How many small, weak states have the resources to send full delegations to each of nearly 200 nation-states? Very few—yet each small state may contact heads of governments or external ministry officers on a need basis during sessions at the U.N. headquarters in New York each fall. Another high-priority organization for both regions is the African, Caribbean, and Pacific group (ACP), which carries a special economic trade linkage to the EC. In addition, there is the Group of 77 (G-77), a major economic advocate for the Third World, and the nonaligned movement, whose membership includes seven of the larger Caricom states, albeit but one Pacific state, Vanuatu.

As noted in the section on regionalism, there are approximately 200 regional organizations functioning in the Pacific, including the (British) Commonwealth, the French Agency de Coopération Culturelle et Technique the South Pacific Commission (SPC), and the South Pacific Forum (SPF). In their promotion of trade and development goals, the Anglophone Caribbean states have placed major emphasis on closer integration via their own regional political and economic organizations.

Conclusion: Comparisons and Suggestions

Economic marginality and resultant sobering levels of unemployment and underemployment continue to be serious concerns in many Caricom states, with unemployment levels exceeding 20 percent in most states and nearing 90 percent for youths, according to one prime minister in the region. As a local editor commented in 1987, Caricom political leaders who managed to get on the U.S. "bandwagon after the 1983 Grenadian invasion by promises [from Washington] of vast monetary aid . . . [are] now either falling apart or are under 'heavy manners.'"[72] The result is a vulnerability that impacts both domestic order and regime longevity. In most states, generations of the never-to-be-employed now walk the streets. Such systemic and regime stress is all the more poignant in the "Big Four" Caricom states in view of their long histories of relatively steady economic growth. The only alternative for 5 to 18 percent of the Caricom populace, writes Aaron Segal, has been to migrate to the European or North American metropole—a pattern that is often followed by financial remittances to family remaining in the Caribbean.[73]

In the south Pacific, much this same "escape" pattern exists for the beleaguered citizens of the smaller islands, though in this case it is to Australia and New Zealand that the migrating unemployed turn, or to Hawaii in the case of the northern Pacific. Such migration is a needed escape valve and an important source of remittance income, but it also is a negatively felt brain drain, according to Robert Pastor. Once initiated, even economic growth often fails to stop the population outflow.[74]

The economies of the Pacific countries are less developed and nearly as fragile as those in the Caribbean, but their very lack of industrialization appears to have cushioned the impact of crisis. Further, as hypothesized, when political systems in the insular Pacific are under "heavy manners," it is the economies that tend to respond adversely to the instability and turmoil. In the Caribbean, in contrast, especially among the Caricom Big Four, the instability and turmoil created by depressed or declining economies appear to influence directly the political system—to impact the very survival of political regimes. Notwithstanding this difference, in all small, weak states, the margin for error is extremely slim.

The advancement of regional integration in the Caribbean is second only to the European Community (EC). Somewhat ironically, as the economies of the Caricom Big Four continue to suffer, new attempts to develop a genuine common market are appearing. In the early 1990s, the subregion is poised for a level of political integration as well. In the Pacific, institutional aspects related to regionalism are less developed than in the Caribbean, but substantial economic, cultural, and political cooperation is under way both informally and within the South Pacific Forum. In both regions, these developments have been encouraged by the intermediate or middle powers, with Australia and New Zealand presenting the most appropriate models. Both regions can learn from each other with respect to the advancement of integration, and certainly both need to take action in the 1990s in the face of metropolitan integration.

In the bilateral sphere, the member states of both regions continue to be dependent on economic assistance from external powers. The Pacific countries, however, are much more integrated with their middle-power neighbors, Australia and New Zealand, than are the Caribbean nations with states such as Venezuela, Mexico, and Canada. This appears to be changing: Venezuela, although not able to continue the high level of financial assistance given to the small Caribbean states during the 1970s and 1980s, continues to promote trade links with them and has proposed joining Caricom as part of the general hemispheric movement toward freer trade. However, given its geopolitical position, the Caribbean will continue to be more dependent than the Pacific on the United States. Both regions are eager to receive more U.S. assistance, but such aid is more crucial for the Caribbean, at least until such time as greater progress is made in diversification of economic ties.

As contact among the small states of the Caribbean and the Pacific expands, the respective leaders of these two regions appear increasingly to perceive common needs and interests that are becoming apparent within organizations such as the United Nations and the African-Caribbean-Pacific (ACP) grouping of former colonies that is renegotiating access to and export stabilization with a consolidating European Community. Despite the cultural and geographical distance that separates them, the Caribbean and Pacific have numerous commonalties. The small states of these two regions can benefit by pooling their information and resources to promote understanding and cooperation that will ensure an audience for and a response to their common concerns within the international community. As will be seen in the next chapter, these concerns are not merely economic but also social and political.

Notes

1. "One sign of the growing prosperity that [East Asian] regional integration is bringing is that Australia, which has long resisted identifying itself with Asia because of its European roots, is now more concerned about being left out of the boom. We now see ourselves as part of the Asia-Pacific region, but we have to work hard to remain a part of it, said [an Australian diplomat]." See *New York Times*, May 8, 1990, p. D18.

2. *New York Times*, December 14, 1987, p. A14. As elaborated later, not all Indonesian-PNG contacts are positive, given that these countries share a common frontier on the island of New Guinea.

3. Ali Mazrui makes the distinction between "strategic" and "organic" (primarily economic interpenetration) relations among developing countries. See "The New Interdependence," in Guy F. Erb and Valeriana Kallab, eds., *Beyond Dependency: The Developing World Speaks Out* (Washington, D.C.: Overseas Development Council, 1975), p. 49.

4. Quoted by Hans Morgenthau, *Politics Among Nations: The Struggle for Power and Peace* (New York: Alfred A. Knopf, 1961), p. 167.

5. James Pope-Hennessy, quoted in Hector Bolitho, ed., *The British Empire*, (London: B. T. Batsford, 1947), p. 174.

6. See Alan Burns, *History of the British West Indies* (London: Allen and Unwin, 1965); Gordon K. Lewis, *The Growth of the Modern West Indies* (New York: Monthly Review, 1968); Eric Williams, *Capitalism and Slavery* (Chapel Hill: University of North Carolina Press, 1944); and Anthony P. Maingot, "The English-speaking Caribbean," in Mark Falcoff and Robert Royal, eds., *The Continuing Crisis: U.S. Policy in Central America and the Caribbean* (Latham, Md.: University Press of America, 1987), p. 133.

7. For basic history of the 1958–1962 federation, see John Mordecai, *The West Indies: The Federal Negotiations* (London: Allen and Unwin, 1968); and Hugh W. Springer, "Federation in the Caribbean: An Attempt That Failed," *International Organization*, Autumn 1962, pp. 758–777. Failure of the WIF may be attributed largely to Britain's hesitance, during its three-plus centuries of tutelage, to establish adequate interterritorial communication linkages among its Caribbean colonies and also persistently to support sufficient central governmental authority in the federation. I do not wish to suggest, however, that there was no fault among insular leaders, from Adams and Bustamante to Williams, because there most certainly was. Also see Great Britain, Colonial Office (GBCO), Cmd. 1679, *Report of a Visit [by E.F.L. Wood] to Certain West Indian Colonies and to British Guiana* (London: H.M.S.O., 1922); GBCO, Cmd. 6607, *West India Royal Commission Report, 1938–1939* (London: H.M.S.O., 1945).

8. Anguilla, initially linked with St. Kitts/Nevis, opted to return to colony status in 1967. The federation of St. Kitts/Nevis continues as a weakly integrated unit under a constitution that permits dissolution at the option of either island.

9. Annette Walker, "Is Puerto Rico at a Crossroads?" *Caribbean Contact*, July/August 1990, p. 14. There are problems with the proposals for each status option. The Popular Democratic Party representing the commonwealth status is seeking an enhanced commonwealth, e.g., authority to negotiate agreements with

foreign nations, the right to levy tariffs, jurisdiction over marine resources, and the right to name federal officials assigned to Puerto Rico. Also see Peter Passell, "Debate on Puerto Rico Rests on a Bottom Line," *New York Times* (national ed.), May 15, 1990, p. A10. On the decolonization of the Dutch Caribbean, see Rosemarijn Hofte and Gert Oostindie, "Upside-Down Decolonization," *Hemisphere* 1 (Winter 1989): 28–31.

10. Per capita GDP of $22,743 in the Cayman Islands leads both subregions, unless one considers world-leading Brunei and tiny Nauru. Ironically, both the Caymans and Brunei made headlines in early 1987 as a result of U.S. Senate "Iran-Contragate" investigation reports that funding from Brunei had been garnered to support the Nicaraguan contras and that Cayman "offshore" banks were involved in a transfer of contra funds. Detailed information on Anguilla, the British Virgins, the Caymans, and the Turk and Caicos islands appears in *Latin America and Caribbean Contemporary Record* (hereafter *LACCR*), Jack W. Hopkins, ed., 1983–1986, and Abraham F. Lowenthal, ed., 1987 (New York: Holmes and Meier, 1983–). Also see *World Development Report 1987* (New York: Oxford University Press, 1987).

11. Harold C. Hinton, "Clouds over the Pacific," *Pacifica* 1 (January 1989): 1–26, quote on 21.

12. Ibid., pp. 21–22. An indication of Korean thinking is reflected in "Materials on Pacific Community Concept," *Korea and World Affairs* 7 (Summer 1983): 276–303, and accompanying documents, 304–328.

13. When Europeans such as Domeny de Rienzi (1831) began to name and describe such Pacific subdivisions, it was assumed that linguistic, racial, and ethnological factors distinguished the peoples of the "micro" islands from the Melanesians and Polynesians. More recent research, however, indicates considerable cultural overlap. For example, all the indigenous languages appear to have a Malayo-Polynesian root. See Saul Riesenberg, "The Cultural Position of Ponape in Oceania," Ph.D. dissertation, University of California-Berkeley, 1950; and Norman Meller, *The Congress of Micronesia* (Honolulu: University of Hawaii Press, 1969), pp. 1–6. According to Meller, the previously noted boundaries are approximations because Nauru, Guam, and part of what was the Gilbert and Ellice insular group are also technically part of Micronesa.

Another practical approach, as it is in the Caribbean Basin is to divide the Pacific region into those states that are independent and those that are not (see the next section, "From Colonial to Statehood Status"). Two additional insular states, the Philippines and Indonesia, are considered part of Southeast Asia and both are members of the Southeast Asian intergovernmental organization (Association of Southeast Asian Nations)—even though both archipelagoes figured heavily in the original settlement of the new Pacific states. The regional intermediate powers— Australia, New Zealand, and Japan—are more developed countries (MDCs). The primary focus of this chapter and the next is on those nations that have received independence since 1961.

14. In this respect, Latin America is unique among major Third World areas. Africa and South Asia, for example, unlike Latin America, encompass all linguistic national groups, including those from offshore islands, as part of their respective geographically defined area. See W. Marvin Will, "A New Definition for Latin America," *MALAS Noticias*, Winter 1986, pp. 2–4.

15. See Deryck Scarr, *Fiji: A Short History* (Lale, Hawaii: Institute of Polynesian Studies, Brigham Young University-Hawaii Press [BYU-H], 1984), pp. 139–177, esp. 139; Brij V. Lal, *Politics in Fiji* (Lale, Hawaii: BYU-H), 1986; F. J. West, *Fiji, Tahiti and American Samoa* (Melbourne: Oxford University Press, 1961). In the words of Steward Firth, "Sovereignty and Independence in the Contemporary Pacific," *Contemporary Pacific* 1, 1 and 2 (Spring and Fall 1989):

77, "Sovereignty is . . . precluded by the political status of free association."
16. William Roger Louis, *Great Britain and Germany's Lost Colonies 1914–1919* (Oxford: Clarendon, 1967), pp. 118–160. The mandate system of the League of Nations assigned Class A and Class B status to territories lost in World War I for which there was a foreseeable date of independence. Class C status was reserved for the most traditional areas in which independence was extremely unlikely (i.e., the German colonies in southwest Africa and in the southwest Pacific).
17. Firth, "Sovereignty and Independence," p. 75; for probably the best work in English on the French overseas territories see Robert Aldrich and John Connell, *France's Overseas Frontier: Départements et Territoires d'Outre-Mer* (Cambridge: Cambridge University Press, 1992). Note that Réunion, in the Indian Ocean, is also a French Overseas department.
18. Michael R. Ogden, "The Paradox of Pacific Development," *Development Policy Forum* 7 (December 1989): 361–373; John Connell, "Island Microstates: The Mirage of Development," *Contemporary Pacific* 3, 2 (Fall 1991): 256, 261, 270.
19. Several Caribbean states export oil they have refined, but only Trinidad markets surplus production, albeit a declining amount. For Pacific data, see Economist Intelligence Unit (EIU), *Country Report, No. 1, 1988, Pacific Islands: PNG, Fiji, Solomon Islands, Western Samoa, Vanuatu, Tonga* (London: EIU, 1988); John Carter, ed., *Pacific Islands Year Book* (Sydney: Pacific Publications, 1986); and Francis X. Hezel, "Suicide and the Micronesian Family," *Contemporary Pacific* 1, 1 and 2 (Spring and Fall 1989): 43–74. In Article 6, no. 3, the trust agreement commits the United States to promote "the social advancement of the inhabitants . . . without discrimination; protect the health of the inhabitants; control drugs, and alcoholic and other spirituous beverages." Economic and educational advancement and "foster[ing] the development of such political institutions that are suited to the trust territory" were other pledges accepted. See U.S. Congress, *Senate Review of United Nations Charter Collections of Documents*, Senate Doc. no. 87, 83d Congress, 2d Sess., 1954.
20. On Guyana's economy over the years, see Caribbean Development Bank (CDB), *Annual Report 1985* (St. Michael, Barbados, 1986), pp. 36–37. (The annual CDB reports are cited hereafter as CDB, *19xx*.) See also CDB, *1986*, pp. 15–17, 28–29; CDB, *1989*, pp. 15, 31; CDB, *1990*, pp. 15, 30–32. For an assessment of the Guyanese economic model, see W. Andrew Axline, "Integration, Development, and Security in the Caribbean," paper presented to the 28th annual conference of the International Studies Association, Washington, D.C., April 14–18, 1987. Also based on author's observations in January 1992.
21. See CDB, *1985*, pp. 29–31; CDB, *1986*, pp. 15–17, 23–24; CDB, *1989*, pp. 15, 25; CDB, *1990*, pp. 15, 24–25; and W. Marvin Will, "Democracy, Elections, and Public Policy in the Eastern Caribbean: The Case of Barbados," *Journal of Commonwealth and Comparative Politics* 27, 3 (November 1989): 321–346; "Me Na Know," *Economist* 318 (January 19, 1991): 38. Also based on author's observations in September and October 1991.
The Barbadian parliament was expanded by one seat before the 1991 election. Prime Minister Errol Barrow, who led the DLP in its electoral sweep in 1986, died June 1, 1987, and was succeeded by Deputy Prime Minister Erskine Sandiford. It should be noted that the Barbados Labour Party (BLP) and DLP have alternately held power, in cycles of two or three terms, since their preindependence origins.
22. On Trinidad and Tobago's economy, see CDB, *1989*, pp. 15, 38; CDB, *1990*, pp. 15, 36–38. For background on the 1986 election, see Jacqueline A. Braveboy-Wagner's annual reviews "Trinidad and Tobago" in *LACCR*, vols. 1–4; CDB, *1986*, pp. 14–17, 34–35; *New York Times*, December 16, 1986. On the

1990 coup attempt, see *New York Times*, July 30–August 3, 1990; and Selwyn Ryan, *The Muslimeen Grab for Power: Race, Religion, and Revolution in Trinidad and Tobago* (Port of Spain, Trinidad: Inprint Publications, 1991). The leader of the attempted coup was Abu Bakr, a black Muslim and former Trinidadian policeman. In the Caribbean, election day is often spoken of as "the day of reckoning." The author conducted research in Trinidad in November and December 1991.

23. For information on Jamaica, see CDB, *1989*, pp. 32–33; CDB, *1990*, pp. 32–33. For background, see Hopeton Dunn, "J[amai]ca: Whither the PNP?" *Caribbean Contact*, May 1987, pp. 8, 13. Carl Stone, *Democracy and Clientelism in Jamaica* (New Brunswick, N.J.: Transaction, 1980); and polls conducted by Carl Stone for the (Jamaica) *Daily Gleaner* from 1987 to 1989. Data are also drawn from author's observations, June–August 1992.

24. See CDB, *1986*, pp. 15–23; and the essay on the Bahamas in *LACCR*, 1987. It should be noted that among the so-called Caricom MDCs, Guyana also held a general election in the 1980s—in 1985, a year after the death of this independent country's only official national leader, 62-year-old Forbes Burnham. The disastrous economic conditions would most probably have toppled the PNC for the first time (British and U.S. intelligence had been instrumental in installing Burnham and the People's National Congress (PNC) twenty-two years earlier) had it not been for PNC manipulation of the Guyanese electorate.

25. See "The Lady Goes on Ruling," *Economist* 315 (June 2, 1990): 42; CDB, *1982*, p. 24; CDB, *1987*, p. 15; CDB, *1989*, p. 15, 34–37; CDB, *1990*, p. 15.

26. "Belize," *Mesoamerica* 8, 10 (October 1989): 11–12.

27. CDB, *1990*, p. 25.

28. CDB, *1984*, p. 18; CDB, *1987*, p. 15; CDB, *1989*, p. 16.

29. CDB, *1985*, pp. 18, 39–47; CDB, *1986*, pp. 15–17, 23–24; CDB, *1989*, pp. 15, 34–40; CDB, *1990*, pp. 29–30; W. Marvin Will, "From Authoritarianism to Democracy in Grenada," *Studies in Comparative International Development* 26, 3 (Fall 1991): 29–57.

30. See CDB Annual Reports, including *1990*, pp. 16, 23–24. Debt estimate and other information are from *Trinidad Guardian*, January 1, 1992, p. 10.

31. Inter-American Development Bank (IDB), *Annual Report 1989* (Washington, D.C.: IDB, 1990), p. 124. (The IDB annual reports are cited hereafter as IDB, *19xx*.) IDB, *1988;* IDB, *1987;* IDB, *1986; The Universal Almanac 1990* (New York: Andrews and McMeel, 1989), p. 485; Adiante Franszoon, "Crisis in the Backlands," *Hemisphere* 1 (Winter 1989): 36–38.

32. According to a special report of the Pacific Forum, Institute for Foreign Policy Analysis, John C. Dorrance R. T. Thakur, J. Wanandi, L. R. Vasey, and Robert L. Pfaltzgraff, Jr., *The South Pacific: Emerging Security Issues and U.S. Policy* (Washington, D.C.: Brassey's, 1990), p. vii, "only Papua New Guinea, Fiji, . . . Nauru, and possibly the Solmons and Vanuatu, appear to have a resource base offering hope of future economic self-sufficiency." Michael P. Hamnett and Robert C. Kiste, *Issues and Interest Groups in the Pacific Islands* (Washington, D.C.: U.S. Information Agency, Office of Research, 1988), pp. 15, 20; Sir Julius Chan, "A Prime Minister's Reflections on Papua New Guinea's Constitution," *Pacific Perspectives* 3 (c. 1984): 55–56; and "Bright Future for Agriculture," *Pacific Islands Monthly* 59, 10 (October 1988): 24–26; *World Development Report 1990* (New York: Oxford University Press 1990), p. 243; "Peace in Prospect," *Economist* 318 (January 26, 1991): 34–36.

33. Jemima Garrett, "Bougainville," *Pacific Islands Monthly* 62, 1 (January 1992): 20–21. According to Terence Wesley-Smith, "Papua New Guinea," *Contemporary Pacific* 3,2, (Fall 1991): 407–413, the "war" was enlarged by both sides until brokered in 1991 by Peter Wallensteen with assistance from

international observers.

34. Garrett, "Bougainville"; Wesley-Smith, "Papua New Guinea"; Michael P. Hamnett, *Donor Assistance in the South Pacific* (Suva, Fiji: Regional Development Office, USAID, 1988). Garrett, "Bougainville," writes: "The dismissal of deputy prime minister Ted Diro after the leadership commission found him guilty of 81 charges of misconduct proved the resilience and the strength of PNG's democratic institutions" (p. 20). See also "PNG's New Government," *Pacific Islands Monthly* 62, 8 (August 1992): 93–94.

35. In "Fiji: The Future," a special report by Stan Ritova in *Pacific Islands Monthly* 59, 7 (July 1988): 35–36, Ritova concluded that although "Fiji remains politically scarred by her 1987 coups, investor confidence would soon return." He appeared to be correct, and foreign capital is returning. See also Michael P. Hamnett and Michael R. Ogden, "Fiji," country paper commissioned by the U.S. Information Agency (USIA) under contract to the Pacific Islands Association, Honolulu, Hawaii, November 1988; Fiji Government, *Fiji's Ninth Development Plan, 1986–1990* (Suva, Fiji: Central Planning Office, 1985), p. 88; R. S. Milne, *Politics in Ethnically Bipolar States* (Vancouver: University of British Columbia, 1981); and Scarr, *Fiji; World Development Report 1990* p. 243; Greg Fry, "The Region in Review," *Contemporary Pacific* 3, 2 (Fall 1991): 397–399.

36. Hamnett and Ogden, "Fiji"; Fry, "Region in Review"; and Sandra Tarte, "Fiji," *Contemporary Pacific* 3, 2 (Fall 1991): 401–405.

37. See John Roughan, "Solomon Islands," country paper commissioned by USIA under contract to the Pacific Islands Association, Honolulu, Hawaii, November 1988; EIU, *Country Report 1988 Pacific Islands;* "Kari's a First for Women," *Pacific Islands Monthly* 60, 7(July 1989): 15; *World Development Report 1990*, p. 243.

38. See Lindstrom, "Vanuatu," country paper commissioned by USIA under contract to the Pacific Islands Association, Honolulu, Hawaii, November 1988; *World Development Report 1990*, p. 243.

39. See Lindstrom, "Vanuatu"; and David Clark Scott, "Coup Attempt in S. Pacific Nation," *Christian Science Monitor*, December 20, 1988. For details regarding an early coup attempt, see "A Bow-and-Arrow Rebellion," *Newsweek*, June 16, 1980, pp. 42–43; Hamnett, *Donor Assistance*. On the question of drugs, see "Vanuatu: Vila's Big Drug Bust," *Pacific Islands Monthly* 60, 7 (July 1989): 26; and "Crackdown on Drugs," *Pacific Islands Monthly* 60, 7 (July 1989): 48–49. Also see "Sope, Sokomanu Guilty of Mutiny and Sedition," *Pacific Islands Monthly* 60, 3 (March 1989): 10–13.

40. See Garrett, "Bougainville," p. 20; Ron Adams, "Vanuatu," *Contemporary Pacific* 3, 2 (Fall 1991): 418–421.

41. Donald H. Rubinstein, "The Federated States of Micronesia," country paper commissioned by USIA under contract to the Pacific Islands Association, Honolulu, Hawaii, October 1988; Hamnett and Kiste, *Issues and Interest Groups*, pp. 15ff; Neal Spivack, "U.S. to Divest Pacific Trusteeship," *The Interdependent* 12 (January/February 1986): 3; "Palau: New Chapter in Bid for Compact," *Pacific Islands Monthly* 60, 7 (July 1989): 21.

42. "Spendthrift's Lament," *Economist* 318 (January 19, 1991): 33, notes that Nauru, with an annual per capita income estimated at up to $20,000, imports excessive quantities of consumer goods and "junk" food that have contributed to absenteeism and deterioration of physical health. Quote by President Dowiyogo.

43. Rodney C. Hills, "The 1990 Election in Tonga," *Contemporary Pacific* 3, 121 (Fall 1991): 357–376.

44. Michael R. Ogden, "The Paradox of Pacific Development," *Development Policy Research* 7 (December 1989): 361–373, quote on 369; see also B. Knapman, "Aid and the Dependent Development of Pacific Island States," *Journal*

of Pacific History 21 (1986): 149.

45. "The Right to Development," *Pacific Islands Forum* 59, 7 (July 1988): 27; "Palau: Voicing Approval for the Compact," *Pacific Islands Forum* 60, 8 (August 1989): 16; "Power Plant Fall-out Leaves Islands in Debt," *Pacific Islands Monthly* 57,8 (August 1986): 12; "Small-Scale Industry Boost for Kiribati," *Pacific Islands Monthly* 59, 12 (December 1988): 38; "Rethinking Pacific Constitutions," *Pacific Perspectives* (special issue) 13 (c. 1984): 1–108. Drawing on developmental lessons gleaned from high-growth countries on the Pacific Rim, we find a recipe for economic development that combines high investment levels, expanded mass education (especially in the technical fields), Keynesian theory, and fiscal conservatism in international loan practices. See Goy Keng Swee, "Asia After Independence," *Straits Times Weekly* (overseas ed.), November 10, 1990, p. 14.

46. The Caribbean Commission was sponsored by the metropolitan colonial powers (the United States, Britain, France, the Netherlands), much as is the South Pacific Commission. This organization and its auxiliary bodies—the Caribbean Research Council and the West Indian Conferences—withered and terminated before the singular independence movement in the Caribbean. Eric Williams, the first prime minister of Trinidad and Tobago, was a staunch opponent of the commission, perceiving it to be overly paternalistic. See Bernard L. Poole, *The Caribbean Commission* (Columbia: University of South Carolina Press, 1951), esp. pp. 207–255.

47. Mike Richards, "A Successful Summit," *Caribbean Contact,* August 1987, pp. 1, 4, 14. *Communique of the Conference of Heads of Government of the Caribbean Community, June 29–July 2, 1992* (Port-of-Spain, Trinidad, 1992).

48. Quotation in Doreen Hemlock, "Eastern Caribbean Nations Try to Form One New Nation," *Caribbean Business,* July 23, 1987, p. 17; personal interviews with selected OECS leaders, Belize City, Belize, May 26–30, 1987; "OECS Federation: Yes or No?" *Caribbean Contact,* August 1987, pp. 8–9. According to Dominica's prime minister, Eugenia Charles, a successful vote in the referendum on unity would "spur the other OECS islands, and even the larger Caribbean Community (Caricom) members, to consider political unification." See "Ms. Charles Prefers a Unitary State," *Caribbean Contact,* January/February 1991, p. 1; also W. Marvin Will, "Seizing the Moment," in Congressional Research Service for the Joint Economic Committee, *United States Economic Relations with the Caribbean and Latin America* (Washington, D.C.: Government Printing Office, forthcoming 1992).

49. The best potential for political integration in the Caribbean currently appears to be a Windward Island subset of St. Vincent, Grenada, Dominica, and possibly St. Lucia. Island leadership, too often provincial, and U.S. policy will be the final determinants.

50. G. E. Fry, "South Pacific Regionalism," M.A. thesis, Australian National University, Canberra, 1979; Hamnett and Kiste, *Issues and Interest Groups,* pp. 89–90, quote on p. 90. Also see H. E. Maude, "The South Pacific Commission," in *Australia's Neighbors* (Australia: n.p., 1963), p. 3. The comparative data on the Caribbean Commission is from Herbert Corkran, *Mini-Nations and Macro-Cooperation: The Caribbean and the South Pacific* (Washington, D.C.: North American International, 1976), pp. 18–22.

51. The Australian economy was also in decline by 1991, raising questions as to how long such largesse will continue. See Chapter 8; see also *Pacific Islands Monthly* 62, 1 (January 1992): 23.

52. Sam Pearsall, "The Emergence of the South Pacific Regional Environment Programme," University of Hawaii, Honolulu, 1988 (unpublished manuscript); Hamnett and Kiste, *Issues and Interest Groups,* p. 98.

53. Robert C. Kiste, "Economic Security Issues in the South Pacific," *Economics and Pacific Security* (Washington, D.C.: National Defense University Press, 1987), pp. 169–187; Hamnett and Kiste, *Issues and Interest Groups*, pp. 91–99. For the history, analysis, and text of Lomé III, see *The Courier* (special issue), January–February 1985, esp. pp. 28–32. Also see Corkran, *Mini-Nations*, chs. 6–7. Lomé IV is now operational.

54. B. Knapman, "Aid and the Dependent Development of Pacific Island States," *Journal of Pacific History* 21, 3 (1986): 149. Also see the writings of Tongan Epeli Haúofa, including his novel *Kisses in the Niderends* (Auckland, New Zealand: Penguin, 1987), which is discussed in Chapter 8.

55. Andrés Serbin, "The Caricom States and the Group of Three," *Journal of Inter-American Studies and World Affairs* 33, 2 (Summer 1991): 53–89, sees an even greater future role for Venezuela and other intermediate powers, albeit the 1992 coup attempt against President Andrés Pérez suggest there may have to be limits to Venezuelan assistance.

56. Ronald Reagan, speech on February 25, 1986.

57. See Anthony Payne, *The International Crisis in the Caribbean* (Baltimore, Md.: The Johns Hopkins University Press, 1984), especially ch. 3.

58. See U.S. House of Representatives (HR), *Caribbean Basin Economic Recovery Act*, Report 98-266 (Washington, D.C.: U.S. Government Printing Office [GPO], 1983); HR, *Caribbean Basin Initiative*, Hearings, Subcommittee on Trade, Committee on Ways and Means, 92d Congress (Washington, D.C.: GPO, 1982). For details on preliminary meetings, see W. Marvin Will, "Reagan and the Caribbean," Jack W. Hopkins, ed., in *Latin America and Caribbean Contemporary Record*, vol. 1 (New York: Holmes and Meier, 1983), pp. 90–100. For details on legislation, see Emilio Pantojas-Garcia, "The U.S. Caribbean Basin Initiative and the Puerto Rican Experience," *Latin American Perspectives*, Fall 1985, esp. pp. 105–108; also see Payne, *International Crisis*.

59. *Caribbean Contact*, June 1986.

60. Two-Tenths of One Percent," *New Republic* 195 (October 27, 1986): 5–7, quote on p. 5; *Christian Science Monitor*, March 19, 1987, pp. 5, 7, quoting Stephen Hellinger (p. 7), opined that the CBI was not sufficiently "built on the productive structure of the region" and encouraged offshore assembly production "that has few backward linkages into the local economies." Historical Barbados data are given in International Monetary Fund (IMF), *Direction of Trade Statistics Yearbook 1991* (Washington, D.C.: IMF, 1991) p. 98.

61. *Christian Science Monitor*, March 19, 1987, p. 7.

62. Ibid.

63. *Remarks Announcing the Enterprise for the Americas Initiative*, White House press release, June 27, 1990.

64. Michael Manley, in John Hearne, ed., *The Search for Solutions: Selections from the Speeches and Writings of Michael Manley* (Oshowa, Canada: Maple House, 1976), p. 196.

65. Payne, *International Crisis;* Tony Thorndike, *Grenada: Politics, Economics, and Society* (Boulder, Colo.: Lynne Rienner, 1985).

66. For example, Prime Minister Robinson of Trinidad presented a variation of this theme in his "Budget Speech 1987": "The imperatives for 1987 are threefold: (1) We must at all cost escape the debt trap and dependence on the IMF. (2) We must avoid . . . inflation, hyper-inflation, successive devaluations and institutionalised misery. (3) We must resist the temptation to spend more than we earn; we must . . . control imports and . . . the balance of payments." Trinidad went on to negotiate an IMF deal and borrow heavily from abroad. For some troubling and prescient projections, see Regino Diaz, "The Unpayable Debt," in Susan Jonas and Nancy Stein, eds., *Democracy in Latin America* (New York: Bergin and

Garvey, 1990), pp. 117–143.

67. Steve C. Ropp, "Cuba and Panama: Signaling One Way, Going Another," in Barry B. Levine, ed., *The New Cuban Presence in the Caribbean* (Boulder, Colo.: Westview, 1987), pp. 59–73. Ironically, portraits and statues of Torrijos and even his burial ashes disappeared after the U.S. intervention.

68. L. R. Vasey and Robert L. Pfaltzgraff, Jr., "U.S. Policy Toward the South Pacific," in Dorrance et al., *South Pacific*, p. 96.

69. "France Reconquers the Pacific," *Economist* 315 (May 19, 1990): 33.

70. Andrew Axline, "Lessons for the Caribbean from Small States in Other Regions," in Anthony T. Bryan, Edward Green, and Timothy Shaw, eds., *Peace, Development, and Security in the Caribbean* (New York: St. Martin's, 1990), pp. 306–319, provides excellent coverage of the role of intermediate or middle powers in counterbalancing the United States. For a discussion of economic cooperation and fears of Australian cutbacks, see *Pacific Islands Monthly* 62, 1 (January 1992): 21.

71. George L. Reid, *The Impact of Very Small Size on the International Behavior of Microstates* (Beverly Hills, Calif.: Sage, 1974), quote on pp. 30–31.

72. Quoted from *Caribbean Contact*, May 1987, p. 1; also see Yussuff Haniff, "Antigua and Barbuda," ibid, pp. 8–9; Mark Hamlet, "Grenada: Period of Uncertainty," ibid, pp. 1, 12. "Heavy manners" is a Caribbean term for stress or strain.

73. Aaron Segal, "The Caribbean Exodus in Global Context," in Barry B. Levine, ed., *The Caribbean Exodus* (New York: Praeger, 1987), pp. 44–64.

74. Robert A. Pastor, "Migration and Development: Implications and Recommendations for Policy," *Studies in Comparative International Development* 24 (Winter 1989–1990): 46–64. Pastor concludes that emigration costs the sending countries and often impedes development. And even more discouraging, in the short term, rapid development tends to exacerbate the pressures of migration.

8
Security Problems of the Newer Caribbean and Pacific States

W. Marvin Will

As with the proverbial apples-and-oranges analogy, there are obvious differences between the communities of newer states in the Caribbean Basin and the Pacific Basin: in geographic size and location; in natural resources; in racial-ethnic composition; and in patterns of colonization. There are also recognizable similarities, and these are greater in number and importance than are the interregional differences. Each Basin, for example, has nearly equal numbers of small, newly independent states that are, for the most part, relatively open political democracies; the total population among states that gained independence in the two decades after 1962 is remarkably similar in each region (fewer than 6 million) and includes both very small, poor LDCs—or SICs, smaller island countries—and larger states with greater developmental potential. In addition, each Basin faces many similar tasks in coping with regionalism, security concerns, and economic development; these include the problems of contending with great distances, the pros and considerable cons of tourism, the appropriate technological needs of small insular societies, shared fishing and agricultural concerns, and the strategies and problems of markets and trade that are intensified by increasing trade and investment competition from an expanding Europe.

In the previous chapter, the common economic concerns of the Caribbean and Pacific small states and the strategies adopted in the pursuit of economic security were addressed in detail. In this chapter, the focus is on noneconomic security issues within two basic themes: First, a major hypothesis of the chapter is that the security of the small states of both the Caribbean and the Pacific has been intimately linked to the security concerns of external powers; moreover, in the case of the United States—and also Europe to some degree—post-1970s policy toward the newer states of these two regions has been formulated and implemented without sufficient sensitivity to the needs of these small countries. Second, the security of Caribbean and Pacific small states is multifaceted in nature, involving a number of military, political, and social issues, aside from the economic issues already discussed in Chapter 7.

Security Interests and Issues

The Problem of Misperceptions

At the turn of the century, U.S. essayist O. Henry humorously illustrated an important theme apropos both to this chapter and to this book: the need for improved cross-cultural understanding between the United States and its adjacent geopolitical basins of the Caribbean and the Pacific, and between the two basins as well, if serious misperceptions are to be averted. In the O. Henry essay, an impoverished Caribbean native seeking medical assistance for his very infirm spouse approaches a white North American doctor. Finding the native's indigenous dialect incomprehensible, the doctor misperceives not only the malady but also who is ill and proceeds to prescribe his stock, premixed "cure-all." To the accompaniment of many forceful gestures about the medication schedule, the doctor concludes by holding up his watch and making a circling motion with first one, then two extended fingers. "Take one every two hours!" he shouted—"two!" The native sadly handed his cherished silver watch to the doctor and mumbled in a barely discernible dialect that he would procure a second watch for the doctor as soon as possible.[1]

U.S. and European policy toward the newer states in both the Caribbean and the Pacific Basins, especially since the late 1970s, has been prepared and administered in the same fashion as was the doctor's premixed elixir: after misperceiving the real "health-maintaining" development needs of these two regions and without comprehending that genuine long-term interests of the United States are congruent with such overall development. Instead, there appears to have been a pattern of focusing too much attention on narrow security-oriented "medication," administered with a view to the East-West conflict. It is my contention in this chapter that there is much the United States and the European powers can learn from the emerging intermediate powers of the two regions. Perhaps more important, both small and large states of the Caribbean and the Pacific Basins can benefit from a better understanding of cross-Basin similarities, differences, and policy concerns.

Objects of Strategic Interest

For centuries, the small territories of both the Caribbean and Pacific regions have possessed considerable strategic and even economic importance to metropolitan powers. The Caribbean was a jumping-off point for Third

World colonization, and its slave-driven plantations fueled much of the industrial revolution. Its sea lanes, strategically important to Washington throughout the twentieth century, took on added significance when a spate of Marxist revolutions swept the area beginning in 1979. The insular Pacific territories, though not widely colonized as early as the Caribbean, have served as vital strategic posts for overseas empires since the 1521 voyage of Magellan. Both Basins, but especially the Pacific, also played vital roles in World War II.

Regional impact of World War II. Although, in comparison to the Pacific, the Caribbean region had only peripheral involvement in World War II, units from the islands served with the British against the Axis powers. Moreover, the United States leased land from Britain to construct military bases in a number of countries from the Bahamas in the north to Guyana in the south. Installations remain today in Antigua, the Bahamas, and Bermuda.[2]

The Pacific islanders were more directly impacted by World War II.[3] New Guineans saw their state alternate between Australian and Japanese rule during the war years; ethnic divisions that are still existent between Indians and natives in Fiji were intensified as a result of differing views of patriotism; many areas suffered extraordinary losses: for example, in the Solomon Islands and Micronesia, up to ten in every hundred people sacrificed their lives in the battles for their territories; and throughout the region, the remains of wartime battles continue to clutter the landscape. On a positive note, many of the colonized, such as the traditional warriors from New Guinea, distinguished themselves and were highly praised for their role as modern soldiers, and according to a Samoan author, the Pacific islanders were often treated as equals for the first time in their contact with the West. The resulting sense of equality paid dividends just a few decades later when the young independent nations of the Pacific emerged as small but vibrant—and at times boisterous—democracies.[4]

The war in the Pacific not only gave U.S. citizens and Pacific islanders startling headlines and disparate shared memories—in contrast to the Caribbean, where the citizenry was less involved militarily—but it also brought the United States and other metropolitan actors additional Pacific colonies, islands acquired from Japan as U.N. trust territories. This new role of trustee was instrumental in preventing the return of the United States to its isolationist stance that characterized the prewar years. But there was a downside—and often intragovernmental disagreement as well. In one instance, the U.S. Navy sought to annex Micronesia outright as a spoil of war, agreeing to a U.N. trusteeship only when President Harry Truman, who was pressuring the British and French to decolonize, expressed sensitivity to potential charges of inconsistency. As discussed later, two intermediate metropolitan actors, Australia and New Zealand, would assist—and sometimes lead—the move for increased decolonization. Increased roles were also played by the former USSR, by revolution-impacted China, and by an emergent Japan, all in pursuit of security, prestige, and markets.

The postwar period. Since the 1960s, decolonization has significantly impacted the Caribbean and the Pacific, and these two regions now contribute to the world its largest groupings of small states and its largest pools of Third World democracies. As was noted in the last chapter, the first Pacific and Caribbean states to gain their independence were Western Samoa, Jamaica, and Trinidad and Tobago, all in 1962. Even the Pacific trust territories have moved toward independence, including the Federated States of Micronesia (FSM), the Commonwealth of the Northern Mariana Islands, the Marshall Islands, and, on a more wavering path, the Republic of Palau. The "free-association" status of the FSM and Palau has been a source of confusion,[5] as has the "commonwealth" status chosen by the Northern Marianas.[6] In addition, American Samoa, another trust "assignment," remains a "U.S. unorganized unincorporated territory," and Guam, a former Spanish colony taken by the United States in 1898, is officially an "organized unincorporated territory" seeking to become a Puerto Rico–like commonwealth or an independent state.

From the late 1970s through the 1980s, both the Caribbean and Pacific were objects of an ongoing struggle for East-West strategic leverage. With the breakup of the USSR and the Eastern bloc, this competition has diminished, but is not expected to disappear completely. Even with a potential "new world order," Russia will continue to have major trade and security interests in the Pacific, and the United States may well continue to consider both the Caribbean and Pacific as "its lake," thereby contributing to persisting rivalry.[7] Still, the leverage accruing to small, strategically positioned islands is likely to be much diminished in the post–Cold War period.

Decades of neglect by the great powers have alternated with periods of visibility and prominence for both insular groups, and frequent bouts of economic deprivation have been commonplace in the face of rapid technological change. As countries look ahead to the twenty-first century, each Basin not only needs to be understood better by the metropolitan actors, but the small states of the two regions also need to understand better both the metropole and each other in order to address their shared problems, goals, and strategies.

The historically greater U.S. intervention in and paternalism toward the Caribbean Basin, for example, plus greater U.S. emphasis on potentially divisive unilateral policies in the Caribbean during the 1980s (as opposed to a more flexible policy in the 1970s), represent a point of reference for the Pacific. Before Caribbean states officially opt for a nuclear-free policy (as did at least one country during the 1980s), greater cognizance of the extreme difficulties encountered by Pacific Basin states engaged in such activity would benefit their effort. Likewise, the important role played by intermediate (or middle) powers in the Pacific could be a beneficial model for both middle and major powers functioning in the Caribbean.

Security Issues in the 1990s

The security problems of the Caribbean and Pacific extend, of course, beyond the role of external powers. For the most part, the newer states are relatively open political democracies, but each region faces internal social, racial-ethnic, economic, and political threats to democracy. Moreover, problems of smuggling, drug trafficking, and environmental degradation are primary concerns to both sets of countries. In the economic arena, discussed in the last chapter, regional cooperation has played a major role in countering economic difficulties. In the sociopolitical arena, the small states of both regions have begun to address the need to establish and maintain security forces that expeditiously and economically control smuggling, drug trafficking, and terrorist acts—and yet most important, do not pose a direct threat to their political democracies. (In this regard, see Chapter 6 for a discussion of the role of the Regional Security System in the eastern Caribbean.) Furthermore, these states have begun to work together on environmental issues that have a unique impact on island territories.

The security commonalities between the Caribbean and the Pacific have already been the subject of a major (British) Commonwealth study on the security and vulnerability of small states.[8] As contact between the two regions expands, common interests—economic, social, political, and military—will become more apparent and are likely to lead to greater cooperation, especially within the framework of the United Nations and other organizations.

Power, Democracy, and National Security

Size, Power, and Weakness

Potential national power—the ability to induce other actors to perform in an involuntary manner—traditionally has been associated with geographical and population size and a significant level of raw-material resources. By these criteria, the small-state Caribbean and Pacific Basins are extremely weak, individually and collectively, despite their strategic locations astride major trade and transit routes. But size and traditional power conceptualizations may not be the alpha and omega of development or the trading games of the twenty-first century: Indeed, they may be inimical to national democratization and communication. According to Richard Rosecrance, access to and use of appropriate technology and the ability to exploit international markets represent alternative levers for the modern state in an increasingly "globalist" and trade-oriented reality.[9]

For today's small states, factors of highest importance are the sociopolitical and socioeconomic quality of society, the national level of organization and leadership, the degree of institutional development and legitimacy of governance, national security, and the quality of domestic services such as education and health. In both Basins, insular status appears to offer protection from outside threats, according to security specialist Richard Herr—although such status also appears to present a vulnerability to subversion and to outside intervention, especially by drug cartels.[10] Open political systems are also the rule in both Basins.

The Democratic Process

Advocates for each Basin routinely classify their area as "the Third World region where democracy is the strongest." And indeed, nearly all of the newly independent Caribbean and Pacific nations may be categorized as plural democracies. Exceptions include the Kingdom of Tonga, which remains a traditional monarchy; Suriname in the early 1990s has alternated between periods of civilian and military rule; and Fiji, in accordance with the constitution drafted after its two 1987 coups, limits Fijians of Indian ancestry to only twenty-seven of seventy parliamentary seats and ten of thirty-four senate seats.[11] Coups and insurrections are rare, however, and it is interesting to note that almost all of the exceptions to democratic openness among these states are the ex-colonies in which indentured foreign workers were imposed in large numbers on an existent population of natives and former slaves, the result being to create the potential for societal cleavages. To paraphrase Eric Williams, prime minister of Trinidad and Tobago at the time of independence in 1962, the country had become a sovereign state but was not yet a nation because of the diversity of race, class, and religion.[12] This challenge continues to frustrate nation building from Guyana, Suriname, and Trinidad to Fiji. In the nation-building process, it must be noted, each colony reproduced variations of the relatively advanced political and economic systems of its respective colonizers. The only exports the Europeans had left to send to their colonies when decolonization was at hand, in the words of Ronald Robinson, were their constitutions.[13]

Indeed, nearly all the newer states of both the Pacific and Caribbean possess fairly open democracies with consistent patterns of government by law and independent judiciaries, and most possess competitive parties that recruit potential leaders and conduct regular elections. Both regions have elections to select heads of government, and most states have experienced not only regime change via the ballot but alternating governing parties as well. Indeed, such partisan rotation has become routine in several small countries. In Jamaica, for example, governing parties have alternated every two terms since the 1930s.

In the independent Pacific, Papua New Guinea (PNG) has experienced perhaps too much political change (often by way of parliamentary no-confidence votes), including an attempted separatist move by Bougainville. Coups in Fiji in 1987 and short-lived rebellions in Vanuatu in conjunction with its independence in 1980 and again in 1986 have broken the orderly pattern in these insular states. Among the twelve independent Caribbean states, only Grenada and Suriname have experienced extraconstitutional governmental change, and Dominica and Trinidad and Tobago have experienced two coup attempts.

All the newer states in the Caribbean and Pacific in the early 1990s have elected leadership, and the vast majority have open political systems. Such openness can be a great source of political legitimacy in both regions, but it also contributes to vulnerability, particularly (1) when the party system overlaps ethnic tensions instead of crosscutting them, as in Fiji, PNG, Guyana, Trinidad, and Suriname; (2) when the British-style two-party system is perceived to be at variance with traditional customs, as in the Kingdom of Tonga; or (3) when there are demands for a so-called "people's democracy," as in Grenada during the 1970s.[14] We turn now to some specific issues of national security.

The Caribbean and National Security

In formulating security goals, small states must remain cognizant of great limits and great vulnerability, whereas large states may appear oblivious to such factors. Most English-speaking Caribbean states have experienced both real and perceived threats to national security since the 1970s involving (1) subnational plotting, such as attempted coups in Trinidad and Tobago in 1970 and 1990, in Barbados in 1976, and in Dominica twice in the late 1970s; attempts by mercenaries to overthrow the Barbadian and Dominican governments in the late 1970s and early 1980s; reported military and opposition plotting in Jamaica between 1979 and 1981; secessionist activity in St. Vincent and Antigua in 1979; and a successful coup in Grenada in 1979 and subsequent antigovernment activity up to the U.S. intervention in 1983; and (2) external "excursions," such as Cuba's attack on Bahamian ships and territory in 1980; Venezuela's unresolved historic claim to two-thirds of the state of Guyana; an unsettled border between Guyana and Suriname; and Guatemala's total claim to Belize, a claim that has been substantially neutralized as a result of diplomatic pressures, including actions by Mexico and Venezuela, followed by direct negotiations between Guatemala and Belize.

The Caribbean subregion faces yet a third and more menacing threat to national security: a sea literally awash with drug and gun runners, mobsters, and terrorists—and even, as in the case of Dominica in April 1981, mercenaries (in this case, U.S.-based) planning to overthrow legitimately elected governments. Barbadian sovereignty was severely compromised when a Cubana DC-8 turboprop was destroyed in midair by anti-Castro terrorists as it departed Barbados on October 6, 1976, killing all seventy-eight passengers and crew members on board. In none of these activities has the United States, the hemispheric superpower, demonstrated an enviable track record for militarily protecting the region, just as many islanders recall the United States could not fully protect them from Axis submarines in World War II. Nor has the United States any more effectively countered drug trafficking in the region during the 1990s than it intercepted rum-running from Bahamaian cays a half century earlier.

With exceptions such as Guyana, militarization of the Anglophone states in the Caribbean, a particular concern in the 1970s and 1980s, was modest and balanced positively by socioeconomic expenditures during the pre-Reagan/Bush era. Cuba offers a comparison: After its 1959 revolution, Cuba showcased its efforts in education, especially at the elementary and middle levels. Yet in the mid-1970s, Cuba spent U.S.$114 per capita on the military as contrasted with $162 on education. The ratio for Barbados, on the other hand, was only $36 for military, $223 for education (14:228 in 1978); for Trinidad 14:170; and for Jamaica 9:76 (9:113 in 1978). Whereas Cuba has maintained in excess of 200,000 soldiers since 1977 and Castro, in the words of one-time Castro apologist Herbert Matthews, has been something of a Caribbean Napoleon, Barbados, Trinidad, and Jamaica have maintained forces of only 1,000–2,000. Cuba spent 9 percent of its GDP on the military; the bulk of the English-speaking Caribbean historically disbursed less than 2 percent. In the 1980s, in fact, most Anglophone states disbursed less than 1 percent—only Guyana, Trinidad, and Jamaica exceeded the 2 percent level, and this reflects an increase over the late 1970s. The increases in military expenditures resulted partially from Washington-induced militarization during the Reagan administration, especially after 1982 when U.S. funding was substantially responsible for development of the Regional Security System (RSS) in the eastern Caribbean. As noted, much impetus for the increases also resulted from drug/gangster activity and Cuban adventurism in the region during the 1970s and 1980s.[15] With the end of the Cold War in the 1990s, notwithstanding increased Caribbean attention to the narcotics issue, military expenditures are expected to decline as economic difficulties absorb increasingly greater energies. This scenario applies even to Cuba, where continuing U.S.-Cuban antagonisms are no match for the greater security issue of economic viability.

In sum, if small states are permitted to determine their own military budgets, appropriate militarization can be expected in the Caribbean (and also in the Pacific). Gargantuan military budgets in these states would threaten the very development process that provides the principal antidote to insurrection—and could threaten civilian institutions as well. To quote Vaughan Lewis, general secretary of the OECS:

> The reinforcement of local security systems leads to an upsetting of the balance between the various socio-political sectors . . . suggest[ing] to the military a sense of their own particular status as the only virtuous sector—as the guardians of the system. . . . This sets the basis for the coup and counter-coup syndrome.[16]

Long ago the philosopher Thomas Hobbes noted that "clubs are trump" when no other countervailing force is present.[17] And it matters little whether the guardians of the dynasties are called soldiers or police, Gordon Lewis reminds us, for to accept the myth that the English-speaking Caribbean will never emulate the man-on-horseback models so often found in Hispanic America (as well as Haiti and, more recently, Suriname) is but "charming conceit!"[18]

The Pacific and National Security

Several of the trust territories held by the United States and, in particular, the several remaining French colonies in the Pacific have been sites for weapons testing, military maneuvers, and other general security interests. Such activity, especially by France, has been perceived as severely damaging to health, ecology, and international peace and has led to escalating hostilities in French Polynesia and a growing antinuclear policy throughout the region: from Palau to the Solomon Islands to Papua New Guinea to New Zealand. In the mid-1980s, New Zealand largely forfeited its membership in ANZUS (a pact among Australia, New Zealand, and the United States) in the face of Washington's paranoia regarding its antinuclear policy and also sustained the indignity of insults and threatened sanctions from the French after the sinking of a visiting ship, Greenpeace's *Rainbow Warrior,* by French special forces in Auckland harbor in 1985.[19] By the early 1990s, ten nations, including the People's Republic of China and Russia, had signed a nuclear-free pact for the south Pacific. Considerable effort has been made to mollify U.S. objections to the pact but to no avail.

There were still 167 U.S. military bases scattered throughout the north Pacific and along the Asian coast in the 1980s. In the 1990s, the damaged Clark Air Force base in the Philippines and Subic Bay have been closed. The uncertainty of the bases in the Philippines induced the United States to be inordinately protective of its military holdings in its small Pacific territories. Such bases are perceived as a mixed blessing by the islanders—a plus economically but a negative from the perspective of insular sovereignty compromised on the grounds of alleged metropolitan security interests, as is frequently the case in the Pacific region.

The increased U.S. attention to the Pacific Basin that occurred after 1978 and 1979[20] was prompted largely by strategic interests and perceived Soviet penetration of the region, particularly a fishing pact negotiated between impoverished Kiribati and the (former) USSR. Such concerns triggered U.S.

attempts to build new relationships in the region, as exemplified by a call from Richard Holbrooke, assistant secretary for East Asian and Pacific Affairs, for the creation of an Office of Pacific Affairs in the U.S. Department of State[21] and the upgrading of diplomatic status with Fiji and Papua New Guinea (PNG). An annual Pacific symposium at the National Defense University in Washington, D.C., also has been initiated.[22]

Many leaders in the Pacific Basin would not have agreed that there was a real security problem in the Pacific before the 1980s. There was no perceptible international drug trafficking, and the U.S.-predicted domino theory had not materialized on the Pacific–Southeast Asian littoral. But perceptions modified, and change for the worse came to the region after two coups that toppled civilian governments in Fiji in 1987, largely as a result of lost political power by native Fijians to the emerging Indian majority. Fiji's political future has remained clouded despite the promulgation of a new constitution. But probably more serious for regional security is the near-war status in French Caledonia and the serious border conflicts and secession problems in PNG.

Papua New Guinea and Indonesia share the lone land frontier among the new states in the Pacific Basin. This border, extending 760 kilometers over poorly marked and extremely rugged terrain, has been—and will probably remain—a long-simmering source of friction. The high degree of sensitivity each government attaches to the dispute makes this a serious flash point, according to Australian political scientist F. A. Mediansky. Indonesia must prove its ability to hold intact its far-flung state; much weaker Papua New Guinea must muster special tenacity to maintain its sovereignty. Following much the same pattern as Belize and Guyana in the Caribbean, the earlier Michael Somare government of PNG attempted to internationalize the dispute by interjecting the issue at numerous multilateral forums, including the United Nations.[23]

The Caledonian independence movement and the Legionnaire-led French resistance, fresh from unlearned lessons in Algeria and Vietnam, represent another serious security concern and test of will in the Pacific. The Caledonians are not (yet) in the league that could handle Dien Bien Phu (Vietnam) or the Battle of Algiers, but the Front de Liberation National Kanak et Socialiste (FLNKS) is serious, and it appears the struggle will be lengthy despite a temporary moratorium on independence negotiated in 1988. This, potentially, is the Pacific region's most destabilizing crisis, one that could bring the area into the fray because the Kanaks have strong support from PNG, the Solomons, and Vanuatu.

Militarism is less intrusive among the new states of the Pacfic than of the Caribbean. Only four states in the Pacific maintain defense forces: Fiji (5,000), NG (3,000), Tonga (200), and Vanuatu (300). Correspondingly, military budgets are low, with Australian aid monies supporting most of this activity, except in postcoup Fiji. Continued conflict, plus the attraction and involvement of outside participants, could exacerbate the disputes and arms buildups in ways similar to what has been noted regarding the Caribbean. Despite apprehension among Pacific policy officials, this has not occurred.[24]

The New Environmental Threat to the Caribbean and Pacific

The island states of both the Caribbean and Pacific consider the environmental threat to be perhaps the greatest survival issue of the 1990s. Their prime concern is global warming: Emissions of carbon dioxide and other greenhouse gases have contributed to a rise in the ocean's level estimated at 4 to 5 inches in the last century. Already tourist beaches are shrinking, and flooding is becoming a major problem. Warmer climates will also intensify tropical weather patterns and adversely affect coral reefs and fishing grounds. As Vanuatu's U.N. representative has noted: "It's a question of survival, it's that simple. At the very least, sea level rises of a foot or so could wipe out island ecosystems. At worst, whole islands could disappear under water."[25]

Aside from concern about the rise in the ocean's level, the island nations of the Caribbean and Pacific worry about the possible fallout to the tourist industry—a major provider of foreign exchange for many of them—stemming from the depletion of the ozone layer and consequent public concern about exposure to high levels of unfiltered solar energy. This is already providing an impetus for citizen and government action in the south Pacific. Environmental concerns are also beginning to affect domestic politics: For example, the civil war in Papua New Guinea, according to John Connell, has been fueled by environmental problems from the Bougainville gold and copper mines that escalated into a secession movement.[26]

In preparation for the June 1992 U.N. Conference on Environment and Development in Brazil, the Caribbean and Pacific small states formed the Alliance for Small Island States through which they have voiced their concerns at the United Nations. The group's main focus has been to persuade the industrial and industrializing countries to reduce harmful emissions. For them, the environmental struggle is viewed as a cause for which a portion of the so-called peace dividend must be expended.[27] Their efforts have proved only partially successful.

Major and Intermediate Powers: Differing Interests and (Mis)Perceptions

Both Caribbean and Pacific governments have been concerned that the United States, a major player in both regions, is inordinately insensitive to the long-term real security needs of the subregion. For them, the United States has historically placed too much emphasis on militarism at the expense of economic and social issues. Although this is changing in the post–Cold War era, there is a new concern that U.S. financial largesse will be directed elsewhere, away from the traditional recipients.

Although any kind of attention may have advantages over policy neglect, there are significant concerns that the developmental needs of much of the insular Caribbean and Pacific are being ignored in the name of security. Prime minister Kennedy Simmonds of St. Kitts/Nevis feels that real long-term security "can't be won at all with the force of arms,"[28] and Trinidadian Anthony Maingot agrees, especially in light of the historic suspicion of militarism and of armies among West Indians. Real security requires that priority be given to the promotion of economic development, with all that portends for programs in education and health.[29] Sir Peter Kenilorea, then foreign minister of the Solomon Islands, reminded the Washington establishment in 1988 that real security requires far more than mere militarism and military solutions. National integration, societal well-being, and economic prosperity are also factors in overall long-term national security, he stressed.[30]

Australia, the major intermediate power in the south Pacific, whose security interests are directly tied to its emerging Pacific neighbors, basically agrees with Sir Peter. This faithful ally of the United States, demonstrating some continuity with the legacy of Herbert Vere Evatt[31] (the underdog champion and anticolonialist attorney general and minister of external affairs in Australia during the post–World War II period), has not only resisted the temptation to annex or otherwise incorporate the former trust territories, but officially states, in terms of its security interests in the region, that "where aspirations can be assisted and economic development supported, the ensuing political stability is an important strategic asset."[32] Such considerations are particularly relevant to the south Pacific. Even if militarism and military solutions were found to produce a satisfactory end result, it would not be cost-effective for Australia or New Zealand to give primary security emphasis to such a course in view of their relatively modest population and resource base. Partly for this reason, "Australia seeks to promote its political/security interests through persuasion—through political and diplomatic exchanges in association with our aid, trade, defence co-operation and other programs designed to promote economic development as well as confidence in Australia as a concerned, reliable partner."[33] In stating it another way, Pacific islander Michael Ogden suggests that long-term development assistance is "virtually the price [Australia and New Zealand] are prepared to pay in order to ensure that the . . . [south Pacific islands] remain friendly and stable, as well as to prevent 'slums' developing in their own 'backyard.'"[34]

Perhaps the United States—and Japan, China, and Russia—could glean a positive lesson from these regional intermediate powers. For the United States, a more sensitive policy toward the emerging Pacific states would signal a return to the positive policy path it pursued during the bipartisan period of the Truman presidency, when "the Australians and New Zealanders helped ultimately to tilt the balance of interpretation of trusteeship more toward the view adopted by the State Department in Washington."[35] These two relatively large Commonwealth countries (Australia and New Zealand) also treated the islanders with greater respect than accorded them by France and, to a lesser extent, Britain.

It is a rare national leader who does not seek prestige and dignity for his or her nation and, certainly, the avoidance of national and personal humiliation. "With dignity," the president of one Basin country has stated, "we can accomplish many things; without it nothing."[36] Given the legacy of racial-ethnic division and dependency in the former Caribbean and Pacific colonies, it is understandable that their leaders are especially sensitive to affronts to their collective or individual dignity, which many feel has occurred too frequently, both directly and indirectly.

The United States, of course, has its own national interest agenda: Not always will U.S. policy align cooperatively with the interests and perceptions of its small neighbors in the Caribbean and Pacific Basins, just as there are differences between Washington and its other allies, including relatively small states in areas such as Europe and the Middle East. This divergence is why nations pursue diplomacy, both bilateral and multilateral, and why the Foreign Service Institute of the U.S. Department of State concludes in its negotiating manual that effective influence of fellow states requires the projection of (1) clear and legitimate U.S. objectives; (2) cognizance of the history and cultural sensitivities of those to be influenced; and (3) care to avoid or at least reduce real or perceived affronts to dignity.[37]

And yet U.S. policy too often has represented no clear vision—or even demonstrated consistency between the executive and legislative branches or between political parties—while being singularly neglectful of regional history and unnecessarily disrespectful of local dignity. William Fulbright, former chair of the Senate Committee on Foreign Relations, warned in his *Arrogance of Power* that the United States too often appears to pursue this pattern as it implements short-term goals at the expense of long-term interests and the sensitivities of small nations. Such arrogance and ethnocentrism also contribute to misperceived communications and misaligned policies.

Still, past associations and cultural transfers spawned a residue of goodwill toward the United States and other metropolitan powers in much of the Pacific, but this goodwill began to wear thin in the wake of perceived inordinate militarization during the 1980s, including the testing and transport of nuclear weapons. Public support for the United States and France has been negatively impacted by their steadfast refusal to endorse the region's nuclear-free treaty, and the United States receives particularly negative reactions for its continuing support of French nuclear testing in the region. In the past, there has also been distaste within the region for the sometimes onerous strings attached to the trust territories and the refusals to discuss full decolonization, particularly by the United States and (still continuing) France. In response to such metropolitan activity, there has been a thrust among the small Pacific states toward a more closely knit society that focuses on common regional problems.[38]

For the Caribbean, with its greater dependence on the United States, the "heavy hand" of the United States has been strongly felt, with U.S. assistance openly linked to the region's support for U.S. policy and strategies. One notable case of U.S. disregard for local sentiment was the attempt by the Reagan administration to manipulate the Caribbean Development Bank (CDB). (This regional bank includes all sixteen former British colonies in the subregion; Anguilla, Venezuela, Colombia, and Mexico as "other regional" members; and Canada, France, the United Kingdom, Italy, and Germany as nonregional members.) A representative of the U.S. Agency for International Development (USAID), in testimony to Congress in 1980, praised the CDB as a most effective and desirable institution for the promotion of stable Caribbean governments that, in turn, provides a "basis for cooperative U.S.-Caribbean relations."[39] Giving substance to such words, the Carter administration in 1979 and 1980 contributed 32 percent of the total resources of the institution. By 1986 and 1987, however, the Reagan administation had reduced U.S. contributions to the CDB nearly 10 percent—to just 22.5 percent of CDB income, more than 4 percent beneath the contribution level of the French and the British.[40]

Although the reduced U.S. financial support presented a serious obstacle, the most reverberating impact of U.S. policy on the CDB occurred in 1981 in conjunction with Washington's attempts to destabilize the Grenadian revolution. The Reagan administration stipulated then that any U.S. financial grant to the CDB was conditional on the institution's exclusion of educational loans to Grenada. The foreign ministers of Caricom collectively protested this action as an effort "to subvert Caribbean regional institutions."[41] Even Tom Adams, the conservative prime minister of Barbados who was probably the greatest foe of the Bishop regime among Caricom leaders, was so outraged that he instructed the Barbadian representative to the CDB board of directors to organize opposition to acceptance of the conditional grant. Karl Hudson-Phillips, then leader of the conservative National Organization for Reconstruction (ONR) in Trinidad, wondered aloud why the United States would attempt to "destroy our institutions by forcing a violation of the [CDB] constitution."[42] The conditional U.S. grant was rejected unanimously, but U.S. efforts to isolate the Grenada regime continued to 1983 when political factionalization in Grenada facilitated U.S. military intervention.[43]

Caribbean states have suffered similar affronts from the United States at the more personal diplomatic level. Cultural slights and outright discourtesies were visited on the Caribbean subregion by Ambassador Milan Bish, a Reagan appointee to the then Eastern Caribbean embassy in Barbados; his cultural inattentiveness and personal insults became legend. A different kind of insensitivity was reflected in a speech presented in Guyana by the U.S. ambassador after Guyana began to infuse market capitalism into its economy in 1986. In this speech, the ambassador underscored not once, but twice, the economically beleaguered Desmond Hoyte administration's consistent plea for PL-48—wheat, wheat the United States had been withholding from Guyana for five years because of dissatisfaction with its policy. The ambassador made a point of stressing that the United States was only approving shipment of the much-needed grain because the Guyanese government was consenting to welcome U.S. private investment and to pursue a "balanced" foreign policy. Guyanese could not help but question the quality of such diplomacy.[44]

Similar problems are encountered by the Pacific states in requesting aid from the metropole, according to the speeches of former Prime minister Peter Kenilorea of the Solomon Islands,[45] and are noted also in the pleas of South Pacific Forum leaders opposing U.S. attempts to parlay the Johnston toll into a depository for garbage, nerve gas, and chemical waste.[46] The writings of Tongan development specialist Epeli Haúofa capture such island frustrations in a fictional format. In a recent work, he describes a request for medical assistance made beseechingly by a small-island politician from the New Zealand high commissioner "because our hospitals are no good."[47] In this account, cross-cultural misperceptions by officials of both the metropole and the small islands lead to major misunderstandings about the patient's illness (the thrust is reminiscent of the O. Henry tale discussed earlier), and these cause needless delay before the request is eventually identified and resolved with an appropriate mix of traditional and modern technology funded by a mix of assistance from the intermediate powers and the metropole. Perhaps it is such misperceptions which Prime minister Eugenia Charles of Dominica made reference in her often-cited comment that "poor countries . . . must learn to beg carefully," a remark that hints at the metropolitan insensitivity against which former Senator William Fulbright warned.

Nonetheless, it is inaccurate to suggest that a large number of U.S. diplomats project insensitivity or that little historical affinity extends toward the United States from the Caribbean and Pacific regions. Indeed, the United States remains something of a shining light on a very visible hill to the peoples of these regions, thanks in part to their three-century colonial tie to close U.S. allies, to the fact that there have been no long-term and delegitimizing U.S. military occupations (such as regularly occurred in Hispanic parts of the Caribbean Basin), and to the positive role played by the United States during World War II, especially in the Pacific. Because of this reservoir of goodwill, eastern Caribbean leaders could openly invite U.S. forces to enforce militarily a dubiously legal treaty in neighboring Grenada and still receive applause on their return home, a reaction unlikely to occur in most areas of Hispanic America. Much the same can be said of the new states of the south Pacific, where the United States maintains a generally positive image despite negatives relating to its weapons testing and reluctant decolonization.

Being small neighbors of the United States and other metropolitan powers, however, has meant for these states being lavishly embraced in one historical moment and rejected or taken for granted in the next—a legacy dating to the colonial era in both basins. The U.S. administrations of Presidents Reagan and Bush cannot be accused of neglecting either basin; however, it is not the level of attention that is at issue, writes Robert Pastor, a former member of the National Security Council, but rather the consistency and sensitivity of such attention.[48] How the strong relate to the weak is not only a moral issue but also an issue that evinces the essence of leadership.

Conclusion: Comparisons and Suggestions

Conspiciously astride vital sea lanes and representing the two largest communities of Third World democratic governments, the Caribbean and Pacific small states have much to learn from each other, not the least of which is how many similarities they share, including their great vulnerability. Although there are major differences between the two regions as well, including variations in political and economic development, there are surprising similarities, such as common patterns of settlement, governance, developmental options, and the manner in which Washington and other metropolitan centers relate to these adjacent basins.

Each region shares with the United States an adherence to a high level of democratic pluralism; modernizing but conservative values, including substantial support for the free-market system; a long mutual friendship, with increasing familial links; cultural and economic ties; and relative proximity—although the Pacific Basin does not have front-yard proximity to the United States as does the Caribbean. On the one hand, the United States has had a longer track record of relations in and with the Caribbean, and thus the Pacific Basin actors can learn much from observing their Caribbean counterparts. On the other hand, the Pacific nations have a better track record in dealing with intermediate powers (e.g., Australia and New Zealand), and thus can serve as a model for the Caribbean in its relations with regional powers such as Canada, Venezuela, Mexico, and Colombia.

Indeed, Caribbean and Pacific nations can work together to urge the United States and relevant European powers to move in the direction of the positive leadership demonstrated by the aid policies of intermediate powers Australia and New Zealand in the Pacific Basin, as well as by the somewhat similar practices of Canada, Venezuela, and Mexico in the Caribbean. For example, there is much to consider in the argument that south Pacific intermediate powers advance—that persuasion, diplomacy, and international law should be employed before significantly advancing militarization or resorting to arms, and that the need to resort to arms occurs less frequently among orderly, self-reliant, democratic neighbors. There is a great reservoir of such nation-states in both basins, although they are small and weak and occasionally must solicit assistance from their metropolitan friends. Assistance in promoting these ends would prove far less costly than military arrangements—and would have a more lasting payback. This is especially so with the end of the Cold War and the emergence of equally valid new security concerns such as preserving the ecosystems come into play.

There are valid politico-military security concerns among the approximately two dozen nations in each basin that have gained independence since 1962. Cases of international intrigue have impacted Dominica, Antigua, and Barbados, and a spate of seemingly political-related murders has swept Palau. Rebellions and/or coup attempts have occurred in Fiji, Papua New Guinea, and in Trinidad and Tobago, and an independence struggle is ongoing in New Caledonia. There is an increasing incidence of infiltration by drug cartels, smuggling rings, and terrorists, and foreign fishing fleets are penetrating the territorial seas and economic zones of these insular states. Finally, there are direct threats across frontiers by countries sharing borders—Belize, Guyana, Suriname, and Papua New Guinea—and at least one example of military penetrations of an archipelago (the Bahamas by Cuba).

From the insular perspective, perhaps the most important security concern is the need to balance security needs with socioeconomic demands. There is genuine fear in both basins that militarization will weaken real security by diverting funding for domestic needs and, in the process, create such a powerful military that it can overwhelm countervailing civilian institutions. Another military-related concern of the Pacific islanders, and also of the intermediate powers in the south Pacific, is the nuclear policies of the United States, France, and Russia, because these policies have, in the past, usually involved naval forces that represented the most "hardened" fulcrum of the strategic triads of these countries.

The United States has a legacy of respect in both regions, due in part because it has never intervened militarily in the non-Hispanic Caribbean (at least not until Grenada) and acted in the Pacific only as a direct result of World War II. And yet there have been increasing patterns of frustration with U.S. cycles of paternal attention and neglect and with the U.S. tendency to perceive security as a military issue while slighting the economic issue; most damaging has been a perception of cavalier or insensitive treatment by Washington—a sense that the needs, pleas, and time-honored institutions of the small states of the Caribbean and the Pacific are too frequently of little consequence to the colossus. Sensitivity to and respect of the rights of all, including the very weak, is a time-honored constitutional principle in the United States, and an external policy reflective of this principle should again receive greater attention in this post–Cold War era.

Given their common problems of vulnerability, the small states of the Caribbean and Pacific Basins can learn from each other: Although both groups of newer states are weak and vulnerable, in numbers they are strong, and in the game of multilateral diplomacy, any bloc of more than two dozen states can have considerable clout. Discussion and sharing of mutual security concerns will be beneficial to both the Caribbean and Pacific, and collective solutions to common problems can be worked out in international and regional forums. In the economic area, discussed in the last chapter, effective collaboration has occurred between the regions with respect to negotiation of the ACP-Lomé accord. In the noneconomic security arena, such collaboration is occurring in the environmental area within the Alliance for Small Island States. In the political and military fields, however, beyond the commitment to democracy, both regions will continue to depend on external powers to fulfill their security needs and provide the necessary climate for development. Through a unified effort, the Caribbean and Pacific states may encourage the metropolitan powers to demonstrate positive leadership and cooperation with their allies in both Basins in the post–Cold War era.

Notes

1. O. Henry [William Sydney Porter], *Cabbages and Kings* (New York: Doubleday, Post, 1904), pp. 55–56. Although the setting for this prescient tale supposedly was the Caribbean Basin, it could just as well have been in the Pacific. Enormous opportunities for grievously dysfunctional misperception remain within and between both regions today, misperception that is largely an outgrowth of ethnocentrism. One specialist argues that the reason U.S. "policy so often flounders or ends up on the shoals, is a fundamental lack of understanding and empathy about the Third World . . . countries," which results from ethnocentrism. See Howard Wiarda, *Ethnocentrism in Foreign Policy: Can We Understand the Third World?* (Washington, D.C.: American Enterprise Institute, 1985), p. 1.

2. James Pope–Hennessy, *West Indian Summer* (London: B.T. Batsford, 1943), p. vi, credited the trade of U.S. destroyers for bases as putting the islands back in the news.

3. Although a familiarity with the Pacific region among the U.S. citizenry during the World War II era has dimmed, a war/security image of the Pacific remains etched in the perceptions of many U.S. policymakers and diplomats, as evidenced by gifts Ambassador Vernon Walters presented to leaders in the Pacific during his mid-1980s tour of the region: albums of World War II photos.

4. Lelei LeLaulu, "Political, Economic, and Social Developments and Their Effects on Pacific Basin Security," luncheon address to 1987 Pacific Symposium, reprinted in Dora Alves, ed., *Pacific Security Toward the Year 2000,* (Washington, D.C.: National Defense University Press, 1988), p. 309. Also see J. D. Legge,

Australian Colonial Policy: A Survey of Native Administration and European Development in Papua (Sydney: Angus and Robertson, 1956), esp. chs. 9–14. Many residents of the Republic of Palau feel the "new equality" has been severely tested by U.S. demands that this trust territory overturn its antinuclear constitutional stipulations in exchange for home rule and substantial financial reward; by mid-1989, the 10,000 voters in Palau had defeated such a referendum seven times! See "Compact Vote Likely . . . Again," *Pacific Islands Monthly* (April/May 1989): 10. World War II also impacted popular culture in the Pacific, as Lamont Lindstrom and Geoffrey White note: "The War is still the gist of good talk today. Many personal recollections dating from the war have frozen into narrative accounts. Formalized by frequent retellings, these war stories compose a historical archive. . . . Sitting in a village clearing on certain islands, one may be taken aback to hear older men and women burst into 'God Bless America' or Japanese anthems from the 1940s." See "War Stories," in Lindstrom and White, eds., *The Pacific Theater: Island Representations of World War II* (Honolulu: University of Hawaii Press, 1989), p. 3.

5. Palau has yet to ratify its association agreement, despite seven attempts, primarily because of the U.S. demand for military bases with nuclear weapons. Because of alleged misappropriation of funds by the Palau government, all of the island's major expenditures must currently be approved by the U.S. secretary of the interior, a requirement leading to charges by the Palau legislature that this action is undercutting the island's democracy and self-determination. See *Contemporary Pacific* 4, 1 (Spring 1992): 178–179. Both the Marshall Islands and FSM are now members of the U.N.

6. To seal the U.S.-Marianas bargain, the covenant with Washington grants the Marianas various exceptions from U.S. laws, notably the protectionist Jones Act that requires use of U.S. ships between U.S. ports—a law that very much rankles neighboring Guam. The Northern Marianas also receive $33 million annually from the United States to promote development. As *The Economist* notes, a confused status remains: "Talk to an American official and he will tell you the [Northern Marianas] are very much like other American territories. Talk to one of the 21,000 islanders and he will speak of 'internal sovereignty,' as if they were all but independent." See "The American Empire," *Economist* (May 6, 1989): 17–20, quote on 20. Also see Steward Firth, "Sovereignty and Independence in the Contemporary Pacific," *Contemporary Pacific* 1, 1 and 2 (Spring and Fall 1989): 79–93, which underscores past official confusion and carries President Reagan's statement that Micronesia and the Marshall Islands are "sovereign" and that as of November 3, 1986, the U.N. trusteeship no longer existed. In a U.N. Trusteeship Council meeting in May 1987, however, the U.S. representative correctly stated that the "Trusteeship Agreement remained in force" (p. 80). The agreement was eventually terminated in 1990. *Contemporary Pacific* 4, 1 (Spring 1992): 181 notes that on December 22, 1990, the Marianas were formally discharged from Trusteeship Council purview by the U.N. Security Council. Also see Lindstrom and White, "The Pacific Theater: Island Representation of World War II."

7. During the 1980s, U.S. executives routinely referred to the Caribbean as "our lake." Author Greg Fry projected that in the post–Cold War era, the Pacific is likely to remain an "American lake—one in which the United States plays the role of balancer providing regional order." See "The Region in Review," *Contemporary Pacific* 3, 2 (Fall 1991): 394.

8. *Vulnerability: Small States in the Global Society*, report of a Commonwealth Consultative Group (London: Commonwealth Secretariat, 1985).

9. See Richard Rosecrance, *The Rise of the Trading State* (New York: Basic Books, 1986); and E. F. Schumacher, *Small Is Beautiful* (New York: Harper &

Row, 1973).

10. Richard A. Herr, "Alignment and Alliance: Security in the South Pacific," in *Pacific Regional Security: The 1985 Pacific Symposium* (Washington, D.C.: National Defense University Press, 1986), pp. 565–566.

11. On Fiji, see "Born to Rule," *Economist* 316 (August 11, 1990): 38; and "Shameless in Fiji," *Economist* 317 (December 1, 1990): 34. Suriname was under military rule between 1979 and 1989 and again in 1991. Other countries that could be considered less than open political systems include Grenada (during portions of both the Gairy and the 1979–1983 revolutionary regime); and Guyana (during the lengthy metropolitan-imposed Burnham era, although Guyanese elections in late 1992 were the most democratic since U.S.–British intervention in the early 1960s). The negotiating skill of former U.S. President Jimmy Carter is credited with the latter development. See Festus Brotherson, Jr., "Hoyte Takes the Other Road," *Caribbean Contact,* November/December 1990, p. 8.

12. Eric Williams, *History of the People of Trinidad and Tobago* (New York: Praeger, 1964), pp. 280–82.

13. Ronald Robinson, speech on British decolonization presented to faculty seminar, Harry Ransom Humanities Research Center, University of Texas, Austin, Texas, August 3, 1990.

14. Laurence Whitehead, "International Aspects of Democratization," in Guillermo O'Donnell, Philippe C. Schmitter, and Laurence Whitehead, eds., *Transitions from Authoritarian Rule: Prospects for Democracy* (Baltimore, Md.: The Johns Hopkins University Press, 1986), sec. 3, pp. 3–46; for critique of the implanted two-party system in the Pacific, see David Stanley, *South Pacific Handbook* (Chico, CA: Moon Publications, 1985) p. 33.

15. Anthony P. Maingot, "The English-speaking Caribbean," in Mark Falcoff and Robert Royal, eds., *The Continuing Crisis: U.S. Policy in Central America and the Caribbean* (Latham, Md.: University Press of America, 1987), pp. 134–143, esp. 143; Arms Control and Disarmament Agency, *World Military Expenditures and Arms Transfers, 1986* (Washington, D.C.: U.S. Government Printing Office, 1987), pp. 66–96; and Dion E. Phillips, "The Increasing Emphasis on Security and Defense in the Eastern Caribbean," in Alma H. Young and Dion E. Phillips, eds., *Militarization in the Non-Hispanic Caribbean* (Boulder, Colo.: Lynne Rienner, 1986), pp. 42–64.

16. Quoted in *Christian Science Monitor*, April 11, 1977.

17. See Thomas Hobbes, *A Dialogue Between a Philosopher and a Student of the Common Laws of England*, ed. Joseph Cropsey (Chicago: University of Chicago Press, 1971), p. 122.

18. Quoted in *Christian Science Monitor*, April 11, 1977.

19. France threatened major economic sanctions against New Zealand if the French saboteurs were not returned to France. To add insult to injury, the French government granted promotions to the extradited saboteurs. Even with a change of governments, the New Zealand public still supports a nuclear freeze.

20. Michael P. Hamnett and Robert C. Kiste, *Issues and Interest Groups in the Pacific Islands* (Washington, D.C.: U.S. Information Agency, Office of Research, 1988), p. 101. Despite greater U.S. attention to the small-state Pacific, LeLaulu, "Political, Economic, and Social Developments," correctly feels the United States has displayed too little attention too late. Having the Pacific islands lumped in with China, as in the previous State Department breakdown for the region, is in LeLaulu words, "an absurd arrangement—it's like putting a mongoose with an elephant" (p. 314). Although China has had a presence in the Pacific for only ten years, its number of embassies in the region already equals that of the United States. Some feel France may eventually scale back its

nucleapolicy in the region policy in the region if for no other reason than that its nuclear policy in the region if for no other reason than that its test site, Mururoa, is in danger of being blown to bits. See "France reconquers the Pacific," *Economist* 315 (May 19, 1990): 33.

21. William Langer, ed., *An Encyclopedia of World History* (Boston: Houghton Mifflin, 1948), pp. 88ff; Neal Spivack, "U.S. to Divest Pacific Trusteeship," *Interdependent* 12 (January/February 1986): 3; and David Stanley, *Micronesia Handbook* (Chico, Calif.: Moon Publications, 1985), pp. 27-28.

22. An exception was made in 1990, however, when the symposium focused on the Caribbean.

23. F. A. Mediansky, "Threat Perception in the Southwest Pacific Region," in Alves, *Pacific Security Toward the Year 2000*, pp. 291-293.

24. Robert C. Kiste, "Economic Security Issues in the South Pacific," in *Economics and Pacific Security: The 1986 Pacific Symposium* (Washington D.C.: National Defense University Press, 1987), pp. 181-184; also see John Carter, ed., *Pacific Islands Yearbook* (Sidney: Pacific Islands Yearbook, 1986), pp. 392, 407, 477; interview with Sir Peter Kenilorea, National Defense University, Washington, D.C., February 25, 1988. The then foreign minister of the Solomon Islands voiced concerns regarding inordinate arms expansions he feared could not be checked by available countervailing institutions. The Fijian coups in 1987 induced the late Errol Barrow of Barbados to question the political costs of maintaining a permanent defense force in Barbados.

25. Information and quote from *New York Times*, February 17, 1992, p. A3.

26. John Connell, "Island Microstates: The Mirage of Development," *Contemporary Pacific* 3, 2 (Fall 1991), esp. p. 261. Connell also notes that pollution from the island's phosphate industry is creating problems in Nauru.

27. Jemima Garrett, "Bougainville," *Pacific Islands Monthly* 62, 1 (January 1992): 20-21.

28. Maingot, "The English-speaking Caribbean," p. 134.

29. Ibid.

30. Sir Peter Kenilorea, plenary speech to annual Pacific Symposium, and personal interview by W. Marvin Will, National Defense University, Washington, D.C., February 25, 1988. Sir Peter in his speech was most blunt, citing the New Testament appeal to destroy weapons and promote peace.

31. William Roger Louis, *Imperialism at Bay: The United States and the Decolonization of the British Empire, 1941-1945* (New York: Oxford University Press, 1978), pp. 290-308. Louis writes that "Evatt . . . had drawn the moral from the Cairo Declaration that the great powers would disregard the smaller nations unless bludgeoned into paying attention." Evatt bludgeoned and Roosevelt and the Department of State fumed, even though Evatt's view was that Australia's interests were also in Washington's long-term best interests. Although Australia can be praised for its anticolonial policy, one variable in its failure to push for annexation of Papua New Guinea was its own racial policy.

32. Quoted by Firth, "Sovereignty and Independence," p. 88 from a 1987 Australian Defense Department report.

33. Australia Department of Foreign Affairs, Submission to the Joint Committee on Foreign Affairs and Defence Enquiry into Australia's Relations with the South Pacific, *Hansard Report*, vol. 5, April 27, 1987; also cited by Firth, "Sovereignty and Independence," p. 89; Andrew Axline, "Lessons for the Caribbean from Small States in Other Regions," in Anthony T. Bryan, Edward Greene, and Timothy Shaw, eds. *Peace, Development and Security in the Caribbean* (New York: St. Martin's, 1990).

34. Michael R. Ogden, "The Paradox of Pacific Development," *Development*

Policy Review 7 (December 1989): 368; L. R. Vasey and Robert L. Pfaltzgraff, Jr., "U.S. Policy Toward the South Pacific," in John C. Dorrance, P. T. Thakur, J. Wanandi, L. R. Vasey, and Robert L. Pfaltzgraff, Jr., *The South Pacific: Emerging Security Issues and U.S. Policy* (Washington, D.C.: Brassey's, 1990), p. 99; Dorrance and colleagues note that both "Canberra and Wellington also accept the possibility of an island state internal crisis requiring their armed intervention, if only to provide support to a friendly government under domestic siege, or to evacuate their nationals."

Economic declines in the early 1990s may force the Pacific intermediate powers to constrict their external roles. According to Garrett ("Bougainville," p. 21) should the incumbent Labour Party be defeated in the 1993 Australian election, as current polling projects, "the [opposition] Liberal/National party coalition plans to slash A$209 million from the foreign aid budget in its first two years. That includes a cut of $112 million from country programmes, $83 million from contributions to international financial organisations and a 25 percent cut in money spent on the government's Australian International Development Assistance Bureau (AIDAB)." Proposed across-the-board cuts in public spending also would include reductions in aid and support services for the approximately 2000 students from the Pacific islands studying in Australia.

35. Louis, *Imperialism at Bay,* ch. 18, esp. pp. 290–303, quote on 290. Anticipating the 1980s, Louis wrote in 1978 that "New Zealand and Australia, as their real fears of invasion have receded, have now, like most of the Latin American states, grown alarmed of the United States embrace" (p. 303).

36. *Mexico Today* 30 (May 1985): 1.

37. Hans Binnendijk, ed., *National Negotiating Styles* (Washington, D.C.: Center for the Study of Foreign Affairs, Foreign Service Institute, U.S. Department of State, 1987).

38. See Stanley, *South Pacific Handbook,* pp. 25–37; also his *Micronesia Handbook,* pp. 28–36; Langer, *Encyclopedia of World History.*

39. U.S. Agency for International Development (USAID), *Congressional Presentation,* Fiscal Year 1980, Annex III, Latin America and the Caribbean, pp. 10–11; data on organizations from U.S. Department of State, *Atlas of United States Foreign Relations* (Washington, D.C.: U.S. Government Printing Office, 1986), pp. 16–37.

40. Caribbean Development Bank (CDB), *Annual Report 1979* (St. Michael, Barbados, 1980), pp. 5–7; CDB, *Annual Report 1986,* pp. 5–7.

41. The Reagan administration had sought support within the U.S. government and in the Caribbean for militarily overthrowing the Grenada government, beginning with Operation Ocean Venture '81 in which 12,000 troops, 240 warships, and 1,000 planes conducted a "warm-up" operation to rescue U.S. citizens from "Amber and the Amberdines"—a clear reference to Grenada and the Grenadines. See *Washington Post,* November 24, 1981; and Anthony Payne, *The International Crisis in the Caribbean* (Baltimore, Md.: The Johns Hopkins University Press, 1984), p. 55.

42. Karl Hudson–Phillips, personal interview with W. Marvin Will, Port of Spain, Trinidad, October 8, 1981.

43. As to the effects of the intervention on Caricom, Errol Barrow, independence prime minister and then leader of the Barbadian opposition, harbored deep anxiety that damage to mutual trust and institutional self-respect imposed on an already economically debilitated Caricom would be irreversible. In his judgment, the Grenadian action was yet another instance in which the United States sacrificed the long-term interest of the region for its own short-term interests, including the sending of "a message to Nicaragua, Cuba . . . and other

left-leaning forces!" Errol Barrow, "The Danger of Rescue Missions," *Caribbean Review* 12 (Fall 1983): 2–4. For an accurate account of the U.S. intervention in Grenada, see Judy Woodruff, "Operation Urgent Fury," Frontline, Public Broadcasting Service, 1984, 60 min. videocassette.

44. See *Caribbean Contact,* October 1986, pp. 4–5. For background to U.S. racial-cultural "slights" in the Caribbean, see Noam Chomsky, *Turning Point* (Boston: South End Press, 1985), esp. pp. 87–89; and Lester D. Langley, *The United States and the Caribbean* (Athens: University of Georgia Press, 1980).

45. Kenilorea, plenary speech and interview with author, February 25, 1988.

46. "A Foul Peace Dividend for the Pacific," *Economist* 317 (October 27, 1990): 36; "A Bit of a Smell," *Economist* 317 (November 3, 1990): 39; "South Pacific Dump," *World Press Review* (October 1990): 48; and Editorials, *Sydney Morning Herald,* September–October 1990.

47. Epeli Haúofa, *Kisses in the Niderends* (Auckland, New Zealand: Penguin, 1987), esp. pp. 127–153. Before the infirm islander in the story can be healed, a good deal of cross-cultural misperception, resultant bad policy, and attempts to save face are recounted as a way for Haúofa to demonstrate both the awkward and dependent position small islanders face. But, as in the Caribbean, when survival is at stake, one does what one must to survive.

48. See the following sources by Robert A. Pastor: "U.S. Immigration Policy and Latin America: In Search of the 'Special Relationship,'" *Latin American Research Review* 19, 2 (1984): 35, 53–54; "The Impact of U.S. Immigration Policy on Caribbean Emigration: Does It Matter?" in Barry B. Levine, ed., *The Caribbean Exodus* (New York: Praeger, 1987), p. 258; and "Migration and Development: Implications and Recommendations for Policy," *Studies in Comparative International Development* 24 (Winter 1989–1990): 46–64. Pastor concludes his 1987 essay with a plea for U.S. policies that "will be sensitive to the originating country and to the evolving relationship between the United States and the Caribbean."

Part 4
Conclusion

9
Strengthening the Links
Jacqueline A. Braveboy-Wagner

In the early 1990s, those concerned about global affairs are mulling over the implications of what seems to be a new world order: one in which the United States is the dominant military (if not economic) power, the former Soviet Union is no longer a global power, and the great powers and other middle powers are joining with the United States in a harmony of interest to foil regional aggressors and promote democracy within the framework of the multilateral United Nations. For most First World observers, there is hope in the breakdown of bipolarity, the demise of communism, and the harmonization of global interests. Notwithstanding the continued bitterness of regional and civil conflicts and a shift toward Germany in the European balance of power, the new order offers the stronger nations a chance to manage power in the international system in the way originally envisaged in the Charter of the United Nations. Nevertheless, political harmony among the richer nations is fast being upstaged by dissension on economic matters, as seen, for example, in U.S.-Japan, U.S.-EC differences. Moreover, the economic future seems to be one characterized by global megablocs in North America/Latin America, Europe, and Asia Pacific.

In this environment, the more subdued Third World countries have some particular concerns: They worry about being left out of political decision-making; they are concerned about being even more marginalized in a world of large free-trade blocs; and they fear that traditional financial donors, especially the United States, will neglect them because of the preoccupation with newly liberated Eastern Europe, commitments to Middle Eastern nations hurt by the Gulf war of 1991, and the decreased strategic value of Third World allies in a post–Cold War world. The early 1990s are therefore a time for reassessment and planning on the part of the developing nations.

For the nations of the Caribbean, this reassessment may usefully include a consideration of the diversification of their relations in the direction of the Far East. Understanding that region, learning from the nations of that region, and ultimately strengthening links with them can be a helpful part of a strategy that also ought to include closer integration in the Caribbean (its subregions as well as the wider Basin) and closer integration between the Caribbean and Latin America. Indeed, the trek of Caribbean policymakers to the Far East in search of new markets and new sources of aid has begun. Notwithstanding the consolidation taking place in Europe and in North America, the Pacific will continue to be, overall, the fastest-growing world region into the next century. Although developed-country markets are contracting, the Asian-Pacific nations not only are boosting domestic demand but also are exploring new markets and increasing their competitive edge by advancing technologically; indeed, they are thriving in an atmosphere of competition—from within the region as well as from outside. Even if growth slows in this region, as it has been doing, the Pacific will remain highly important in world trade for the foreseeable future.

How, then, can the Caribbean countries benefit from the Asian-Pacific experience, and how can they strengthen their relationship with those countries? In the exploration of the subject in this book, several possibilities have been raised.

Caribbean countries and Pacific countries share quite a few characteristics, despite the geographical differences and vast cultural differences. If we define the Caribbean to include the Basin countries, we find there are widely differing levels of development in the region, as in the Pacific. There are NICs such as Venezuela and Mexico (comparable in some ways to the Asian NICs); NIC-aspirants such as Trinidad and Tobago (comparable to some of the ASEAN countries); a majority of middle-income countries (as in Southeast Asia); numerous island economies dependent on agriculture and tourism (as are many Pacific island countries); some resource-rich countries, such as Trinidad and Tobago, Jamaica, Guyana, and Suriname (comparable in resources if not in GNP to Brunei, Nauru, Indonesia, and Papua New Guinea); some service economies, such as Bahamas and Panama (comparable in some ways to Hong Kong and Singapore); and some highly aid-dependent/indebted economies—Jamaica, for example—that share this characteristic with Pacific countries (e.g., the Philippines). Yet what distinguishes the Asian area of the Pacific from the Caribbean is assuredly the developmental successes of the East Asian and (some) Southeast Asian states, a successful pattern of export-led development that began in Japan and has diffused through the region. Why similar successes have not occurred in Latin America is the subject of quite a few scholarly works. In this study, the focus was on the English-speaking Caribbean.

Analysts of Latin America have cited both cultural and policy differences in comparing East Asia with Latin America. In the English-speaking Caribbean, literacy levels are high; entrepreneurship levels are not particularly low, although opportunities may be limited and, at the collective level, there is considerable room for improvement with respect to the work ethic. But there are arguments for discounting the Confucian heritage as the key to Asian development. Rather, a policy focus is seen here as a more productive perspective.

In the Asian NICs, domestic protectionism gave way to export promotion fairly quickly. Governments, almost all of them authoritarian, played a role in promoting infrastructural development and instituting incentives to export. Export production moved fairly rapidly up the technological ladder so that electronics, steel, and automobiles competed with garments and toys. Land reform was also undertaken in most countries. In the Caribbean, as in Latin America, there has been prolonged emphasis on import substitution, although export promotion is now the norm. Exported manufactures remain relatively "low-tech." Foreign investment and foreign aid have also played stronger roles in Caribbean than in Asian NIC development (aid was important to the Asians primarily in the initial years). There have been varying degrees of government regulation in the Caribbean—Guyana compares with South Korea in this regard—but planning has been far less efficient. Although the East Asian model's success depends on open markets elsewhere and therefore the NICs (and upcoming NICs) are vulnerable to protectionist sentiment in the developed world, they have shown a capacity to shift to more competitive sectors. Nevertheless, the products of Caribbean countries do not have a competitive edge. The level of foreign involvement in Caribbean economies (investment as well as aid) and a geopolitically derived dependence on the United States leaves these countries far more vulnerable than Asia Pacific to changes in the international economy. Also an important conclusion reached in Chapter 5 was that the various economic growth models employed by the Caricom countries "have been implemented under the constraints of pluralistic democracy (aside from the anomaly of Guyana). . . . Given that the prototypical pluralist political system is composed of constantly changing coalitions and cross-cutting interest groups, [the] syndrome of policy failure might seem both readily summarized and intractable."

Indeed, political pluralism is a key distinction between East Asian and English-speaking Caribbean political systems. Korea, Singapore, and Taiwan have resorted to varying levels of repression, supposedly in the interest of their economic and political security. Now that they are all democratizing in varying degrees, the comment made in Chapter 5 to "reflective East Asian leaders" is also in fact a reminder to Caribbean leaders: that even "if the linkage of market capitalism and political pluralism often produces unsatisfactory results, such a union beyond the short term might best guarantee that growth and development will ultimately underpin rather than undermine each other."

What can the Caribbean borrow from the East Asian model? Clearly, the model cannot be adopted wholesale: Specific factors, including the experience of physical truncation, pushed the East Asian NICs into a development strategy that was outward-oriented and carefully planned. Despite some similarities, quite different circumstances characterize the Caribbean experience, including the aforementioned tradition of political pluralism, proximity to the United States, early adoption of open-economy models, unequal results from attempts at state planning, and heightened vulnerability to the international economic environment. But the conclusion in Chapter 5 is that Caribbean policymakers, having delved into a variety of economic development models (including selective elements of the East Asian experience advocated by international economic agencies), might usefully take note of the following from the East: "the centrality of market incentives to work, save, and invest; largely unrestricted currency convertibility; agricultural reform; significant resource commitment to health and education; and policy continuity."

Few Caribbean countries can aspire to the standard of the East Asian NICs, but many find themselves in comparable economic straits to the island nations of Oceania. Although the prime focus of this book has been on Asian-Pacific–Caribbean relations, the similarities between the two primarily island regions led to inclusion of a comparative analysis of the Caribbean and Pacific. A study done by the (British) Commonwealth highlighted the similarity between the two regions in terms of military, political, economic, technical, social, and cultural vulnerability.[1] In the political-economic sphere, W. Marvin Will observed in Chapter 7 that "the small, highly dependent states of the Caribbean and Pacific basins find their economic development options severely restricted and their socio-economic–political vulnerability exacerbated by their limited natural-resource base and an often frustrating international economic climate. In addition, systemic vulnerability is fostered by the relatively high degree of political openness these states enjoy." Clearly, two economically weak regions cannot assist each other in technical or financial areas. But the similarities engendered by size and history offer opportunities for these nations to learn from each other's development experiences. One major strategy of both regions is economic integration. One major difference is that in the Pacific, the intermediate powers of Australia and New Zealand are formally and deeply involved in regional institutional affairs. In the Caribbean, however, although the Caribbean Development Bank (CDB) is heavily funded by the United States and includes as members the intermediate regional powers of Mexico, Colombia, and Venezuela as well as Canada, decisionmaking is dominated by the English-speaking members themselves. In the Caribbean Community (Caricom) and the Organization of Eastern Caribbean States (OECS), membership is confined to the small Caribbean states. In another area of difference, Caricom and OECS institutional mechanisms are more advanced than those of the South Pacific Forum (SPF). Nevertheless, the Caribbean might well learn from the Pacific in at least a few areas, including the following: the successes of the SPF in negotiating arrangements with external powers; the benefits of the relationship with the intermediate powers, especially Pacific access to Australia's and New Zealand's markets through the SPF (in this regard, a recent promising development is the acceptance by Caricom in 1992 of a Venezuelan offer of one-way free trade; a study of the Pacific islands-Australia/New Zealand arrangement could help Caricom as it negotiates with Venezuela on the various trade issues encompassed by this offer); and the SPF members' effectiveness in offering common positions on important policy matters (Caricom, in particular, has until recently had a record of inaction on important regional political issues).

Economic security can only be built on a base of political and territorial security. In this regard, the Caribbean, Asian-Pacific, and newer Pacific nations have all experienced a range of problems. Asian-Pacific states have been faced with the threat of communist contagion and internal insurrection. Korea, Taiwan, and Hong Kong have ended up as truncated states because of communist expansion. Asian-Pacific states have also been vulnerable to internal ethnic divisions (for example, Fiji and Singapore, where ethnic rivalries contributed to its forced separation from Malaysia); power rivalries (for example, between Indonesia and Malaysia); military coups (especially in Thailand); and other forms of civil instability (for example, the Philippines). The Caribbean region has suffered from similar problems, notwithstanding the reputation of the English-speaking Caribbean for stability. Fears of the spread of communism led to regional polarization in the late 1970s and early 1980s; ethnic instability has characterized Guyana and, to some degree, Trinidad and Tobago; territorial disputes and secessionist attempts have increased the sense of vulnerability; there have been power rivalries among the Basin middle powers; and, in the wider Caribbean, there has been a great amount of civil instability in the Central American region as well as in Jamaica, Grenada, Trinidad and Tobago, and Suriname.

In Chapter 6, the institutional mechanisms and security strategies of the Caribbean and Asia Pacific were examined and compared. Both regions have relied on external assistance as well as regional initiatives. As larger states, ASEAN members have been able to build up their individual military capabilities adequately. They have adhered to the principles of national and regional "resilience," by which increased national capabilities are seen to benefit not only the nation but the region. In contrast, the English-speaking Caribbean nations (and, indeed, the wider Caribbean) have been too small and/or too geopolitically circumscribed to develop a purely indigenous protective capacity and have relied heavily on the United States. Despite the dangers of excessive militarization, the Caribbean countries might do well to develop their own policies of regional resilience. A regional emphasis, presumedly one that reduces the heavy reliance on external powers, is particularly appropriate in the post–Cold War era when the United States is disengaging from areas not considered to be of the highest strategic importance.

ASEAN states appear to have benefited economically from enhanced regional security (and ASEAN does a good job of security cooperation), but Caribbean security cooperation is still limited, given differences in the perception of the need for enhanced security mechanisms. The main regional mechanism in the English-speaking Caribbean, the Regional Security System (RSS), is seen by many as diverting attention and scarce moneys away from much-needed economic development. Nevertheless, in 1992 a mood of cooperation seems to be prevailing in the Caribbean, even in this somewhat controversial military area. In mid-1992, RSS members were moving to improve their joint security arrangements by allowing "interoperability" among the member states, that is, the ability to operate more fully in one another's territory, as a means of combating such threats to economic security as the drug trade, environmental pollution, and smuggling.[2] Indeed, Caribbean decisionmakers can learn from analyzing the way in which ASEAN states have been able to benefit economically from security harmonization.

There is something to learn from the Pacific small states as well. In security, as in the economic arena, the role of the intermediate powers Australia and New Zealand is important to Pacific nations. In the Caribbean, Canada can be persuaded to play a larger role. Venezuela has been called on a few times by English-speaking states to assist in defense of beleaguered governments. Although the small states of the Caribbean are rightly cautious about deepening their security linkages with their large Latin neighbors, selective ties may be in order, as may be a strengthening of the Organization of American States (OAS) to better meet the needs of small states. These needs include enhancement of organizational mechanisms to better safeguard members' territorial integrity against both Latin American and U.S. encroachment, and determination of the limits to which the organization will go in support of democratic governments in the hemisphere—limits currently being tested in the Haitian situation. As for the United States, its continued importance to both the Pacific and the Caribbean was stressed in Chapter 8. Similar problems of insensitivity and misperception were discovered in U.S. relations with both regions. The suggestion was made that the United States might learn from the intermediate powers in this regard and that the Pacific and Caribbean might learn from each other how best to deal with the superpower and other intrusive powers.

The final conclusions relate to the question that was posed and discussed at the beginning of the book: What linkages can we expect between the Caribbean and Asian-Pacific regions in the near future? For the foreseeable future, Japan will remain the center of attention of all the developing countries, including those of the Caribbean region. Japan has established itself as the world's strongest economic power and has also begun to redefine its world role, moving away from a passive self-interested foreign policy toward a (somewhat shaky) partnership with the United States in fostering global cooperation and development. Japan's trade links with the circum-Caribbean countries are already moderately strong, and links with the English-speaking Caribbean began to be developed in the 1970s. If Caribbean countries offer attractive incentives, Japanese joint venture investment may be forthcoming. With adequate lobbying, both directly with Japan and with its partner the United States, the Caribbean may also be able to benefit from the recycled Japanese surplus. Although Japanese aid has in the past been primarily tied or conditional aid, Japan is making great strides in increasing the grant and untied elements of its aid. Moreover, its aid, with a few exceptions, is not given with a view to political interests. Again, Japan is busily engaged in promoting technical assistance activities, including environmental assistance, that can be of great value to Caribbean nations, at least those that wish to achieve a balance between developmental needs and preservation of the environment. In this regard, an offer made by Japan at the global environmental conference in Brazil in 1992 to recycle $7.7 billion in environmental aid can be of significance to the Caribbean. It should be noted, however, that Japan's environmental aid is expected to be targeted toward energy and industry rather than nature conservation. Finally, the Asian NICs are likely to exhibit an interest in precisely those regions that have already had successful experiences with the Japanese. One caveat, however: Caribbean success in courting the Asians (even more so than U.S. success) depends on the extent to which negotiators are trained in the cultural nuances and negotiating postures of the Eastern nations.

As for the Pacific island region, the Caribbean has already benefited from the formation of the African-Caribbean-Pacific group (ACP), which is associated with the European Community and has negotiated four Lomé conventions governing the preferential treatment of ACP products on the EC enlarged market. As demonstrated by the formation of the Alliance for Small Island States,[3] Caribbean and Pacific states can benefit by deepening their links at the United Nations, where measures to help developing island states are instituted, and in other common institutions such as the (British) Commonwealth where these small states share a concern about promoting their special economic and political needs and are more than likely to meet with a sympathetic reception.

In sum, then, if Caribbean states, especially the very small states, are to survive within the new world order, they will need to diversify their relations and enhance their competitiveness. In both these areas they cannot go wrong by looking to Asia and the Pacific. It is hoped that this book is a first step in assisting in this movement toward diversification.

This book has deliberately explored a wide number of areas of actual and potential cooperation between the Caribbean (broadly and narrowly defined) and Pacific (broadly and narrowly defined). A lot has been bitten off, perhaps more than we have been able to chew. But at least the following recommendations can be made to Caribbean policymakers: First, the Caribbean can definitely gain by deepening links with Japan and the East

Asian NICs through a structured, realistic, and culturally sensitive approach. Second, in the best scenario, some aspects of the East Asian model of development can be identified and adopted by the Caribbean countries, and in the worst, Caribbean policymakers can take note of and be helped by analyzing the differences between that model and Caricom's. Third, if military security enhances economic security, as the ASEAN states attest, then Caribbean policymakers, faced with threats to their countries' social security, should not be viewing expenditure on military matters and on development as mutually exclusive. Finally, although this post–Cold War era is emerging as an era of individualism and regionalism among states, it would be unwise to abandon South-South solidarity altogether. In this regard, the Caribbean has nothing to lose and certainly something to gain by strategic cooperation and bargaining with the similarly small Pacific states.

Notes

1. See *Vulnerability: Small States in the Global Society*, report of a Commonwealth Consultative Group (London: Commonwealth Secretariat, 1985), esp. p. 4.
2. Sunday *(Trinidad) Guardian*, July 5, 1992, p. 4.
3. The Alliance of Small Island States (AOSIS), formed in November 1990, is still debating the scope of its membership. By 1992, the group included Cyprus and Malta as well as Indian Ocean, Pacific, and Caribbean islands.

About the Author and Contributors

Jacqueline A. Braveboy-Wagner is professor of political science at the Graduate School and University Center and The City College of the City University of New York. She is author of *The Venezuela-Guyana Border Dispute*, *Interpreting the Third World*, *The Caribbean in World Affairs*, and numerous articles on Caribbean foreign policy and development. She is also president of the Caribbean Studies Association (1992/1993) and past editor of the association's newsletter.

W. Marvin Will is associate professor of political science at the University of Tulsa. He is coeditor of (with Richard Millett) *The Restless Caribbean* and has published numerous articles in journals including *Journal of Commonwealth and Comparative Politics*, *Latin American Research Review*, and *Studies in Comparative International Development*.

Dennis J. Gayle is associate professor in the College of Business Administration and head of international programs at Florida International University.

Ivelaw L. Griffith is assistant professor of political science at Lehman College of the City University of New York. He is the editor of *Strategy and Security in the Caribbean* and author of *The Quest for Security in the Caribbean* (forthcoming), as well as articles in *Caribbean Affairs* and *Journal of InterAmerican Studies and World Affairs*, among other publications.

Index

Adams, Tom, 115, 184
African-Caribbean-Pacific group, 69n7, 152, 155, 161, 162–163, 203
Agriculture: acreage increase, 92; dependence on, 129; export, 36; Haitian, 41; Indonesian, 24; peasant, 140; plantation, 77, 131; production, 89; reform, 94; subsidized, 19; subsistence, 146, 148; Taiwanese, 20; Thai, 25
Aid, economic, 10, 77; Canadian, 63; Japanese, 4, 10, 18, 63, 64; untied, 56
Aid, environmental, 67, 203
Aid, military, 157
Alliance for Small Island States, 181, 203
Antigua and Barbuda, 39; armed forces, 121*tab*; economy, 145; gross domestic product, 121*tab*, 133*tab*; gross national product, 35*tab*, 145; growth rates, 143; life expectancy, 133*tab*; membership in Caricom, 113; membership in OECS, 114; Official Development Assistance, 60*tab*; political stability, 145, 177; population, 35*tab*, 121*tab*, 133*tab*; in RSS, 115
Aquino, Corazon, 26
Aristide, Jean-Bertrand, 41
ASEAN. *See* Association of Southeast Asian Nations
Asia, East: development model, 75–94; development pattern, 12n9; economic interdependence, 4
Asia, Southeast: development pattern, 12n9; Japanese investment in, 27, 28
Asian Development Bank, 154
Asia Pacific Economic Forum, 7, 8, 61
Association of Southeast Asian Nations, 5, 108*tab*, 109–112; economic integration, 23; exports to Pacific Basin states, 9*tab* growth rates, 23; Japanese investment in, 28; membership in PECC, 8, 61; political ties, 29; relations with Japan, 8; relations with United States, 29; security concerns, 101–103, 109–112; technical committees, 110
Australia, 5; exports to Pacific Basin states, 9*tab*; membership in PECC, 61; Pacific role, 149, 154–155, 159

Bahamas, 39; armed forces, 121*tab*; economy, 41–42, 142–143; exports, 47*tab*, 48*tab*, 63; financial services, 42; gross domestic product, 121*tab*, 133*tab*, 143; gross national product, 35*tab*, 41; imports, 47*tab*, 52*tab*, 63; independence, 130, 132; industry, 42; Japanese investment, 56*tab*, 58, 63; Japanese trade, 52*tab*; life expectancy, 133*tab*; membership in Caricom, 113; Official Development Assistance, 60*tab*; population, 35*tab*, 121*tab*, 133*tab*; relations with Taiwan, 46; trade with Pacific Basin states, 47–49*tab*, 51
Baker, James, 7, 8-9
Barbados, 39; armed forces, 121*tab*; economy, 42, 89, 90, 142; education budget, 177, 178; exports, 47*tab*, 48*tab*, 88*tab*, 90, 158; foreign investment dependence, 90; gross domestic product, 87, 89, 121*tab*, 133*tab*, 142; gross national product, 35*tab*, 87, 88*tab*; growth rate, 88*tab*; imports, 47*tab*, 50, 52*tab*, 63, 88*tab*; independence, 130, 132; Japanese trade, 52*tab*; life expectancy, 133*tab*; membership in Caricom, 113; membership in OECS, 86; military budget, 177, 178; Official Development Assistance, 60*tab*; political stability, 115, 177; population, 35*tab*, 88*tab*, 121*tab*, 133*tab*; in RSS, 115;

207

tourism, 89; trade with Pacific Basin states, 47–49*tab*; unemployment, 89
Barrow, Errol, 118, 166*n21*, 191*n24*, 192*n43*
Belau. *See* Palau
Belize, 39; armed forces, 121*tab*; economy, 42, 144; exports, 47*tab*, 48*tab*; gross domestic product, 121*tab*, 133*tab*; gross national product, 35*tab*; growth rates, 42; imports, 47*tab*, 52*tab*; income, per capita, 144; independence, 130, 132; Japanese trade, 52*tab*; life expectancy, 133*tab*; membership in Caricom, 113; Official Development Assistance, 60*tab*; population, 35*tab*, 121*tab*, 133*tab*; relations with Taiwan, 46; trade with Pacific Basin states, 47–49*tab*
Bird, Vere, 145, 153
Bishop, Maurice, 159
Blaize, Herbert, 144
Bouterse, Desi, 146
Brady Plan, 59
Brathwaite, Nicholas, 144
Brunei: armed forces, 121*tab*; economy, 15, 27; gross domestic product, 121*tab*; gross national product, 16*tab*; income, per capita, 31*n40*; independence, 26; membership in ASEAN, 5, 9*tab*, 23, 109; nonalignment, 111; population, 16*tab*, 27, 31*n40*, 121*tab*
Burnham, Forbes, 87, 89, 159, 166*n24*, 190*n11*
Bush, George, 7, 144, 158, 186

CACM. *See* Central American Common Market
Canada, 5; Caribbean trade agreement, 86; membership in PECC, 61; in North American Free Trade Area, 4
Canberra Agreement, 154
Capital: equipment, 91; foreign, 71*n48*, 114; goods, 78; investment, 156; private, 65
Caribbean Basin, 34*fig*; concept, 33–43
Caribbean Basin Economic Recovery Act, 86, 157
Caribbean Basin Initiative, 122, 156, 157, 158
Caribbean-Canadian Trade Agreement, 86
Caribbean Commission, 151, 155, 168*n46*
Caribbean Community and Common Market, 39–40, 42, 43, 78, 86–87, 108*tab*, 113, 139–140, 200; Program for Agricultural Development, 86
Caribbean Court of Appeals, 153
Caribbean Development Bank, 38, 39, 122, 152, 184, 200
Caribbean Export Bank, 153
Caribbean Festival, 156
Caribbean Free Trade Association, 152
Caribbean Multilateral Clearing Facility, 153
Caribbean states: bilateralism, 156–159; colonial history, 130–134; dependence on United States, 158–159, 201; developmental models, 85–94; diversification of economies, 11; economic integration, 42; economic processing zones, 46; economic relations with Pacific Basin states, 45–68; foreign investment, 76; foreign policy coordination, 42; free trade arrangements, 35, 46; institutional development, 42; intraregional relations, 33–43; language subdivisions, 35*tab*, 36, 39–40; links to Pacific Basin states, 11; political economies, 139–146; potential ties with Pacific Basin states, 42–43; relations with Japan, 52–68; relations with United States, 43; security concerns, 103, 106, 112–119; ties with Europe, 43; United Nations membership, 152; Venezuelan investment, 39
CARIBCAN. *See* Caribbean-Canadian Trade Agreement
Caricom. *See* Caribbean Community and Common Market
Carifta. *See* Caribbean Free Trade Association
Carlot, Maxime, 149
Carter, Jimmy, 156, 184, 190*n11*
Cayman Islands: gross domestic product, 164*n10*; income, per capita, 134; Japanese investment, 56*tab*, 58, 63
CBERA. *See* Caribbean Basin Economic Recovery Act
CDB. *See* Caribbean Development Bank
Central America: extraregional trade, 36–37; intraregional trade, 36
Central American Common Market, 36, 43; economic coordination, 66
Charles, Eugenia, 144, 168*n48*, 185
Chiang Ching-kuo, 21
China, 5; gross domestic product, 77; Japanese investment in, 27; membership in PECC, 8, 61; trade with Japan, 28
Chun Doo-Hwan, 19
Clientelism, 142
Cold War: demise, 4, 112; redefinition of security interests, 15, 112; and reduction of superpower economic assistance, 10
Colombia, 5; duty-free zones, 71*n48*; economic processing zones, 66; exports, 38, 47*tab*, 49*tab*, 58; gross national product, 35*tab*; imports, 47*tab*, 50, 52*tab*; income, per capita, 38; intraregional trade, 38; Japanese trade, 52*tab*; membership in Caricom, 113; Official Development Assistance, 60*tab*; population, 35*tab*, 38; trade with Pacific Basin states, 47–49*tab*, 50, 51
Colonialism, 36, 43, 76, 77, 84, 85, 102, 129, 130–134, 152, 154, 159, 173
Commonwealth of Independent States. *See* Soviet Union
Communism, 201; ASEAN actions, 29; demise, 197; economic considerations, 4; Indonesian, 24; Philippine, 26
Competition: Japanese, 17; Pacific-Caribbean, 129

Compton, John, 117, 145, 153
Conflicts: ethnic, 104, 112, 173, 177, 183; regional, 54, 113
Confucian values, 76, 79, 80, 81
Cook Islands, 5, 139, 150; economic dependence, 141*fig*; gross domestic product, 137*tab*; population, 137*tab*
Cooperation: industrial, 107; regional, 107, 154
Costa Rica, 5; exports, 47*tab*, 49*tab*; foreign debt, 37; gross national product, 35*tab*; growth rates, 37; imports, 47*tab*, 52*tab*; income, per capita, 37; independence, 36; Japanese trade, 52*tab*; Official Development Assistance, 60*tab*; population, 35*tab*, 36; trade with Pacific Basin states, 47–49*tab*, 51
Cuba, 39; economic crisis, 40; education budget, 177, 178; exports, 40, 47*tab*, 48*tab*, 50; gross national product, 35*tab*; imports, 47*tab*, 52*tab*, 63; influence in Caribbean, 39; Japanese trade, 52*tab*; loss of socialist markets, 63; military budget, 177, 178; Official Development Assistance, 60*tab*; population, 35*tab*, 40; relations with Caribbean states, 40; trade with Japan, 62–63; trade with Pacific Basin states, 47–49*tab*, 51
Cultural issues, 68, 81, 84, 93, 164*n13*, 183, 184–185, 203
Currency, 114; appreciation, 17, 82; convertibility, 94; devaluation, 89, 91, 92, 99*n88*, 142; eastern Caribbean, 152; floating, 81; values, 17, 82

DAC. *See* Development Assistance Committee
Debt: equity conversions, 62; external, 87, 90, 91, 92, 142; relief, 67; rescheduling, 38, 58; service, 76
Decolonization, 154, 174, 184; Caribbean, 131–132, 134; Pacific, 136, 139, 155
Dependence, 77
Development: Asian-Pacific models, 75–94; assistance, 50; Caribbean Development Bank in, 152; Caribbean model, 85–94; distance obstacles, 136; emphasis on distribution, 78; export-led, 12*n9*, 198; infrastructure, 23, 199; patterns in Asia, 12*n9*; productivity as measure, 78; relation to security, 106; rural, 92; security and, 101–123; social costs, 26; technocratic model, 97*n50*
Development Assistance Committee, 55
Dominica, 39; armed forces, 121*tab*; exports, 47*tab*, 48*tab*; gross domestic product, 121*tab*, 133*tab*; gross national product, 35*tab*; growth rates, 144; imports, 47*tab*, 50, 52*tab*; Japanese trade, 52*tab*; life expectancy, 133*tab*; membership in Caricom, 113; membership in OECS, 114; Official Development Assistance, 60*tab*; political stability, 112, 115, 177; population, 35*tab*, 121*tab*, 133*tab*; relations with Taiwan, 46; in RSS, 115; trade with Pacific Basin states, 47–49*tab*, 50, 51
Dominican Republic, 39; exports, 40, 47*tab*, 48*tab*; focus on United States, 40; gross national product, 35*tab*; imports, 47*tab*, 50, 52*tab*; income, per capita, 40; Japanese trade, 52*tab*; membership in Caricom, 113; Official Development Assistance, 60*tab*; political stability, 65; population, 35*tab*, 40; relations with Caribbean states, 40; trade with Pacific Basin states, 47–49*tab*, 50
Dowiyogo, Bernard, 150
Drug trafficking, 118, 120, 143, 148, 175, 177, 178, 202
Duvalier, Jean-Claude, 41

Easter Islands, 136
EC. *See* European Community
ECLAC. *See* Economic Commission for Latin America and the Caribbean
Economic Commission for Latin America and the Caribbean, 38
Economic processing zones, 19, 20, 38, 46, 66
Economy: diversification, 11; export, 17; global, 4, 11, 15; liberalization, 19–20, 141; open, 19; plantation, 36, 131; service, 37, 198; subsistence, 130
Education: emphasis on, 79; levels, 77; mass, 168*n45*; reform, 17; resource commitment, 94, 177, 178
EFTA. *See* European Free Trade Area
Ellice Islands, 139
Emigration, 84, 85, 89, 94, 122, 161–162, 170*n74*
Enterprise for the Americas Initiative, 158
Entrepôt trade: Hong Kong, 22; Singapore, 21
Environmental: assistance, 203; dangers, 150–151, 181; degradation, 26, 175; pollution, 85, 202; treaties, 156
Esquivel, Manuel, 144
Ethnonationalism, 3
Europe: balance of power, 3; economic integration, 7; import restraint, 10; ties with Caribbean states, 43; United States investment in, 10
Europe, Eastern: conflict in, 3; impact on lending to Caribbean states, 62
European Community, 3, 77, 122, 152, 155, 162, 163, 203; trade barriers, 3; trade deficits, 18
European Free Trade Area, 3
Exchange rates, 79, 83
Export processing zones, 83
Exports: agricultural, 36; Bahamas, 47–48*tab*, 63; Barbados, 47–48*tab*, 88*tab*, 90, 158; Belize, 47–48*tab*; capital-intensive, 92; Caribbean states, 47*tab*, 48–49*tab*; Colombia, 47*tab*, 49*tab*, 58; construction, 81; Costa Rica, 47*tab*, 49*tab*; Cuba, 47–

48tab; diversification, 86; Dominica, 47–48tab; Dominican Republic, 47–48tab; expansion, 80; Grenada, 47–48tab; Guatemala, 47tab, 49tab; Guyana, 47–48tab, 63, 88tab; Haiti, 47–48tab; Honduras, 47tab, 49tab, 61; Hong Kong, 18, 84, 88tab; incentives, 79, 80, 83; intra- Pacific, 9tab; Jamaica, 47–48tab, 63; Japan, 18, 62; Kiribati, 151; Malaysia, 25; markets, 64; Mexico, 47tab, 49tab; microincentives, 84; Micronesia, 149; Nicaragua, 47tab, 49tab, 58; Pacific Basin states, 47tab; Panama, 47tab, 49tab, 58; Philippine, 26; preferences, 86; primary product, 25, 36, 37, 40, 65, 77, 86, 91; promotion, 20, 75, 76, 77, 79; St. Vincent, 47–48tab; Singapore, 18, 88tab; Solomon Islands, 148; South Korea, 18, 81, 88tab; Suriname, 47tab, 49tab; Taiwan, 88tab; Thailand, 25; traditional, 25, 42; Trinidad and Tobago, 47–48tab, 63, 88tab; Vanuatu, 148; Venezuela, 47tab, 49tab, 62

Federation of Malaya, 25

Federation of Malaysia, 21, 22, 76

Fiji, 5, 136; armed forces, 180; economy, 147; gross domestic product, 137tab; independence, 136, 155; military rule, 147; political stability, 147, 180; population, 137tab

Five-Powers Defense Arrangement, 112

"Flying goose" pattern, 5, 12n9, 15

Fraser, Malcolm, 7

Fukuda, Takeo, 28

Gairy, Eric, 159, 190n11

GDP. See Gross domestic product

Gilbert Islands, 139

GNP. See Gross national product

Goh Chok Tong, 22

Government: authoritarian, 19, 76, 77, 79, 87, 93, 199; democratic, 36, 78, 94, 171, 175; democratic socialist, 91; military, 36; plural democratic, 176; relation to population, 104; technocratic authoritarian, 84

Grand Anse Declaration, 114

"Greater Asian Co-Prosperity Sphere," 28, 54

Grenada, 39; armed forces, 121tab; economy, 145; exports, 47tab, 48tab; gross domestic product, 121tab, 133tab; gross national product, 35tab; imports, 47tab, 52tab; Japanese trade, 52tab; life expectancy, 133tab; membership in Caricom, 113; membership in OECS, 114; militarization, 112–113; Official Development Assistance, 60tab; political stability, 41, 112, 177, 201; population, 35tab, 121tab, 133tab; relations with Taiwan, 46; in RSS, 115; trade with Pacific Basin states, 47–49tab, 51; United States' intervention, 40

Gross domestic product: Antigua and Barbuda, 121tab, 133tab; Bahamas, 121tab, 133tab, 143; Barbados, 87, 89, 121tab, 133tab, 142; Belize, 121tab, 133tab; Brunei, 121tab; Cayman Islands, 164n10; China, 77; Cook Islands, 137tab; Dominica, 121tab, 133tab; Fiji, 137tab; Grenada, 121tab, 133tab; Guyana, 89, 121tab, 133tab, 141; Hong Kong, 18, 77, 85; Indonesia, 121tab; Jamaica, 87, 92, 99n91, 121tab, 133tab; Japan, 18, 30n10; Kiribati, 137tab; Malaysia, 121tab; Marshall Islands, 137tab; Micronesia, 137tab; Nauru, 137tab; Niue, 137tab; Palau, 137tab; Papua New Guinea, 137tab, 146; Philippines, 121tab; St. Kitts/Nevis, 121tab, 133tab; St. Lucia, 121tab, 133tab; St. Vincent, 121tab, 133tab; Singapore, 18, 77, 83, 84, 121tab; Solomon Islands, 137tab; South Korea, 18, 77; Suriname, 133tab; Taiwan, 18, 77; Thailand, 121tab; Tonga, 137tab; Trinidad and Tobago, 87, 90, 121tab, 133tab; Tuvalu, 137tab; Vanuatu, 137tab; Western Samoa, 137tab

Gross national product: Antigua and Barbuda, 145; Barbados, 87, 88tab; Brunei, 16tab; Guyana, 87, 88tab; Hong Kong, 16tab, 22, 87, 88tab; Indonesia, 16tab; Jamaica, 87; Japan, 16, 16tab; Malaysia, 16tab; Philippines, 16tab; Singapore, 16tab, 21, 88tab; South Korea, 16tab, 81, 87, 88tab; Taiwan, 16tab, 81, 82, 88tab; Thailand, 16tab; Trinidad and Tobago, 87, 88tab, 90

Group of 77, 161

Group of Seven, 7

Growth, economic: Association of Southeast Asian Nations, 23; Barbados, 88tab; and export expansion, 80; export-led, 79, 85; Guyana, 88tab; Hong Kong, 18, 88tab; Indonesia, 24; Japan, 17; negative, 37; newly industrializing countries, 17; relation to militarization, 106; Singapore, 83, 88tab; South Korea, 18, 82, 88tab; Taiwan, 18, 82, 88tab; Trinidad and Tobago, 88tab

Guam, 136, 139, 174

Guatemala, 5; exports, 47tab, 49tab; gross national product, 35tab; growth rates, 37; imports, 47tab, 52tab; income, per capita, 37; independence, 36; industrialization, 37; Japanese trade, 52tab; Official Development Assistance, 60tab; population, 35tab, 36; trade with Pacific Basin states, 47–49tab, 51

Guyana, 39; armed forces, 121tab; economy, 42, 141, 153; exports, 47tab, 48tab, 63, 88tab; government, 87, 93; gross domestic product, 89, 121tab, 133tab, 141; gross national product, 35tab, 87, 88tab; growth rate, 88tab; imports, 47tab, 52tab, 88tab; income, per capita, 42, 93; independence, 130, 132; Japanese investment in, 63; Japanese trade, 52tab; life expectancy,

133*tab*; membership in Caricom, 113; membership in OECS, 86; militarization, 112–113; Official Development Assistance, 60*tab*; political stability, 104, 112; population, 35*tab*, 88*tab*, 121*tab*, 133*tab*; socialism in, 40; trade with Pacific Basin states, 47–49*tab*

Haiti, 39; agriculture, 41; exports, 47*tab*, 48*tab*; gross national product, 35*tab*; imports, 47*tab*, 50, 52*tab*; income, per capita, 41; Japanese trade, 52*tab*; membership in Caricom, 113; military coup, 41; Official Development Assistance, 60*tab*; political stability, 41, 104, 114; population, 35*tab*, 41; relations with Caribbean states, 41; trade with Pacific Basin states, 47–49*tab*, 50, 51

Heglegam, John, 150

Honduras: exports, 47*tab*, 49*tab*, 61; gross national product, 35*tab*; growth rates, 37; imports, 47*tab*, 52*tab*; income, per capita, 37; independence, 36; Japanese trade, 52*tab*; Official Development Assistance, 60*tab*, 61; population, 35*tab*, 36; trade with Pacific Basin states, 47–49*tab*, 51

Hong Kong: economic strength, 15; exports, 84, 88*tab*; foreign investment, 23; gross domestic product, 18, 77, 85; gross national product, 16*tab*, 22, 87, 88*tab*; growth rates, 18, 88*tab*; imports, 48–49*tab*, 88*tab*; industry, 22–23; infant mortality, 79; interregional trade, 29; Japanese investment, 27, 56*tab*; life expectancy, 79; political insecurity, 23; population, 16*tab*, 22, 88*tab*; trade surpluses, 4; trade with Caribbean states, 46, 48–49*tab*, 50, 51; trade with Japan, 28; transfer to China, 22, 85, 102; unemployment, 85

Hoyte, Desmond, 89

Imports: Bahamas, 52*tab*, 63; Barbados, 52*tab*, 63, 88*tab*; Belize, 52*tab*; Caribbean states, 47*tab*; Colombia, 52*tab*; Costa Rica, 52*tab*; Cuba, 52*tab*, 63; dependence, 92; deregulation, 91; Dominica, 50, 52*tab*; Dominican Republic, 52*tab*; Grenada, 52*tab*; Guatemala, 52*tab*; Guyana, 52*tab*, 88*tab*; Haiti, 52*tab*; Honduras, 52*tab*; Hong Kong, 48–49*tab*, 88*tab*; Indonesia, 48–49*tab*; Jamaica, 52*tab*, 63; Japan, 58, 61, 62, 63; Korea, 48-49*tab*; liberalization, 91; Malaysia, 48–49*tab*; Mexico, 52*tab*; Nauru, 167*n*42; Nicaragua, 52*tab*; Pacific Basin states, 47*tab*, 48–49*tab*; Panama, 52*tab*, 61; Philippines, 48–49*tab*; restraining, 10; restrictions, 114; St. Vincent, 52*tab*; Singapore, 48–49*tab*, 88*tab*; South Korea, 88*tab*; Suriname, 52*tab*; Taiwan, 48–49*tab*, 88*tab*; Thailand, 48–49*tab*; Trinidad and Tobago, 52*tab*, 63, 88*tab*; Venezuela, 52*tab*, 62

Income: distribution, 79, 81, 92, 94; inequalities, 97*n*50; remittance, 162; rural, 92; tax, 71*n*48, 89

Indonesia: agriculture, 24; armed forces, 121*tab*; economy, 15, 24; gross domestic product, 121*tab*; gross national product, 16*tab*; growth rates, 24; imports, 48–49*tab*; income, per capita, 24; independence, 24; industry, 24; infrastructure, 24; internal instability, 24; interregional trade, 29; Japanese investment in, 24, 27, 56*tab*; membership in ASEAN, 5, 9*tab*, 23, 109; nonalignment, 111; oil production, 62; population, 16*tab*, 24, 121*tab*; poverty level, 31n32; trade with Caribbean states, 48–49*tab*, 51; trade with Japan, 28

Industrialization: dependent, 85; import-substitution, 19, 37, 75, 76, 77, 85; by invitation, 75, 85; Pacific lack of, 162; subsidization, 20

Industry: auto, 17, 19, 20, 25, 63; capital-intensive, 22; cement, 23; chemical, 24, 37, 81; communication, 62; construction, 22, 24; cottage, 41; electronic, 17, 19, 22, 23, 26; garment, 26; heavy, 19, 20; high-technology, 20, 22, 25; Japanese, 17; labor-intensive, 23, 79; light, 23, 26, 40; localization, 65, 80; petrochemical, 20, 62; petroleum, 22; protectionism, 20, 22, 80; rubber, 24; semiconductor, 82; service, 22; shipbuilding, 19, 20, 22, 23; steel, 17, 19, 20, 62, 63; textile, 23, 24, 37

Inflation, 80, 82, 83, 89, 90, 91, 93, 94, 148, 150

Infrastructure: creation, 80; development, 199; economic, 104; improving, 20, 22; lack of, 24; socioeconomic, 84

Integration: cross-national institutional, 152; economic, 103, 120, 200; European, 7; Pacific Basin states, 7; policy, 153; regional, 7, 85, 92, 151–156, 154

Inter-American Treaty of Reciprocal Assistance, 113

International Bauxite Association, 40

International Monetary Fund: in Barbados, 90, 142; in Grenada, 122, 144; in Guyana, 89; imbalances, 157; in Jamaica, 91, 92; structural adjustment, 142; in Trinidad and Tobago, 142

Investment, 8; barriers to, 10; controls, 76; foreign, 19, 20, 23, 38, 52, 76, 77, 84, 90, 92; incentives, 65; infrastructure, 65; joint, 28, 50, 59; multinational, 22; in Pacific Basin states, 9; private, 65, 145; public sector, 89; regional approach, 66

Islamic fundamentalism, 26

Jagan, Cheddi, 159

Jamaica, 39; armed forces, 121*tab*; economy, 42, 142, 153; education budget, 177, 178;

exports, 47*tab*, 48*tab*, 63; gross domestic product, 87, 92, 99*n91*, 121*tab*, 133*tab*; gross national product, 35*tab*, 87; imports, 47*tab*, 52*tab*, 63; independence, 130, 132, 174; Japanese investment in, 63; Japanese trade, 52*tab*; life expectancy, 133*tab*; membership in Caricom, 113; membership in OECS, 86; military budget, 177, 178; Official Development Assistance, 60*tab*; political stability, 41, 65, 112, 177, 201; population, 35*tab*, 41, 121*tab*, 133*tab*; tourism, 91; trade with Pacific Basin states, 47–49*tab*, 50, 51; unemployment, 91, 99*n88*, 142

Japan: "bashing," 53; cost of living, 71*n57*; economic strength, 8, 10, 15, 64, 102, 202; exports, 9, 9*tab*, 27, 54, 55*tab*, 58, 62; foreign investment, 52; foreign policy, 53, 54, 58–59, 64; global involvement, 10, 57; gross domestic product, 18, 30*n10*; gross national product, 16, 16*tab*; growth rates, 17, 30*n10*; imports, 27, 55*tab*, 58, 61, 62, 63; industry, 17; international pressure on, 10, 18, 55, 65, 66; investment abroad, 56*tab*; investment in Asia, 27, 28; investment in United States, 10, 27, 52, 56*tab*; membership in PECC, 61; Official Development Assistance, 27, 55, 57*tab*, 58, 59, 60*tab*, 61, 62; peacekeeping role, 54; population, 16, 16*tab*; relations with Caribbean states, 46, 52–68; resource needs, 54, 58–59; tourism, 68; trade surplus, 4, 5, 9, 18; trade with ASEAN, 8, 27; trade with Caribbean states, 51, 52*tab*; trade with United States, 8, 27, 55*tab*; trade with Venezuela, 62; United States assistance, 17

Japan External Trade Bureau, 68
Japan Overseas Cooperation Volunteers, 67

Kenilorea, Sir Peter, 182, 185, 191*n24*
Kiribati, 5, 150; economic dependence, 141*fig*; exports, 151; gross domestic product, 137*tab*; income, per capita, 151; independence, 139; population, 137*tab*
Korea, South, 5; economic processing zones, 19; economy, 15, 134; exports, 81, 88*tab*; government, 93; gross domestic product, 18, 77; gross national product, 16*tab*, 81, 87, 88*tab*; growth rates, 18, 82, 88*tab*; imports, 48–49*tab*, 88*tab*; import-substitution, 19; income, per capita, 19, 93; industrialization, 19; interregional trade, 29; investment, 19, 29; Japanese investment, 27, 56*tab*; liberalization of economy, 19–20; membership in PECC, 8, 61; military in, 106; population, 16*tab*, 19, 88*tab*; state role in economy, 19; trade surpluses, 4; trade with Caribbean states, 46, 48–49*tab*, 50; trade with Japan, 28; unemployment, 82

Labor: controls, 77; costs, 23, 25, 28, 65, 79, 87, 93; demand for, 85; legislation, 89; mobility, 114, 153; organized, 84; unions, 81, 105
Land: reform, 17, 19, 20, 92, 93, 199; tenure, 36
Latin American Economic System, 39, 108*tab*
Latin American Energy Organization, 38–39
Lee Kuan Yew, 22, 28, 84
Lee Teng-hui, 21
Lini, Father Walter, 149
Loans: bilateral project, 59; structural adjustment, 59; untied, 62
Lomé conventions, 69*n7*, 86, 155, 203

Maingot, Anthony, 182
Malaysia: armed forces, 121*tab*; economic strength, 15; exports, 25; gross domestic product, 121*tab*; gross national product, 16*tab*; imports, 48–49*tab*; income, per capita, 24; independence, 25; interregional trade, 29; Japanese investment in, 27; membership in ASEAN, 5, 9*tab*, 23, 109; political stability, 109, 110; population, 16*tab*, 24, 121*tab*; trade with Caribbean states, 48–49*tab*, 51; trade with Japan, 28
Manley, Michael, 91, 122, 142, 158
Manufacturing: downstream, 64; exports, 4–5; global, 79; labor-intensive, 22, 79; light, 19, 38; wage costs, 85
Marcos, Ferdinand, 26
Marginalization, 11, 114
Market(s): access, 155; domestic, 10, 76, 79; duty-free access, 157; export, 64; growth, 81; incentives, 94; international, 175; liberalization, 93; open, 12*n9*, 76, 102; penetration, 10; protectionism, 17; resource allocation, 79
Marshall Islands, 136, 139, 150; gross domestic product, 137*tab*; independence, 174; population, 137*tab*
Mexico, 5; economic processing zones, 38, 66; exports, 47*tab*, 49*tab*; foreign investment in, 38; gross national product, 35*tab*; growth rates, 46; imports, 47*tab*, 50, 52*tab*; income, per capita, 38; industry, 38; Japanese trade, 52*tab*; in North American Free Trade Area, 4, 39; Official Development Assistance, 60*tab*; oil production, 38, 62; population, 35*tab*, 38; relations with Cuba, 40; relations with United States, 39; structural adjustment, 38; trade with Pacific Basin states, 47–49*tab*, 50, 51
Micronesia, 136, 139; economy, 149–150; exports, 149; gross domestic product, 137*tab*; income, per capita, 149; independence, 174; population, 137*tab*
Military: aid, 157; budgets, 19, 105, 106, 177, 178; coups, 41, 104, 106, 166*n22*, 201; in decisionmaking, 105; forces, 121*tab*; governments, 26, 36; occupations, 185; presence of United States, 102; resources,

105; resource sharing, 111; rule, 146, 147, 190*n11*; stability, 119–120
Mitchell, James, 117, 122, 143, 153

NAFTA. *See* North American Free Trade Area
Nakasone, Yasuhiro, 7
Nauru, 5, 136; gross domestic product, 137*tab*; imports, 167*n42*; income, per capita, 150, 167*n42*; independence, 139; population, 137*tab*, 139
Neocolonialism, 105
Netherlands Indonesian Union, 24
New Caledonia, 136, 139; economic dependence, 141*fig*
New Hebrides. *See* Vanuatu
Newly industrializing countries, 5, 75; aggressiveness, 10; economic strength, 15; exports to Pacific Basin states, 9*tab*; growth rate, 17
New Zealand, 5; exports to Pacific Basin states, 9*tab*; membership in PECC, 61
Nicaragua, 5; exports, 47*tab*, 49*tab*, 58; gross national product, 35*tab*; growth rates, 37; imports, 47*tab*, 52*tab*; income, per capita, 37; independence, 36; Japanese trade, 52*tab*; Official Development Assistance, 60*tab*; population, 35*tab*, 36; trade with Pacific Basin states, 47–49*tab*
NICs. *See* Newly industrializing countries
Niue, 5, 136, 139, 150; gross domestic product, 137*tab*; population, 137*tab*
Nonalignment, 107, 111, 113, 149, 161
Noriega, Manuel, 3, 37, 64
North American Free Trade Area, 4, 77, 153

OAS. *See* Organization of American States
OECD. *See* Organization for Economic Cooperation and Development
OECS. *See* Organization of Eastern Caribbean States
Official Development Assistance, 27, 55, 57*tab*, 58, 59, 60*tab*, 61
Ohira, Masayoshi, 7
Oil: crisis, 5, 17; prices, 24, 25, 37, 38, 91, 158; production, 38, 39, 42, 62, 63, 99*n83*, 140
OLADE. *See* Latin American Energy Organization
Open Door policy, 17
OPTAD. *See* Organization for Pacific Trade and Development
Organization for Economic Cooperation and Development, 7
Organization for Pacific Trade and Development, 7
Organization of American States, 40, 41, 43, 108*tab*, 113, 152, 157, 202
Organization of Eastern Caribbean States, 41, 42, 43, 86, 108*tab*, 109, 114–115, 152, 200
Overseas Economic Cooperation Fund, 50

Pacific Basin Economic Council, 5
Pacific Basin states: bilateralism, 159–160; cultural groups, 134, 136; economic interaction, 27; economic relations with Caribbean states, 45–68; impact of cooperation on ASEAN, 7; informal relationships, 27; institutionalization of cooperation, 5, 8; intraregional relations, 4, 15–29, 29; links to Caribbean states, 11, 42–43; membership in PECC, 61; obstacles to cooperation, 8; political economies, 139–141, 146–151; political interaction, 27; regional diversity, 8; strategic importance, 11, 172–173; trade with ASEAN, 29; United States security role, 101–103
Pacific Economic Cooperation Conference, 8, 61
Pacific Trade and Development Conferences, 5
PAFTAD. *See* Pacific Trade and Development Conferences
Palau, 136, 139, 189*n5*; gross domestic product, 137*tab*; population, 137*tab*
Panama, 3, 5; economy, 37; exports, 37, 47*tab*, 49*tab*, 58; gross national product, 35*tab*; imports, 47*tab*, 50, 52*tab*, 61; income, per capita, 37; Japanese investment, 56*tab*, 58; Japanese trade, 52*tab*; military regime, 40; Official Development Assistance, 60*tab*; political crisis, 64; population, 35*tab*; relations with United States, 37; trade with Pacific Basin states, 47–49*tab*, 50, 51
Papua New Guinea, 5, 136; economic dependence, 141*fig*; economy, 146–147; gross domestic product, 137*tab*, 146; growth rates, 146; income, per capita, 146; independence, 136, 146; membership in ASEAN, 109; political stability, 146–147, 177, 180; population, 137*tab*
Park Chung Hee, 19
Patterson, P. J., 142
PBEC. *See* Pacific Basin Economic Council
Peacekeeping: force in Caribbean, 118; Japanese role, 54
PECC. *See* Pacific Economic Cooperation Conference
Philippines: agriculture, 26; armed forces, 121*tab*; economy, 15, 25; exports, 26; gross domestic product, 121*tab*; gross national product, 16*tab*; imports, 48–49*tab*; income, per capita, 25–26; interregional trade, 29; Japanese investment in, 27; membership in ASEAN, 5, 9*tab*, 23, 109; political stability, 25, 26, 107, 109, 110, 201; population, 16*tab*, 25, 121*tab*; relations with United States, 26; trade with Caribbean states, 48–49*tab*, 51; trade with Japan, 28
Pindling, Lynden, 143
Pitcairn Islands, 139

Price, George, 144
Price(s): commodity, 37, 140, 150; decline for traditional products, 25; distortions, 79; international, 37; stability, 80
Private sector, regulation, 93
Privatization, 89, 91
Production: agricultural, 20; for domestic market, 10; fatigue, 17; local incentives, 92
Protectionism, 17, 76, 79, 80, 81, 199
Public sector, 89, 91, 93; deficits, 98n71; efficiency, 91; expansion, 90, 93; management, 92
Puerto Rico, 39; dependent industrialization, 85; income, per capita, 86; membership in Caricom, 113

Quayle, Dan, 7

Ramos, Fidel, 26
Raratonga Treaty, 156
Reagan, Ronald, 7, 144, 156, 177, 178, 184, 186, 189n6, 192n41
Recession, effect on Caribbean states, 42
Reform: agricultural, 79, 94; economic policy, 80; educational, 17; institutional, 92; land, 17, 19, 20, 82, 92, 93, 199; political, 89
Regionalism: Asian-Pacific, 154–156; in Association of Southeast Asian Nations, 23; Caribbean, 151–154; and security, 107–119
Regional Security System, 108tab, 109, 115, 116fig, 117–119, 152, 177, 178, 202
Regional stock exchanges, 114, 153
Rent-Seeking, 94
Resources: allocation, 79; exploitation, 28; military, 105; natural, 28; sharing, 111
Rights: civil, 106, 146; political, 104–105, 106
Rio Treaty, 113
Robinson, A. N. R., 90
Roh Tae Woo, 81
RSS. See Regional Security System

St. Kitts/Nevis, 39; armed forces, 121tab; gross domestic product, 121tab, 133tab; gross national product, 35tab; growth rates, 143; life expectancy, 133tab; membership in Caricom, 113; membership in OECS, 114; Official Development Assistance, 60tab; population, 35tab, 41, 121tab, 133tab; relations with Taiwan, 46; in RSS, 115
St. Lucia, 39; armed forces, 121tab; economy, 145; gross domestic product, 121tab, 133tab; gross national product, 35tab; growth rates, 143; life expectancy, 133tab; membership in Caricom, 113; membership in OECS, 114; Official Development Assistance, 60tab; population, 35tab, 121tab, 133tab; in RSS, 115
St. Vincent, 39; armed forces, 121tab; exports, 47tab, 48tab; gross domestic product, 121tab, 133tab; gross national product, 35tab; growth rates, 143; imports, 47tab, 52tab; Japanese trade, 52tab; life expectancy, 133tab; membership in Caricom, 113; membership in OECS, 114; Official Development Assistance, 60tab; political stability, 115, 177; population, 35tab, 121tab, 133tab; relations with Taiwan, 46; in RSS, 115; trade with Pacific Basin states, 47–49tab, 51
Salvador, El, 5; growth rates, 37; income, per capita, 37; independence, 36; population, 36
Samoa, Western, 5, 136, 150; economic dependence, 141fig; gross domestic product, 137tab; independence, 136, 174; population, 137tab
Sandiford, Erskine, 118, 142, 166n21
Seaga, Edward, 64, 91, 157
Security: ASEAN concerns, 109–112; Caribbean states concerns, 112–119; for development, 101–123; internal, 84; internal instability in, 104–105, 120, 123; intervention in, 105, 120, 123; misperceptions, 172, 181–186; national, 76; and power, 175–176; regional, 5; superpower interests in Pacific, 11, 16, 29; Third World, 103–119; vulnerability in, 104, 114, 120, 123
SELA. See Latin American Economic System
Shultz, George, 7
Simmonds, Kennedy, 182
Singapore: armed forces, 121tab; economic liberalization, 22; economy, 15; entrepôt status, 21; exports, 88tab; foreign trade, 21; government role in economy, 21; gross domestic product, 18, 77, 83, 84, 121tab; gross national product, 16tab, 21, 87, 88tab; growth rates, 18, 83, 88tab; imports, 48–49tab, 88tab; infant mortality, 79; interregional trade, 29; Japanese investment, 27, 56tab; lack of agricultural base, 21, 22; life expectancy, 79; manufacturing, 22; membership in ASEAN, 5, 9tab, 23, 109; nonalignment, 111; political stability, 84, 109, 110; political system, 22; population, 16tab, 21, 88tab, 121tab; state planning, 22; trade surpluses, 4; trade with Caribbean states, 48-49tab, 51; trade with Japan, 28; unemployment, 83
Social: expenditures, 19; hierarchies, 36; inequities, 36; norms, 79
Socialism: Guyanese, 40; Nicaraguan, 36
Solomon Islands, 5, 136; economic dependence, 141fig; economy, 148; exports, 148; gross domestic product, 137tab; income, per capita, 148; independence, 139; population, 137tab
Somare, Michael, 180
South Pacific Bureau for Economic Cooperation, 8
South Pacific Commission, 154, 155
South Pacific Cooperation Fund, 160

South Pacific Forum, 8, 108*tab*, 154, 155, 185, 200, 201
South Pacific Regional Trade and Economic Agreement, 155
Soviet Union, 3; impact on lending to Caribbean states, 62; liberalization in, 4; nuclear arsenal, 3
State: intervention, 76, 77, 81, 82, 93; involvement in economy, 19, 21, 22, 23; market socialist, 84; planning, 22, 77, 200; policy failure, 83
"Strengthened Debt Strategy," 59
Super 807 program, 86, 98n59
Suriname: cultural groups, 145; economy, 145–146; exports, 47*tab*, 49*tab*; gross domestic product, 133*tab*; gross national product, 35*tab*; imports, 47*tab*, 52*tab*; independence, 42, 130, 145; Japanese trade, 52*tab*; life expectancy, 133*tab*; membership in Caricom, 113; military rule, 42, 190n11; Official Development Assistance, 60*tab*; political stability, 42, 104, 145, 176, 177, 201; population, 35*tab*, 133*tab*, 145; trade with Pacific Basin states, 47–49*tab*; unemployment, 145

Tabai, Ieremia, 151
Tahiti, 136
Taiwan, 5; agriculture, 20; economic strength, 15; elections, 21; export processing zones, 83; exports, 50, 88*tab*; foreign investment, 20; gross domestic product, 18, 77; gross national product, 16*tab*, 81, 82, 88*tab*; growth rates, 18, 82, 83, 88*tab*; imports, 48–49*tab*, 88*tab*; import-substitution, 20; income, per capita, 20, 82; infant mortality, 79; infrastructure, 20; investment in Asia, 29; Japanese investment in, 27; life expectancy, 79; membership in PECC, 8, 61; military budget, 20; political liberalization, 21; population, 16*tab*, 20, 88*tab*; trade surpluses, 4, 18, 20; trade with Caribbean states, 46, 48–49*tab*, 50; unemployment, 82; United States assistance, 20
Tanaka, Kakuei, 28
Tariffs, 17, 81; common external, 114
Tax: exemptions, 17, 71n48; incentives, 157; income, 71n48, 89; rebates, 83
Technology: adaptation, 17; computer, 67; transfer, 28, 64–65, 68, 83, 146
Thailand: agriculture, 25; armed forces, 121*tab*; economy, 15, 25; exports, 25; gross domestic product, 121*tab*; gross national product, 16*tab*; imports, 48–49*tab*; income, per capita, 25; interregional trade, 29; Japanese investment in, 27; membership in ASEAN, 5, 9*tab*, 23, 109; military rule, 26; population, 16*tab*, 25, 121*tab*; security threats, 26; trade with Caribbean states, 48–49*tab*, 51; trade

with Japan, 28
Tokelau, 139
Tonga, 5, 136, 150; armed forces, 180; economic dependence, 141*fig*; gross domestic product, 137*tab*; independence, 136; population, 137*tab*
Torrijos, Omar, 40, 159
Tourism, 86, 89, 93, 98n67, 129, 142, 143, 144, 148, 156, 181; Bahamian, 42; diversification, 92; downturn, 42; in Hong Kong, 23; Japanese, 18, 68; in Singapore, 22
Trade: agreements, 86; barriers, 113; Caribbean-Asian, 45–68, 69n7; deficits, 9, 90; dependence, 129; diversification, 10, 46, 51; entrepit, 21, 22, 84; extraregional, 36–37; foreign, 21; free, 4, 7, 39, 66, 110–111, 158; imbalances, 156; international, 77, 78, 79, 114; intraregional, 4, 36, 78, 87, 153; liberalization, 107; negative balances, 91–92; patterns, 51, 69n7, 153; policies, 79; preferential arrangements, 5; surplus, 4, 5, 18, 20, 67, 81, 82, 87; U.S. trans-Pacific, 8–9, 11; volume, 79
Treaty of Chaguaramas, 113
Treaty of Tlatelolco, 119
Trinidad and Tobago, 39, 121*tab*; armed forces, 121*tab*; economy, 42, 90–91, 142, 153; education budget, 177, 178; exports, 47*tab*, 48*tab*, 63, 88*tab*; government, 90–91; gross domestic product, 87, 90, 133*tab*; gross national product, 35*tab*, 87, 88*tab*, 90; growth rates, 88*tab*, 90; imports, 47*tab*, 52*tab*, 63, 88*tab*; independence, 132, 174, 176; Japanese investment in, 63; Japanese trade, 52*tab*; labor controls, 77; life expectancy, 133*tab*; membership in Caricom, 113; membership in OECS, 86; military budget, 177, 178; Official Development Assistance, 60*tab*; oil production, 42, 63, 99n83, 140; political stability, 41, 65, 112, 118, 142, 177, 201; population, 35*tab*, 88*tab*, 121*tab*, 133*tab*; structural adjustment, 91; trade with Pacific Basin states, 47–49*tab*, 50; unemployment, 90
Truman, Harry, 173, 183
Tuvalu, 5, 150; aid-dependence, 140; economic dependence, 141*fig*; gross domestic product, 137*tab*; independence, 139; population, 137*tab*, 139

Unemployment, 82, 83, 85, 87, 89, 90, 91, 99n88, 142, 145, 150, 160, 161
United Nations: Caribbean states membership, 152; Conference on Environment and Development, 181; development funds, 150; Food and Agriculture Organization, 161; Japanese contribution, 54; peacekeeping unit, 54; trusteeships, 154, 189n6
United States: exports to Japan, 55*tab*; exports

to Pacific Basin states, 9*tab*; foreign policy, 3; import restraint, 10; imports from Japan, 9, 55*tab*; interest in Pacific Basin states, 7; intervention in Grenada, 40, 105, 112, 118, 144, 161, 184, 192*n41*; investment in Europe, 10; investment in Pacific Basin states, 9; Japanese investment in, 10, 52, 56*tab*; membership in PECC, 61; Nicaraguan intervention, 36; in North American Free Trade Area, 4; relations with Caribbean states, 43, 67, 121–122; security interest in Pacific Basin states, 101–103, 111; Taiwanese investment, 83; trade deficits, 4, 9, 18; trade with Japan, 8, 55*tab*; trans-Pacific trade, 8–9

United States Agency for International Development, 184

Vanuatu, 5, 136, 139; aid-dependence, 148; armed forces, 180; economic dependence, 141*fig*; economy, 148–149; exports, 148; gross domestic product, 137*tab*; independence, 139, 177; political stability, 177; population, 137*tab*

Venezuela: economic processing zones, 66; economy, 62; exports, 47*tab*, 49*tab*, 62; foreign policy, 39; free trade agreements, 4; gross national product, 35*tab*; growth rates, 46; imports, 47*tab*, 50, 52*tab*, 62; income, per capita, 38; industry, 38; investment in Caribbean, 39; Japanese investment, 62; Japanese trade, 52*tab*; membership in Caricom, 113; Official Development Assistance, 60*tab*, 62; oil production, 38, 39, 62; political stability, 62; population, 35*tab*, 38; state intervention, 62; structural adjustment, 38; trade with Japan, 62; trade with Pacific Basin states, 47–49*tab*, 51

Vulnerability: economic, 104; security concern, 104, 114

West Indies Federation, 132, 151, 163*n7*
Williams, Eric, 168*n46*, 176
World Bank: Japanese contributions, 28; structural adjustment loans, 91; in Trinidad and Tobago, 91
World War II, 173–174, 189*n4*

Zone of Peace, Freedom, and Neutrality, 112

About the Book

Despite the current global focus on prospects for the integrated European market, there are many in the policymaking and business communities who believe that the next century will be a Pacific, rather than a European, one. Not only does U.S. trade with East Asia far exceed its trans-Atlantic commerce, but recent figures show that the countries of Asia Pacific account for more than 40 percent of the world's output of goods and services.

As the Pacific century approaches, Caribbean states are moving to diversify their foreign relations away from the traditional focus on Europe and North America. The authors of this book explore the commonalities and current links between the Asian-Pacific and the Caribbean states and examine ways in which ties between the two groups can be deepened to their mutual benefit.